W9-BYN-656

ISHAI SAGI

SharePoint®
2010

HOW-TO

SAMS | 800 East 96th Street, Indianapolis, Indiana 46240 USA

SharePoint® 2010 How-To

ISBN-13: 978-0-672-33335-4

ISBN-10: 0-672-33335-X

Library of Congress Cataloging-in-Publication Data:

Sagi, Ishai.

  SharePoint 2010 how to / Ishai Sagi.

    p. cm.

  Includes index.

  ISBN-13: 978-0-672-33335-4

  ISBN-10: 0-672-33335-X

  1. Intranets (Computer networks) 2. Microsoft SharePoint (Electronic resource) 3. Web servers. I. Title.

  TK5105.875.I6S2425 2011

  006.7—dc22

                                2010028387

Printed in the United States of America

First Printing August 2010

Trademarks

Warning and Disclaimer

Bulk Sales

Sams Publishing offers excellent discounts on this book when ordered in quantity for bulk purchases or special sales. For more information, please contact

U.S. Corporate and Government Sales
1-800-382-3419
corpsales@pearsontechgroup.com

For sales outside the United States, please contact

International Sales
international@pearson.com

Editor-in-Chief
Karen Gettman

Executive Editor
Neil Rowe

Development Editor
Mark Renfrow

Managing Editor
Sandra Schroeder

Senior Project Editor
Tonya Simpson

Copy Editor
Kitty Wilson

Technical Editor
Guy Yardeni

Indexer
Cheryl Lenser

Proofreader
Language Logistics, LLC

Publishing Coordinator
Cindy Teeters

Book Designer
Gary Adair

Compositor
MPS Limited, A Macmillan Company

Contents at a Glance

Table of Contents

About the Author

Ishai Sagi is a Microsoft SharePoint expert who has been working on Microsoft SharePoint products since its initial release in 2001. Since then, Ishai has trained numerous end users, administrators, and developers in using Microsoft SharePoint and in developing solutions on the platform. Ishai is a regular speaker and an "ask the experts" panelist at Microsoft conferences around the world, including in the United States, Australia, Europe, and Israel. Ishai manages a SharePoint user group in Canberra, Australia, speaking about Microsoft SharePoint in free, open-to-the-public events every month. For his effort and contribution to the Microsoft SharePoint community, Ishai has received the Microsoft Most Valuable Professional award (MVP) in 2007, 2008, 2009, and 2010.

Ishai owns his own company, Extelligent Design (www.ExtelligentDesign.com), which is based in Australia and provides training, consulting, and custom development and sells products and solutions for Microsoft SharePoint. He also is the author of a SharePoint blog aimed at developers who want to develop code solutions for Microsoft SharePoint at www.sharepoint-tips.com.

Acknowledgments

Thanks to everyone who reviewed the *SharePoint 2007 How-To* book and encouraged me to write this book by telling me I have done a good job.

A very big thank you goes to the editors of this book: Neil Rowe, Mark Renfrow, Tonya Simpson, and Kitty Wilson, as they were so helpful and this book would have been very different if it hadn't been for their guiding hands and helpful comments.

Thanks to my family for being excited for me, and most of all, thanks to Anja, who had to suffer through many weeknights and weekends without me for the second year in a row.

We Want to Hear from You!

As the reader of this book, *you* are our most important critic and commentator. We value your opinion and want to know what we're doing right, what we could do better, what areas you'd like to see us publish in, and any other words of wisdom you're willing to pass our way.

You can email or write me directly to let me know what you did or didn't like about this book—as well as what we can do to make our books stronger.

Please note that I cannot help you with technical problems related to the topic of this book, and that due to the high volume of mail I receive, I might not be able to reply to every message.

When you write, please be sure to include this book's title and author as well as your name and phone or email address. I will carefully review your comments and share them with the author and editors who worked on the book.

E-mail: feedback@samspublishing.com

Mail: Neil Rowe
Executive Editor
Sams Publishing
800 East 96th Street
Indianapolis, IN 46240 USA

Reader Services

Visit our website and register this book at informit.com/register for convenient access to any updates, downloads, or errata that might be available for this book.

Introduction

Overview of This Book

This book aims to be your companion as you learn how to use Microsoft SharePoint 2010. It lists common tasks that you are most likely to need to do when you use SharePoint as a working tool and shows how to accomplish these tasks in an easy step-by-step manner.

This book is written for people who are unfamiliar with or are unsure how to approach tasks in Microsoft SharePoint 2010. It also covers advanced tasks such as managing sites and security, editing and authoring pages, and using some of the more complex functionality available in Microsoft SharePoint 2010. However, this book is not intended to be administration guide, a developer handbook, or a completed and comprehensive user guide to everything you can do with Microsoft SharePoint. The end result of such a book would be a heavy, intimidating volume that might be harder to read through and learn from. Instead, this book focuses on assisting you with the basic tasks, covering the essentials and making sure you know where to go to do the most common day-to-day tasks that you will encounter as a Microsoft SharePoint 2010 end user. Hopefully, this book will lend you enough of an insight into the workings of SharePoint that you will be able to continue learning more and more about the options and features available in SharePoint.

This book is written with the firm belief that to learn, you must do. You can use this book as a reference tool when you need to perform a certain task that you need help finding out how to perform, or you can use it as a learning guide if you have an environment to perform the tasks outlined in this book one by one. Whatever you choose, it is our hope that this book will be a helpful companion.

How to Benefit from This Book

We've designed this book to be easy to read from cover to cover. It is divided into four parts to make looking up problems easier.

Part I, "Solutions for Readers," includes the most common and basic tasks that do not involve changing anything in SharePoint, but just viewing, browsing, and finding information. This part includes the following chapters:

- ▶ Chapter 1, "About Microsoft SharePoint 2010"
- ▶ Chapter 2, "Finding Your Way Around a SharePoint Site"

- ▶ Chapter 3, "Solutions Regarding Files, List Items, and Forms"
- ▶ Chapter 4, "Searching in SharePoint"
- ▶ Chapter 5, "Social Networking, Personal Sites, and Personal Details in SharePoint Server"

Part II, "Solutions for Authors and Content Managers," teaches you how to perform tasks that involve adding content to SharePoint or changing the way it looks. This part includes the following chapters:

- ▶ Chapter 6, "Creating and Managing Files, List Items, and Forms in SharePoint"
- ▶ Chapter 7, "Creating Lists and Document Libraries"
- ▶ Chapter 8, "Creating List Views"
- ▶ Chapter 9, "Authoring Pages"
- ▶ Chapter 10, "Managing Security"
- ▶ Chapter 11, "Workflows"

Part III, "Solutions for Site Managers," introduces advanced tasks involved in creating and customizing SharePoint sites. This part includes the following chapters:

- ▶ Chapter 12 , "Creating Subsites"
- ▶ Chapter 13, "Customizing a SharePoint Site"
- ▶ Chapter 14, "Managing Site Security"

Finally, part IV, "Appendixes," provides shortcuts and links that will help you find your way and achieve some tasks more quickly.

Ways to Continue Expanding Your Knowledge

This book does not claim to cover all that you can do with SharePoint. If you find yourself in need of more information, check out the built-in help system available in SharePoint itself. Almost every page in SharePoint has a help button that will open the help screen, enabling you to search for the topic you want help on. Additionally, you can find SharePoint manuals, training videos, and help articles from Microsoft on the Microsoft help site at http://tinyurl.com/SP2010Help.

If you cannot find what you want in the aforementioned site and help pages, plenty more help is available on the Internet from the SharePoint community, which is big and helpful, both in blogs and discussion forums. To find solutions to issues, it is recommended to search the Internet (using your search engine of choice) for a solution on the issue. Many blogs and websites have information on how to achieve tasks in SharePoint.

If you have a question for which you cannot find the answer, try posting it on the Microsoft forums that are dedicated to such problems. These forums can be found at http://tinyurl.com/SP2010Forum.

Finally, if you need professional help, the author of this book can recommend trainers and consultants through his company at www.extelligentdesign.com.

CHAPTER 1

About Microsoft SharePoint 2010

What Is Microsoft SharePoint 2010?

SharePoint is a Microsoft platform that allows people to build websites. SharePoint 2010 is the fourth version of SharePoint from Microsoft, and it is also known as SharePoint v4 or Microsoft Office SharePoint Server 2010. It is very different from the versions that came before it.

SharePoint allows people to create websites with different content and different purposes. Its many built-in features and components make it a comprehensive solution that can fit many needs.

One common use of SharePoint in organizations is to create sites that are used for team collaboration. These collaborative sites, also known as *team sites* or *group work sites*, enable team members to better work with one another. They can use the site to share documents, assign tasks, track team events on a shared web calendar, and much more. This use is known as a *team collaboration system*.

Many companies use SharePoint for their central document storage, replacing network folders. This use is known as an *electronic document management system*.

Another common use is as a corporate portal where the corporate employees can go and download forms, read corporate news, fill in surveys, and search for documents. This use is known as an *electronic content management system* or an *intranet*.

Finally, some companies choose the SharePoint platform as the platform for their Internet sites—where visitors from around the world can visit the company's website and read about the company's products, register for events, and do whatever it is the site has been configured to allow them to do. This use is known as a *web content management system*.

This variety of possible uses of SharePoint indicate the flexibility of the SharePoint platform. It is highly customizable—which means that one SharePoint site (for example, the one shown in Figure 1.1) may look entirely different from another SharePoint site (such as the one shown in Figure 1.2). This book shows mostly basic SharePoint sites (sites that have not been customized), and the sites that you will be using may look significantly different. It is important to keep that in mind when following the instructions in this book, as some of the things mentioned in this book and shown in the figures may differ from site to site.

The SharePoint platform is also known as SharePoint Foundation. This book uses *SPF* when referring to a SharePoint site that is built based on this platform.

The SharePoint product family has other products that can be added on top of SPF to enhance the sites in different ways. One of these products is called SharePoint Server, and even that has two versions—standard and enterprise—each adding more features. Often the term *SharePoint* is used to refer to either SPF or to the two extended versions SharePoint Server—and this can be a bit confusing.

Because the SharePoint Server products are extensions of SPF, sites built using those products have all the capabilities of SPF sites, but with extra features. Some of the differences between SharePoint Server and SPF are explained in the following section.

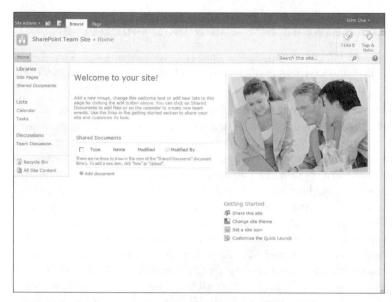

FIGURE 1.1
A standard SharePoint site.

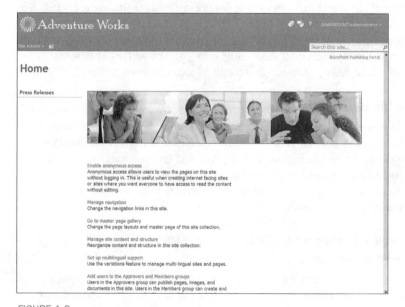

FIGURE 1.2
A customized SharePoint site.

SharePoint sites have many built-in features that make them useful, flexible, and customizable—features such as security management, lists of information, document libraries (places to store and manage files and documents), views, alerts, and searches. All these and more are explained in this chapter.

Difference Between SPF and SharePoint Server

As mentioned earlier in this chapter, SharePoint Server is an extension of SPF. SharePoint Server sites have features that are not available in SPF sites, and they enjoy all the features of SPF sites.

SPF sites work well for collaboration sites. Such a site gives groups of people the ability to upload and download documents, use discussion boards, assign tasks, share events, and use workflows. However, SPF does not have enough features to be a good platform for a corporate portal or for a corporate search solution. SharePoint Server offers extra features that upgrade SPF into a platform that can serve a corporation with enterprise searching (searching from one location across all the sites that corporate has and on documents and external systems that are stored in other locations, not just in SharePoint). It also has features for storing details about people and searching on them, and it enables employees to have their own personal sites where they can store documents (instead of on their machines). SharePoint Server has many more features related to business intelligence and business processes and forms. (For more information about personal sites, see "What Is a Personal Site?" later in this chapter, and see Chapter 5, "Social Networking, Personal Sites, and Personal Details in SharePoint Server.")

Finally, SharePoint Server has a publishing feature that enables site managers to create publishing sites where it is easy to author pages (as opposed to documents) and publish them using workflows. This is very important for large corporations that want to, for example, publish corporate news using an approval workflow or build an Internet site where every page must go through a special approval process.

What Is Microsoft FAST Search?

FAST is an optional component of SharePoint Server that an organization can have installed on top of SharePoint. It adds further intelligence to the regular SharePoint search experience by enhancing the search options and how the search results are returned. If FAST is installed on a SharePoint site, you see more options than you would normally get in SharePoint. Chapter 4, "Searching in SharePoint," provides some examples of these options.

How to Tell Whether a Site Is Based on SPF or SharePoint Server

There is no way to tell just by looking whether a site is hosted on a server that has SharePoint Server installed. Customizations that a company might have developed may cause an SPF site to look as if it has some extensions that come with SharePoint Server. On the other hand, customizations can cause a SharePoint Server site to look simpler; for example, it might remove the SharePoint Server–specific links that help identify a site as a SharePoint Server site.

However, there is one thing you can look for in most SharePoint sites to determine with a fair degree of certainty whether a site is SharePoint Server or SPF: You can look for the My Site link under the name drop-down at the top of the screen (see Figure 1.3). If you see that link, you are viewing a site that is running on a server with SharePoint Server. Not having the link does not necessarily mean that the site does not have SharePoint Server, however, because the administrator can choose to disable that functionality.

FIGURE 1.3
The My Site link under the Name drop-down.

Additional differences between the two versions will become clear as you go through this book. Many topics in this book indicate that they are valid only in SharePoint Server, and you can usually find whether they are available by trying to perform the task described.

What Is a Site?

The structure of SharePoint sites (sometimes referred to as *webs*) is very different from the structure of typical Internet sites that contain only pages. In SharePoint, a site can house more than just pages. It is a container that holds lists and libraries (discussed later in this chapter), and it can have other sites under it.

For example, a corporate portal might have a home site called SharePoint Intranet that contains information that people see when they browse to that site. That portal also might have a subsite called Human Resources that stores forms such as travel requests, expense claims, and other forms. The two sites are linked because the Human Resources site is under the SharePoint Intranet site. The two sites may share some attributes, such as security (who is allowed to do what in the sites) and navigation (so that visitors to the sites can navigate between the sites), but they have separate contents—for example, different pages, libraries, and lists, as shown in Figures 1.4 and 1.5.

Every SharePoint site is a member of a site collection. As the name implies, a site collection is a collection of sites. Every site collection has a single site as its root site, and other sites can be built under the root site. A site collection has some attributes that are common to all the sites in that collection (for example, some search settings, a Recycle Bin for deleted items).

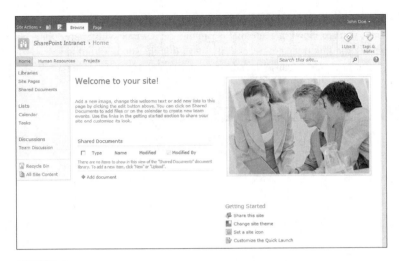

FIGURE 1.4
A site that has subsites. Human Resources and Projects are subsites of the site SharePoint Intranet site.

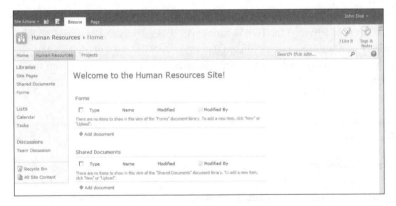

FIGURE 1.5
A site that is a child site. The Human Resources site is under the SharePoint Intranet site.

What Is a Personal Site?

A personal site is a site that belongs to a specific user and is used to show user information that belongs, personally, to that user. The user can upload documents to a personal document library in the personal site, and only that user will be able to see and manage these documents. The personal site is also a place where users can manage their personal favorite items and comments that they have tagged throughout SharePoint or even outside SharePoint (see "What Is Tagging?" later in this chapter). The personal site has special pages with information that might be important to track. A user can track information by using newsfeeds that tell you what your colleagues are up to. In addition, users can run searches and stay up-to-date on those subjects. In addition, the personal site is usually the place from which users can modify their personal details in the corporate directory.

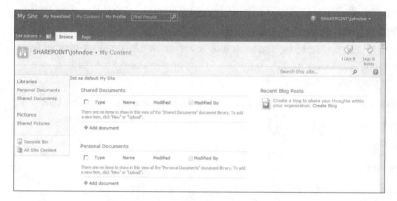

FIGURE 1.6
A personal site showing the content of the site.

A personal site usually has components that display information targeted specifically to that user. For example, it might have components that show the user's e-mail, or upcoming meetings from the person's calendar, and a list of documents the user has recently worked on and tasks assigned to the user.

For more in-depth information about the personal site and what you can do in it, see Chapter 5.

NOTE As mentioned earlier, personal sites are available only with SharePoint Server, not with SPF.

What Is a Ribbon?

As part of the Microsoft Office product family, SharePoint 2010 uses a design concept called a ribbon to display different menus and buttons, depending on what you are looking at. It is important to know how to use the ribbon so you can move around in a site and perform actions in it.

This book covers many different actions available in different ribbons. Part II, "Solutions for Authors and Content Managers," explains how to author content, and Part III, "Solutions for Site Managers," explains how to manage websites. Although these tasks use the ribbon heavily, it is also important for readers who do not need to author information to be familiar with the ribbon concept to avoid getting lost. As you will see in Chapter 2, "Finding Your Way Around a SharePoint Site," and Chapter 3, "Solutions Regarding Files, Documents, List Items, and Forms," you use the ribbon to perform many types of navigational actions on documents and list items.

What Is a List?

A SharePoint list is a container for information, similar to a very simple database or spreadsheet. Using a list is the most common way to manage information in a SharePoint site.

In a list, data is gathered in rows, and each row is known as a *list item*. A list can have multiple columns—also known as *properties*, *fields*, or *metadata*. So a list item is a row with data in those columns.

For example, a list of contacts (shown in Figure 1.7) may have the following columns:

- First Name
- Last Name
- Company
- Phone

FIGURE 1.7
A contacts list with sample data.

These columns may have the following list items:

- First Name: John
- Last Name: Doe
- Company: Extelligent Design
- Phone: 1800-000-000

Lists can be used in many cases. For example, you might use lists for links, tasks, discussions, announcements, or events. In SharePoint, users can create lists and columns. Lists can be used for almost anything that can be described by a group of columns.

The information in lists can be displayed on pages in a SharePoint site. For example, if the site manager wants to display a list of links on the site, that manager can add a web part (See "What are Web Parts?" later in this chapter) that shows that list, as detailed in Chapter 9, "Authoring Pages."

Different lists can have different security settings. For example, list managers can define who is allowed to add items to a list, who is allowed to edit items, who is allowed to read the items, and so on. Similarly, each list item can have its own security settings, so different list items can be visible to different people. For example, an item that is a link to a restricted site can have security settings that prevent users who don't have access to that site from seeing it.

In some lists, you can attach files to list items—very much like attachments in e-mail. For example, in a contacts list, you could attach to each contact a picture and a resume. Or in a list of tasks, you might attach documentation of what needs to be done to the task.

A list can hold different types of content, as explained later in this chapter, in the section "What Is a Content Type?"

For information on how to interact with lists, see Chapters 6, "Creating and Managing Files, List Items, and Forms in SharePoint," and 7, "Creating Lists and Document Libraries."

What Is an External List?

An external list is unlike other SharePoint lists. Strictly speaking, it is not a SharePoint list at all because it doesn't store information inside it. An external list is a view on external data—that is, data that is contained not within SharePoint but in external databases and systems.

When you add external lists to SharePoint sites, they are displayed in an interface that looks almost exactly like a regular SharePoint list. An external list also allows most of the same interactions with the items in the list that are offered with a regular SharePoint list. This book does not cover external lists because they are an advanced feature of SharePoint 2010 that is created and configured by developers while usually looking and feeling the same as regular lists for you, the end user.

What Is a Document Library?

A document library a special instance of a list, in which every list item is a file, as shown in Figure 1.8. Files can be Microsoft Office documents, Adobe Acrobat documents (PDF files), or any other type of file that the system administrator allows. This book often refers to document libraries as simply *libraries*.

Most of the attributes of lists exist in document libraries. In fact, lists and documents libraries are similar in many ways. However, each item in a document library is a file. Therefore, when creating a new item in a document library, you need to either upload a file or create one. This process is explained in Chapter 6.

FIGURE 1.8
A sample document library with several types of documents.

Additionally, unlike in lists, in document libraries, each row can hold only one file. There isn't an option to attach more files to the row. Essentially, the file itself *is* the row.

Also, because a file can be downloaded, visitors to document libraries have different options available to them when browsing a document library than they have with lists.

Because document libraries and lists have so much in common, many instructions throughout this book apply to both. Where appropriate, the text makes clear that the instructions are for both. For example, the section "Add a Column to a List or Document Library" in Chapter 7 covers both document libraries and lists because the principle of how to create them is the same.

Several special document libraries templates are available in SharePoint. These templates are designed for specific types of content, but they are essentially document libraries. Some of these special cases are described later in this chapter.

What Is a Wiki Page Library?

A wiki page library is a special instance of a document library that is designed to store web pages. On those web pages, you can display different types of content—text, images, videos, and web parts. (For more information on web parts, see "What are Web Parts?" later in this chapter.)

What Is a Form Library?

A form library is much like a document library, but it is supposed to host only Microsoft InfoPath forms. Microsoft InfoPath is electronic form-creation software that integrates with SharePoint. Forms created with InfoPath can be published to SharePoint form libraries, and users can then fill out these forms.

With SharePoint Server, you can load some InfoPath forms without having Microsoft InfoPath installed on your machine. In this case, the form opens in a browser, as a web form. If you have a program that can edit InfoPath forms, such as Microsoft InfoPath 2007 or Microsoft InfoPath Filler 2010, the form opens in that program.

If your company uses InfoPath for creating forms, you might want to learn how to read forms that are in form libraries, as explained in Chapter 3. You also might want to learn how to fill forms, as explained in Chapter 6. (This book does not cover creating Microsoft InfoPath forms.)

What Is an Asset Library?

An asset library is a special instance of a document library that is specially designed to store digital assets such as images, audio files, and videos.

This kind of library (shown in Figure 1.9) can be used as a repository for media files that will be used throughout the SharePoint environment—for example, corporate logos, training videos, and podcasts.

FIGURE 1.9
A sample asset library with a music file, a video file, and several stock photos to be added to pages in the site.

For more information on using the asset library as a repository for images and media files, see Chapter 9, "Authoring Pages."

What Is a Slide Library?

A slide library is a special type of library that has features not available in other types. This library type (shown in Figure 1.10) is designed to help people in an organization collaborate to create PowerPoint presentations by sharing slides. One user can allow other users to import those slides into their presentations.

For more information about using slide libraries, see Chapter 6.

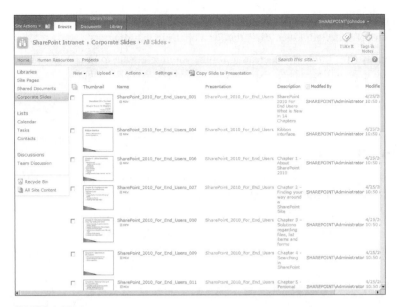

FIGURE 1.10
A slide library with multiple slides available for reuse.

What Is a Picture Library?

A picture library is a special type of a document library that is dedicated to images. A picture library is useful for sharing photos with other people. For example, you can have a picture library as your stock photo repository, as shown in Figures 1.11 and 1.12.

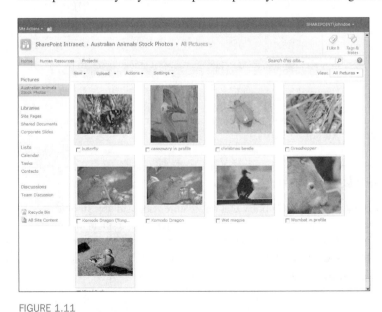

FIGURE 1.11
A picture library showing thumbnails of the pictures in it.

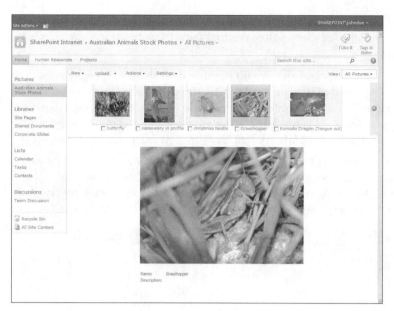

FIGURE 1.12

A picture library showing a filmstrip of the pictures in it.

A picture library includes special views that show the images as thumbnails, as in Figure 1.11, or as a film strip, as in Figure 1.12.

For more information about adding images to a picture library, see Chapter 6.

What Is a View?

Using views is a useful way for a list manager to create different ways to show the information in a list or library. Different views may show different columns and have different sorting and filtering, grouping, and styles.

In SharePoint, views can be either public or private:

▶ **Public**—The list's or library's managers create public views, and these views are available to anyone to use.

▶ **Private**—Users create private views. Only the user who created a private view can use that view. You may, for example, create a private view and customize it to show the information that you usually need to find the items or files that you usually work with.

Chapter 8, "Creating List Views," covers creating views in more details. Chapter 3 covers how to switch between views.

There are several types of views in SharePoint. Most of the views that you will see are the standard tabular views that resemble printed worksheets—with column headers and values in rows but no ability to edit the data directly. However, some special view styles show the information in the list in different ways. For example, the Datasheet view allows directly editing the data, and a Calendar view shows items as part of a calendar.

A Calendar view shows the items in a list based on dates that are set on the items. Other views include the Gantt view and the Datasheet view. The Gantt view is similar to the Calendar view: It shows information based on dates in the list items' properties. The Datasheet view is a Microsoft Excel–like view that allows copying and pasting of data into the list or library. These types of views are covered in detail in Chapter 8.

Let's look at an example of a possible difference between two views. One view for an announcement list may show the title of the announcement and the date that the announcement was changed (see Figure 1.13). A different view of the same list may show the body of the announcement and the date on which it will expire (see Figure 1.14).

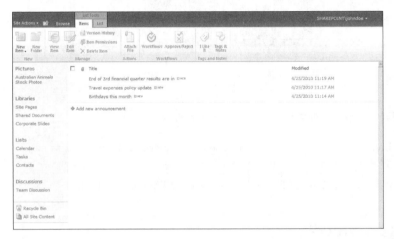

FIGURE 1.13

An announcement list in a view that shows the Title and Modified columns.

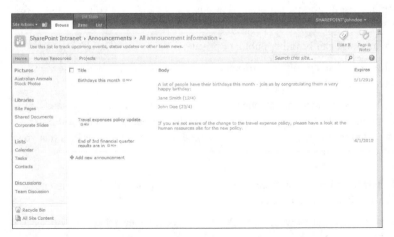

FIGURE 1.14

An announcement list in a view that shows the Title, Body, and Expires columns.

If you have multiple announcements, you can have different views sort the announcements differently. For example, one might sort by the title of the announcement and the other might sort by the modification date. Figure 1.14 shows a view sorting the announcements by their creation date (with the one created first on top). Figure 1.15 shows a view that sorts on the title of the announcement.

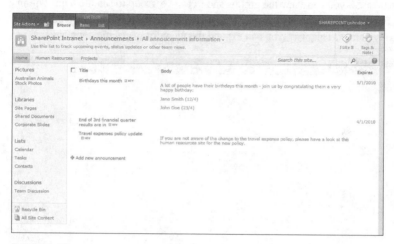

FIGURE 1.15
The announcement list in a view that sorts by the title.

Some views change the style in which the items are displayed. For example, Figure 1.16 shows the announcement list with a different style, called boxed style.

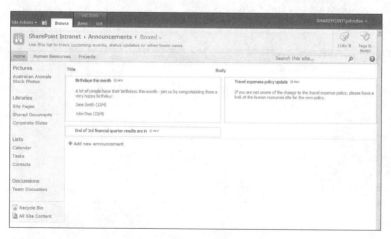

FIGURE 1.16
The announcement list shown with the boxed style.

An announcements list may have a filter applied to it to show only items that have not expired (refer to Figure 1.14). Other views can be configured not to have that filter. If you are viewing a list and the item you are looking for is not showing, consider the possibility that the current view is configured to filter that item.

Finally, some views may display the data grouped by one column, as shown in Figure 1.17. In such cases, you can view the groups and expand a group to see the items within the group. For example, in a contacts list, a view may be set up to group the contacts by their company names. This way, you can expand the view for a specific company.

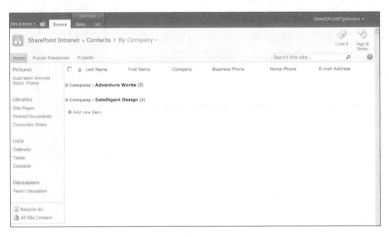

FIGURE 1.17
A contacts list, grouped by company.

To see the items in a group, click the + sign next to the group name or on the group field's name that shows up as a link (in this example, the Company: link). The group expands, showing you the items that belong to that group (see Figure 1.18).

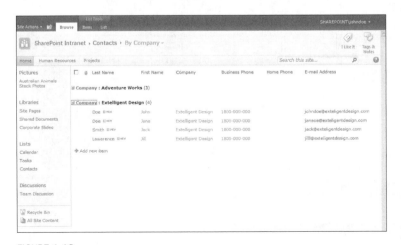

FIGURE 1.18
A contacts list grouped by company, with Extelligent Design expanded.

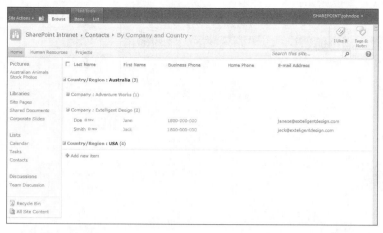

FIGURE 1.19

A contacts list, grouped by country and then by company, with Australia and Extelligent Design expanded.

SharePoint supports up to two grouping levels (for example, by country and then by company, as in Figure 1.19).

As mentioned earlier, picture libraries have their own special views that show the pictures that are in the library as either thumbnails or filmstrips of the pictures.

Some views support paging. *Paging* is a common method in websites used to show large amounts of data without overloading the page. Using paging, the data in a list or library is split into pages, with each page showing only a certain number of the items. The user can navigate back and forth between the pages, using the paging buttons at the bottom of the page or the paging button in the Library ribbon or List ribbon. (See Figures 1.20 and 1.21.)

For example, suppose you have a document library that contains 1,000 documents. Showing all the documents to the user at once might cause the page loading time to be quite slow, and a user might have difficulty finding a particular document. A more sensible approach would be to display the files in batches of 15 (for example), which makes it easier for the reader to see what information is available on the page. This is true even if you don't have thousands of documents! As your document library or list grows to have more and more files or rows, you will want to separate them into pages, as shown in Figures 1.20 and 1.21.

Finally, advanced users can create custom views by using Microsoft SharePoint Designer. Custom views can look totally different from anything that is available for regular views. This book does not cover the use of SharePoint Designer. The book *SharePoint Designer 2010 Unleashed* by Kathy Hughes (Sams Publishing) is a good resource that explains the many uses of SharePoint designer to achieve more complex tasks than the ones described in this book, including creating custom views.

Total number of files in the library

The numbers indicate what documents appear;   Use the paging control to
in this case, the first 15 documents appear.   navigate between pages.

FIGURE 1.20
The first page of a view of a document library with 31 documents, showing the first 15 documents.

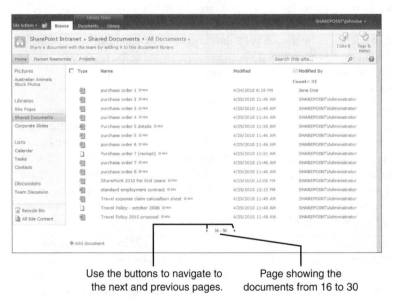

Use the buttons to navigate to   Page showing the
the next and previous pages.   documents from 16 to 30

FIGURE 1.21
The second page of the view shows the next 15 documents.

What Are Web Parts?

Web parts are the building blocks of pages in SharePoint. They are components that show data, and they can be placed in certain regions of a page—known as web part zones. A page can hold many web parts, in different zones or in the same zone. They may be one under another in some zones and side-by-side in other zones.

For example, to show on the home page of a site the contents of a list of links, you can use a web part that displays the content of a list. The web part in Figure 1.22 is one that you have already seen in this chapter—it is the web part that shows views of lists and libraries.

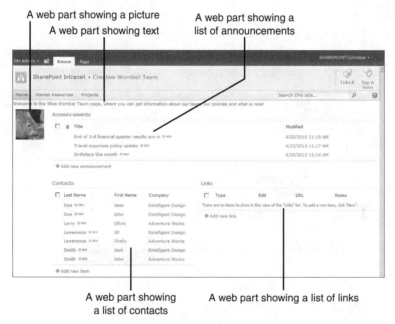

FIGURE 1.22
Different web parts on a page.

SharePoint developers can develop web parts, and the data and functionality that web parts offer to visitors of a SharePoint site is limited only by what developers can create.

The following are some other examples of how web parts could be used:

- ▶ To show search results (see Figure 1.23)
- ▶ To show a picture
- ▶ To show the users of a site
- ▶ To show the content of a site

Although web parts are a part of SharePoint, they can show information that is from outside SharePoint. For example, a special web part may be developed to show information from a corporate application for timesheets or project management. The web part can even offer interaction with the data, allowing users to modify data in the corporate application. In this case, the data itself is not in SharePoint. However, such web parts usually have to be developed, and most of the web parts that come with SharePoint out of the box are used to display data that is stored in SharePoint.

FIGURE 1.23
Search-related web parts.

While web parts might be important building blocks for a SharePoint page, other components also make the pages what they are. Not everything you see on a SharePoint page is a web part, but identifying web parts usually is easy—especially if you have the permissions to edit a page, in which case the page editor shows you the web parts that are on the page, with options to remove them, move them around, and add them.

You will learn to use web parts in Chapter 9.

What Are Alerts?

Using alerts is a great way to be notified by e-mail of changes in lists and libraries or even specific documents or list items.

SharePoint has a built-in alert mechanism that enables users to register for different kinds of alerts. Basically, a user selects the piece of content she wants to be alerted on and requests that SharePoint send her an e-mail when that content changes.

For example, you might use alerts with a document library that is supposed to have documents regarding a specific topic. You might want to know immediately when a new document is added to that document library (see Figure 1.24). As another example, you might want to know when a particular policy document is changed (for example, the corporate travel policy might be very important to people who travel a lot). Alerts enable you to request to be notified when changes like these occur.

FIGURE 1.24
An alert e-mail that is sent when a document has been added to a library.

What Is a Site Column?

A site column is a column for a list or a document library that can be used in all document libraries or lists in the site in which it is created, as well as in the subsites for that site.

A site manager can define a specific column of data once and manage it from a central location instead of creating that column many times in many lists and libraries. In addition, content types can only use site columns. (In lists and libraries, on the other hand, columns can be created separately.)

Using site columns is covered in Chapter 7 and Chapter 13, "Customizing a SharePoint Site."

What Is a Content Type?

As mentioned earlier in this chapter, lists and document libraries can store different kinds of content, known as *content types*. A site manager can create and manage the content types in a site. The content types are then available in that site and in all the sites under it. The different types of content may have different site columns and/or different settings, such as policies and workflows, associated with them.

Content types can use site columns only for column definitions. This means that to create a content type, you must choose what site columns should be included in that content type.

A simple example of a content type is a list of contacts that stores two types of contacts—an internal contact and an external contact. The Internal Contact content type is used for a contact inside the company—and as such does not need the company property because all internal contacts are from the same company. However, the External Contact content type does require the company property because every contact may be from a different company. Hence, a single list has two different column requirements.

As another example of the use of content types, consider a document library where you store many different types of documents. Some documents are presentations, and some are financial reports, while others are user guides and product whitepapers. The differences between those content types are possibly more than just different columns: The content types can also specify different templates that users should use when creating documents of these types. For example, when creating a presentation, a Microsoft PowerPoint template will be used. When creating a financial report, a user will get a specific Microsoft Excel workbook as a template from which to start. User guides may be from a certain Microsoft Word template, while product whitepapers may be PDF documents. Some of these examples are shown in Figure 1.25, which shows the content type options for creating a new document in a document library.

FIGURE 1.25
Choosing a content type when creating a new document in a document library.

Content types can be created in each site, and every subsite under that site can then use the content type. The subsites can either use the content type as it is defined in the parent site or create their own content types.

Content types are hierarchical, which means they can inherit from other content types. For example, the External Contact and Internal Contact content types can both inherit from the Contact content type. This way, if changes are made to the Contact content type (for example, if a property birthday date is added), both child content types may get the update (depending on whether the person who applied the update to the Contact content type chose to apply the update to content types that are inheriting from that content type).

Because the content type of an item or file says a lot about what the item actually is, it is a very important piece of data associated with an item. This makes it very important that authors (that is, people adding information to SharePoint) choose the right content type when creating data in SharePoint. However, sometimes content types are not used. A list may use the basic content type Item or a library may use the content type Document and add columns to the list itself—not impacting the content type itself. This means that all the columns are defined in the list or library and are added to all the items or files in it.

Content types use site columns to define the properties that the files or list items of that content type will have. Site columns are explained later in this chapter, in the section "What Is a Site Column?"

Chapter 7 show how to add and remove a content type to a list or document library.

What Is Tagging?

Tagging is a social web mechanism available in Microsoft SharePoint 2010 Server (not in SPF) that enables you as the user to tag a document or a list item or a even a page—in the SharePoint site or outside it.

You can tag something to help remember it and find it more easily later on.

One tag that SharePoint comes with is the I Like It tag. This tag enables you to signify that you like a document or a page, and then other people can see that you liked it. You can easily find that document or page again by looking at the list of items you've tagged as things you like (usually from your personal site).

Tagging isn't limited to I Like It, however. You can add new tags as shown in Figure 1.26, and you can remove and rename tags. Depending on what the tag manager configured for the site, you might be able to tag objects in your site under different tags.

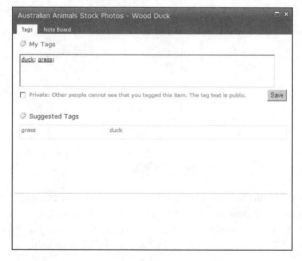

FIGURE 1.26
The duck picture is tagged with two terms—duck and grass—to help users find it based on the terms later on.

You can also add notes to an object, including saying what you like or dislike about it, or any other kind of notes. These notes are displayed to other people who look into the notes that you write, and you can view them as well. You can therefore keep working notes on documents or pages you are working on, without those notes being part of the actual document or page.

Chapter 3 explains in detail how to add tags to content. Chapter 5 explains how to use tags and notes from your personal site to find content you tagged or commented on.

What Is Managed Metadata?

Available only through Microsoft SharePoint 2010 Server (not SPF), managed metadata is a mechanism that enables administrators to create hierarchical term sets that can then be used in document libraries and lists as columns.

A term set is similar to a list that contains items, except that these items can contain more items under them in a hierarchy. For example, if you have a term set called Products, you could have a term for each product that you have in the organization.

By using managed metadata, you can create the list as a hierarchical list, grouping the products into categories (creating terms for the categories and then terms for the products under them) or into product groups, as shown in Figure 1.27.

FIGURE 1.27
A managed metadata list of products.

You can then choose whether the terms that are categories (and not products) are available to the users as options. You can therefore allow the users to tag a document as belonging to a category of products (for example, Books), or you can let them tag a document as belonging to a specific product (for example, SharePoint 2010 How To).

As you can see, managed metadata can be quite useful for tagging and then finding documents and list items. Chapter 7 describes how to create managed metadata columns and how to define term sets for those columns.

What Are Versions?

Document libraries and lists in SharePoint have an option to track versions. This option stores old versions of files or items each time a change is made. For example, if a user uploads a document, and then another user edits the document and saves it, SharePoint saves the original document as a version of the file. Later, users can look at the version history of the file and choose to open a specific version or restore it (that is, make that version the current one).

SharePoint supports two types of versioning. In the first type, each change is regarded as a major change, and the version numbers go from 1 (the first time a document was uploaded) to 2 (after the first change) and then 3 and 4 and so on as shown in Figure 1.28. In the second type, each change is regarded as a minor change, unless the user specifies that it is a major one. The version numbers go from 0.1 (the first time a document was uploaded) to 0.2 (the first change) and so on, until a user selects the option to perform a major change, and the version number changes to 1.0, and subsequent changes raise it to 1.1, 1.2, and so on.

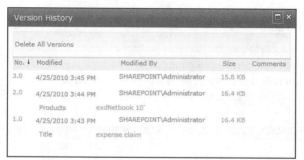

FIGURE 1.28
Viewing the lists of versions for a document.

For information about how to work with versions, see Chapters 3 and 7.

What Does Check-in/Check-out Mean?

Check-in and check-out are common terms in many document management systems, including SharePoint. Their purpose is to prevent conflicts in an environment where multiple people might want to edit the same piece of content (in SharePoint, list items or files) at the same time. The term *check-in* describes the process of adding a new or modified item or file to a document library or a list to replace the previous version. The term *check-out* describes the process of getting a version of a document or list item in a list or library. By checking out an item or a file, a user can prevent others from editing that content. By checking in the item, the user can allow others to edit the content, without needing to worry about overriding changes that others have made.

Usually when an item or a file is checked out to a user, that user can work on that item or file, and other users cannot. Other users must wait for the user to check in the item or file again (that is, perform a check-in) before they can edit the item or file. While the item or file is checked out, other users usually can see only the last version that was checked in; they can't see the changes that the current user has made on the file while it's been checked out.

Pages in SharePoint can be in document libraries—and often are. This means that pages can be checked out and in, allowing page editors to change a page (for example, add or remove a web part), but the users cannot see the changes until that editor is happy with the changes and checks in the page.

> **NOTE** SharePoint does not require a check-in and check-out on all lists and libraries. This is a setting that the list or library manager can set.

When versioning is activated on a document library or list, a check-in creates a new version. See "What Are Versions?" earlier in this chapter.

What Is a Workflow?

In SharePoint, a workflow is a series of steps—some automatic, some manual—that must be performed as part of a business process for a document or a list item.

For example, the most common workflows for documents are review and approval. Some important documents (for example, contracts) need to go through several steps of approval from different people before they can be officially considered final and published. An example of starting such a workflow is shown in Figure 1.29.

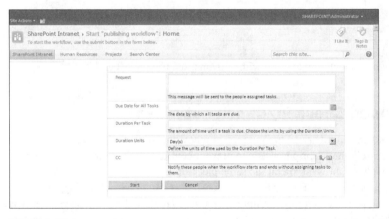

FIGURE 1.29
Starting an approval workflow to publish a page.

Another example is pages in a site itself. In some SharePoint environments, each change to a page needs to be approved by the site's manager to make sure the contents of the page comply with the company's policies.

SharePoint enables developers to develop workflows and attach them to documents or list items. End users might be expected to interact with a workflow, either approving documents or items or triggering a workflow to start or stop.

Chapter 11, "Workflows," covers the common tasks involved with workflows.

CHAPTER 2

Finding Your Way Around a SharePoint Site

IN THIS CHAPTER

This chapter shows you how to get around a SharePoint site, with some common tasks that you might want to do in every SharePoint site you use. It explains how to log on to a SharePoint site and the different navigation options in SharePoint sites.

Get to a SharePoint Site

Scenario/Problem: The most basic thing when working with SharePoint is getting to the SharePoint site and opening it.

Solution: How you get to a SharePoint site depends on the location of that site. Most often, your system administrator will give you the location. Your company might have several sites, and an administrator should supply you with links to the sites you should be aware of. Possible examples of such links are http://*portal* or http://*home* or http://*companyname*. In this book, we use http://sharepoint as the example link.

NOTE SharePoint sites can have subsites. If there is a subsite under sharepoint called sample, for example, the path to the site would be http://sharepoint/sample.

To get to the site itself, you open the link supplied to you in any Internet browser, such as Internet Explorer or Firefox.

Depending on the setup of the site itself, you might be prompted for a password. Because SharePoint often is configured to automatically identify you, it is very likely that you will not be prompted, and SharePoint will log you on with the user name and password you used when you logged on to your computer. If you are prompted, fill in the user name and password that your administrator advised you to use (see Figure 2.1).

FIGURE 2.1
The prompt for credentials when connecting to SharePoint.

If for some reason you do not have permissions to the SharePoint site you are trying to open, SharePoint displays an Access Denied page, telling you that you don't have permissions (see Figure 2.2). This page also allows you to sign in as a different user. When you click the link, you are prompted for a user name and password, which will be used to log you on to the site again.

FIGURE 2.2
The Access Denied screen.

Once you are logged on, the SharePoint site opens. SharePoint sites look different from one another, depending on the way the site mangers set up the sites.

Log On with Different Credentials

Scenario/Problem: Sometimes when you are viewing a SharePoint site, you might want to log on as a different user. For example, you might want to do this when you are using someone else's computer. That user is logged in, but you want to see the site with the permissions that you have for it.

Solution: After you have logged on to a SharePoint site, you might want to switch to a different user. You do this by clicking on the [*your name*] link at the top of the page to open a drop-down menu. Then select Sign In as a Different User from the options (see Figure 2.3). You are then prompted for your user name and password, as if you have not logged on to SharePoint before.

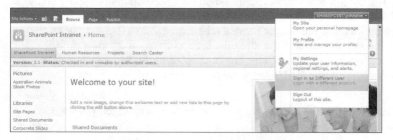

FIGURE 2.3
How to sign in as a different user.

If you change your mind and you want to again log on with the user name and password that you used to log on to your machine, you can either type in the user name and password or close the browser and open the site again.

Sign Out of a Site

Scenario/Problem: Sometimes when you are viewing a SharePoint site, you might want to sign out. For example, say that you logged on as a different user (see the preceding section) and you now want to sign out completely.

Solution: After you have logged on to a SharePoint site, you might want to sign out. You do this by clicking the [*your name*] link at the top of the page to open a drop-down menu, and then selecting Sign Out from the options (see Figure 2.4). After you click on that option, the window shows a message that you have been signed out, and it closes itself if your browser allows it to.

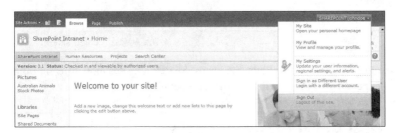

FIGURE 2.4
How to sign out of a site.

Use the Ribbon

Scenario/Problem: Any page in SharePoint may have several ribbons. While SharePoint attempts to detect what ribbon you need to see based on what you select in a page, you often need to manually switch to different ribbons to find the actions or the information that those other ribbons offer.

Solution: The control that allows you to switch between ribbons is usually shown at the top of the page, listing the names of the available ribbons as tabs. For example, in most pages, you see the tab for Browse (see Figure 2.5). (This tab shows the navigation ribbon that contains the site title, breadcrumbs, and top-level navigation. All these concepts are explained later in this chapter, in the section "Navigate Through a SharePoint Site.") This is the default ribbon in most scenarios.

To switch between ribbons, click on the name of the ribbon to which you want to switch. For example, when viewing a site's home page, you can usually switch to the Page ribbon to see buttons that allow you to e-mail a link to the page or make the page your browser's home page.

Some ribbons have several tabs in them, with each tab presenting different buttons. An example of this is the Calendar Tools ribbon in a calendar list. This ribbon has two tabs: Events and Calendar (see Figure 2.6). Because these tabs are also containers of buttons and look like all the other ribbons, we refer to them as *subribbons* in this book. To navigate to a subribbon, simply click on the title for that subribbon, the same way you would with a regular ribbon. The only difference is that you cannot click on the parent ribbon itself; you must click on one of the subribbons.

The ribbons provide links and buttons to different functionality. However, sometimes your screen is not big enough to display all the buttons that appear on a ribbon. This is why the ribbon is split into sections, as shown in Figure 2.6. The sections group various buttons and controls together.

The Browse ribbon, showing the
site's image and breadcrumbs on
the left and the tagging buttons
on the right side.

Buttons to switch to other available
ribbons in this page: Page, Publish,
Documents, and Library.

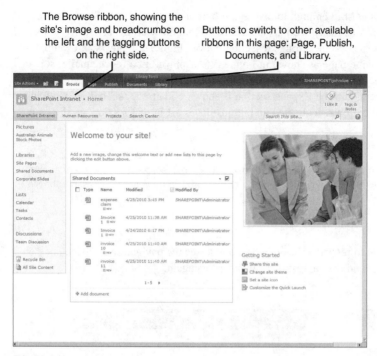

FIGURE 2.5

The ribbon interface, showing the Browse ribbon and buttons to switch to other available ribbons.

The Events and Calendar subribbons
are available as tabs under
the Calendar Tools ribbon.

The Share &
Track section

The Settings section

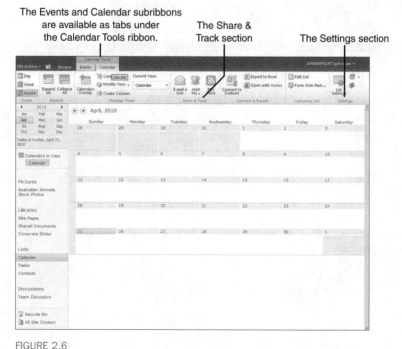

FIGURE 2.6

The Calendar Tools ribbon, with its two subribbons, Events and Calendar.

If the screen is not big enough to display all buttons in all sections, SharePoint automatically shrinks as many sections as needed so that the sections are still visible, and the buttons are accessible through a section button. Figure 2.7 shows an example of this, with the same page as shown in Figure 2.6 displayed in a much smaller screen. As you can see, the Scope section is compressed to display the buttons without their text next to them, and the Expand section is shown collapsed, as a button. Clicking on the Expand button reveals the two buttons that exist in that section, as shown in Figure 2.8.

> **NOTE** The images in this book were taken on a small screen to make them easier to read. If you have a bigger screen, the ribbons shown on your screen will probably show more buttons, and they will be bigger.

When you want to return to the default ribbon to see the navigation toolbars, click on the Browse tab, and the navigation ribbon appears again.

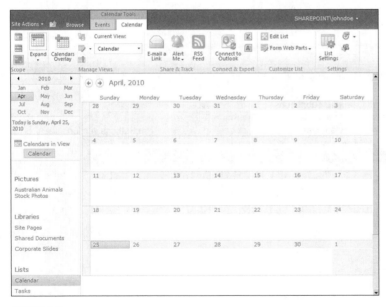

FIGURE 2.7
The Calendar subribbon, in a smaller screen, showing the Scope and Expand sections compressed to save screen space.

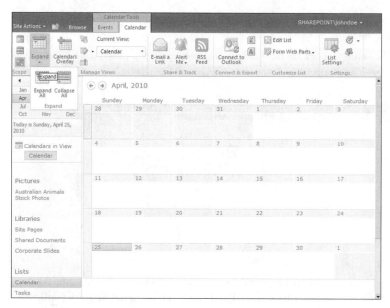

FIGURE 2.8
The Expand section as a drop-down button, showing the buttons under it when pressed.

Change My Regional Settings

Scenario/Problem: When you are working in an environment that has sites from all over the world, you might want to define in a specific site that you want the date formatting to appear in the way you are used to—for example, with the month before or after the day in a date. You also may want to show time data in your time zone, and not in the time zone that the site manager set. For example, when viewing a list of events, you may see an event scheduled to start at nine in the morning. But if the site was created by someone in Japan, and you are in the United States, you need to know if that time is based on the time zone in Japan or in your time zone.

Solution: Depending on the configuration of the site, you might be able to define in that site your own regional settings. Doing this changes the way the site is presented to you, without affecting anyone else viewing the site.

When you change the regional settings, you can define how you want dates and numbers to be shown to you, the default sort order that will be used in the site when you view lists, what calendar format you want to see, and how you want to define your work week days.

For example, in a calendar list of events, when the regional settings are set to Australian regional settings, the events are shown with the day before the month. But if you change the settings to the American regional settings, the date will show the month before the day, and the times for the events will change to show when the events occur in the selected time zone.

To change the settings, click on the [*your name*] link at the top of the page to open a drop-down menu and select My Settings (see Figure 2.9).

FIGURE 2.9
The My Settings link in the drop-down.

SharePoint opens a page showing your details as they are saved in the system. When you click on My Regional Settings, SharePoint opens the Regional Settings configuration screen, where you can choose the settings you want (see Figure 2.10). The default option is to always follow the settings defined for the website. Unless you clear this option, you will not be able to set any personal setting for yourself.

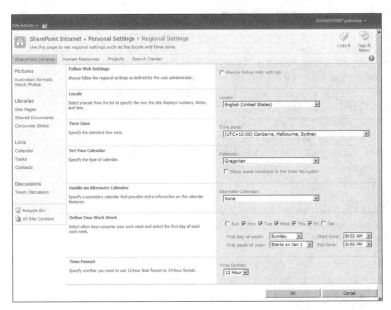

FIGURE 2.10
The Regional Settings page.

The following are the settings you can configure on this page after you disable the Always Follow Web Settings option:

- ▶ **Locale**—Sets the formats of dates, numbers, and sorting order.

- ▶ **Time Zone**—Sets your time zone so that times (for example, time for a meeting) will be displayed to you in your time zone.

- ▶ **Set Your Calendar**—Allows you to select a different calendar format (for example, the Jewish calendar or Arabic calendar) to be displayed instead of the default one.

- ▶ **Enable an Alternate Calendar**—Allows you to select alternative secondary calendar that will be displayed in addition to the default one.

- ▶ **Define Your Work Week**—Allows you to select your work week and working hours (which changes how calendars will be displayed to you).

- ▶ **Time Format**—Allows you to select whether the time format should be in 12-hour format (for example, 01:00 PM) or 24-hour format (for example, 13:00).

Change My Display Language

Scenario/Problem: All the SharePoint menus are in a language different from the one I am most comfortable with. I want to see the menus in my own language, while keeping the content in the language it was written in.

Solution: Sometimes in multinational organizations there are people who are more comfortable with languages other than English. While your content (documents, list items, and page information) is usually in one language as a standard, you might want to see the menus—the actions you can take—in a language that is more familiar to you.

SharePoint has an option for an administrator to install a "language pack" for different languages. When this is installed, users can choose what menu language they want the site to use. For example, an organization based in the United States may employ a lot of employees who are more comfortable with Spanish than with English. Allowing those employees to switch the language of a site's menus will help those employees be more productive; they'll be able to more easily find what they're looking for. Because this setting is user-based, it affects only the user in question, and not other users of the site. This does not change the content of the page—just menus such as the Site Actions menu and the menu that opens when the user clicks on the [*your name*] link. It also changes the commands on the ribbon menu that is displayed

To change a display language, click on the [*your name*] link at the top of the page. If the SharePoint administrator installed a language pack on the server, and the site manager chose to allow users to select an alternate language, the option Select Display Language appears, and when you move the mouse on top of it, you see the available languages for the site (see Figure 2.11).

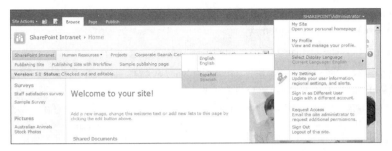

FIGURE 2.11
The Select Display Language menu shows the installed languages you can choose for your display.

When you chose a language, you see all the menus in that language. Depending on what the site manager chose, you might also see certain labels, such as the site's title and description, in the newly chosen language (see Figure 2.12).

FIGURE 2.12
When the display language is changed to Spanish, the title of the page and of some of the list names appear in Spanish.

To switch back to the original language, you perform these actions again and select your original language. Notice that each language in the Select Display Language menu shows up both in the currently selected language and in that language, so even if you change to a language that uses characters you don't understand, reverting to your own language is simple.

Navigate Through a SharePoint Site

Scenario/Problem: Information is the focus of a SharePoint site. Each site may contain different information in different places. You need to know how to navigate a site to find the information you need.

Solution: This section explains the different mechanisms that help you navigate through a site. Most sites use the navigation ribbon (also known as the Browse ribbon) to show navigation controls on the top of the page—including a top navigation bar and the breadcrumbs. Often there is also a side navigation bar that shows more navigation options on the left of the page.

A site manager can change the navigation bars to show different links to different parts of the site. The navigation bars should be your primary source of information about what you can view in the site.

Figure 2.13 shows an example of a site that shows both navigation bars, along with two other navigational aids—the breadcrumbs and the Navigate Up button. In this figure, the top navigation bar shows links to subsites that exist under the current site.

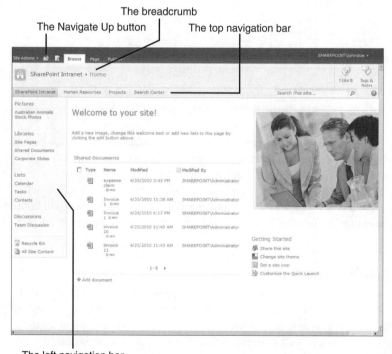

FIGURE 2.13

The four navigational aids: the Navigate Up button, the breadcrumbs, the top navigation bar, and the left navigation bar.

Sometimes the navigation in a site is configured to display the pages and/or the subsites of the subsites, resulting in a hierarchy of sites that is displayed as flyout menus. These menus show the subsites for a site when you hover the mouse over the link for that site, as shown in Figure 2.14.

FIGURE 2.14
The top navigation bar, showing flyout menus for the subsites under the Human Resources site

To navigate to a subsite, you can click on the links to that subsite in either navigation bar. Depending on how your administrator set up the navigation, the subsites may show the same top navigation bar but a different left navigation bar—one that is specific to the current site. However, the administrator can choose that a subsite will display the same left navigation as the top site, making it look as if you are still in the same site, except for the fact that the current site you are on is highlighted in the top navigation bar.

Use the Left Navigation Bar

The left navigation bar is also known as Current Navigation. It is usually used to show content that exists in the current site and sometimes content from subsites. The content is usually (but not always) lists and libraries, and it is usually grouped so that document libraries are shown under a Documents header, lists under a Lists header, discussions under a Discussions header, and so on.

The left navigation bar highlights where you are in the navigation—but only when you are on a page that is shown in the navigation (see Figure 2.15).

The parent site of the current site is highlighted in the top navigation bar.

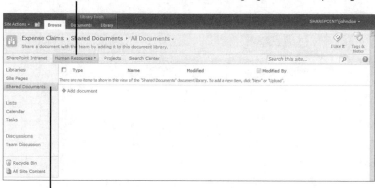

The current document library is highlighted in the left navigation bar.

FIGURE 2.15
The left navigation bar with the current document library highlighted.

The left navigation bar is meant to be used as a quick launch bar—a useful list of links in the current site, and sometimes the sites under it. It may even contain links to content that isn't in SharePoint (for example, an Internet site).

> **NOTE** Some sites and some pages do not show a left navigation bar. In that case, you have to rely on the information on the page to find your way around the site.

Use the Top Navigation Bar

The top navigation bar is also known as Global Navigation, and it is usually used to show links to sites that are at the top level of the site hierarchy. This allows you to quickly see what important sites the site administrator wants you to see that are available globally.

This menu bar supports flyout menus. These are menus that become visible when you hover with the mouse over the parent menu item. You can sometimes tell when menus have flyout menus because they are usually marked with a triangle pointing to the direction in which the flyout menu opens.

> **TIP** The top navigation bar can be customized to show many levels of sites, and sometimes other links. If you see the small triangles or arrows, hover over them with your mouse to find out what navigation items are under them.

Use the Breadcrumbs

Breadcrumbs is a mechanism commonly used to navigate websites. It shows you where you are in the site, so you can go "up" the hierarchy all the way to the home page of the site. For example, if you are viewing a folder in a document library, the bread-crumbs will show you the list of folders that are above the current folder, and then a link to the document library's root folder, and then the link to the site's home page as the first link (see Figure 2.16).

The breadcrumbs showing where you are in the Expense Claims site.

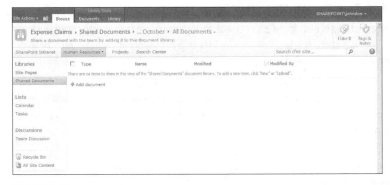

FIGURE 2.16
The breadcrumbs navigation interface for the Expense Claims 2007 folder in the
Shared Documents library in the Expense Claims site.

In some cases (usually with pages in pages libraries), the breadcrumbs do not show that
the page is under a library, but instead display as if the page is directly under the site
itself.

If the hierarchy is too long to be displayed in one line—for example, if you navigate
into the October folder shown in Figure 2.16—the breadcrumbs are automatically
compressed to fit the screen (similarly to the way the ribbons are compressed) and
show only the last item and whatever else fits before it, as shown in Figure 2.17.

FIGURE 2.17
The breadcrumbs in the October folder are compressed to show fewer links in order to fit on
the page.

To use the breadcrumbs, just click on the link you want to navigate to.

TIP When you're in a document library that has folders, using the breadcrumbs is
the best way to go back to the parent folder of the one you are currently in.

Use the Navigate Up Breadcrumbs

In addition to the navigation bars and the breadcrumbs, SharePoint 2010 also has a button dedicated to navigation, called the Navigate Up button. This button solves the problem of very long breadcrumbs. As mentioned earlier, if you are in a folder in a document library with a lot of parent folders, the breadcrumbs may get too long to display the entire hierarchy.

You can usually find the Navigate Up button in the top-left corner of the page (see Figure 2.18). It appears as a folder icon with a green arrow pointing up. Clicking on that button does not take you up but instead shows you a hierarchical view of breadcrumbs showing you where you are on the site and allowing you to navigate up, the same as the breadcrumbs mechanism described earlier in this chapter.

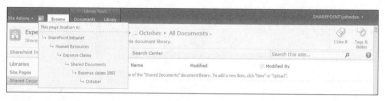

FIGURE 2.18
Using the Navigate Up button allows you to follow the breadcrumb trail all the way to the top site.

The Navigate Up breadcrumbs differ from the normal breadcrumbs navigation mentioned earlier in this chapter in two major ways. First, they show the entire hierarchy all the up to the root site in the site collection, and not just to the current site. For example, if you have a site called Expense Claims inside the Human Resources site, the Navigate Up breadcrumbs show Human Resources above Expense Claims in the hierarchy. Figure 2.18 shows the Navigate Up menu for the October folder shown in Figure 2.17.

Second, compared to the regular breadcrumbs, the Navigate Up breadcrumbs offer more hierarchy detail for pages. Unlike the breadcrumbs mentioned earlier, the Navigate Up breadcrumbs display the entire hierarchy structure for the page you are viewing. For example, if you are viewing a web part page in a pages library, the normal breadcrumbs will show the site name as the parent for the page, while the Navigate Up breadcrumbs show you the library the page is in as the parent of the page. This allows you to go to the library as well as to the site, but it can make the hierarchy in this control very long if the page you are viewing is deep inside the hierarchy.

CHAPTER 3

Solutions Regarding Files, Documents, List Items, and Forms

SharePoint is most commonly used to store information in the forms of either list items or files (which can be documents, forms, or any other type of file).

This chapter explains how to perform common tasks in SharePoint that you as an end user would need to know, such as creating list items, viewing files and their properties, and setting up alerts that let you know when there are new files or list items or when specific files or list items have been modified.

Most importantly, this chapter also covers how to switch between list views so you can see the content in a list in various different ways and therefore find the content you are looking for more easily.

If you are looking for more author-oriented tasks, such as uploading files or creating new list items, see Chapter 6, "Creating and Managing Files, List Items, and Forms in SharePoint."

See What Lists and Document Libraries Are in a Site

Scenario/Problem: When you're in a SharePoint site, you often want to see what is beyond the home page of the site. What document libraries are there to store information, and what lists and surveys exist?

Solution: There are several ways to see what lists and document libraries are available in a site. The following sections demonstrate how you can use various methods to view the content of a site.

Use Direct Links in the Left Navigation Bar

Site managers can use the left navigation bar to show various links in different categories. Document libraries are usually shown under the Documents header, and lists are usually under the Lists header, as shown in Figure 3.1.

View All Lists and Libraries

Not all the document libraries and lists are shown in the navigation bar. Which ones are shown depends on how the site administrator set up the navigation bar.

To see all the libraries and lists available, you use the All Site Content link in the left navigation bar (refer to Figure 3.1). SharePoint takes you to the All Site Content page, which lists all the content in the site. The document libraries are displayed under the Document Libraries header, and the lists are displayed below the Lists header, as shown in Figure 3.2.

A link to a picture library
    A link to a document library
        A link to a calendar list

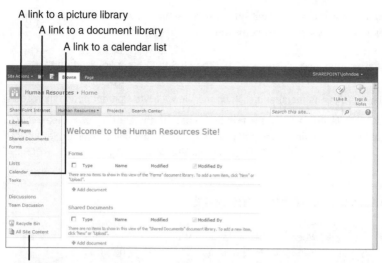

A link to see all available lists and libraries

FIGURE 3.1
The left navigation bar's links to document libraries and lists.

All document libraries in the site

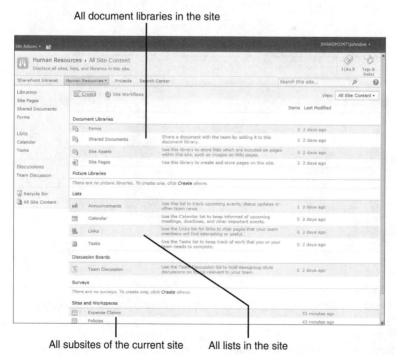

All subsites of the current site   All lists in the site

FIGURE 3.2
The All Site Content page.

You click on the link to the document library to view the documents in them, or you click the link to a list to see the list items in it.

NOTE If the site has been customized and the All Site Content link isn't on the page, you can try to get to this page by using one of the following methods:

▶ Open the Site Actions menu and click on the View All Site Content option there.

▶ Type _layouts/viewlsts.aspx at the end of the path to the site. For example, if your site is at http://sharepoint/sample, you type http://sharepoint/sample/_layouts/viewlsts.aspx in your browser to get to the All Site Content page.

Open a Document for Reading

Scenario/Problem: When viewing a document library, either in the home page or in a library view, you must open a document to see its contents.

Solution: When you're in a document library, just click on the link to the document you are interested in (see Figure 3.3). Depending on your machine's configuration, the document opens either in a new window or in the associated application (Word documents open in Word, Excel workbooks open in Excel, and so on).

FIGURE 3.3
Open a document for reading by clicking the document's file name in the document library.

Also, depending on the installed applications on your machine and on the level of permissions you have, you might be prompted to make a choice about how to open the file (see Figure 3.4). To read the file, click Read Only, and then click OK.

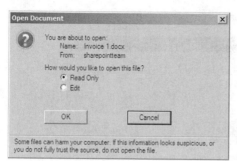

FIGURE 3.4

Choose Read Only to open the document for reading.

View Properties of a Document

Scenario/Problem: When viewing a document library in either a web part on the home page or in one of the list views of that library, you might want to see more details about a document before choosing what to do with it. These details may include who wrote the document, its subject, and maybe additional pieces of metadata describing the document (for example, the client it was written for, the date it expires).

Solution: There are two ways to view the properties of a document: You can use the ribbon interface or use a drop-down menu.

Using the Documents Ribbon

To view the metadata of a file by using the ribbon, you click on the row for that file—but not on the link to the file itself. If you find it difficult to do this, you can hover the mouse over the file's row. The row is highlighted, and you see on the left a checkbox that allows you to select the file more easily.

When you select a file, the Documents ribbon is displayed at the top of the screen, as shown in Figure 3.5. Click the View Properties button to view the file's properties.

In some views, the check box interface is not available, and you cannot use the ribbon interface. In such a case, you need to use a drop-down menu, as described in the following section.

Using a Drop-down Menu

To view the metadata of a particular file, move your mouse over the link to the document. An option to open a drop-down appears (see Figure 3.6).

The View Properties button

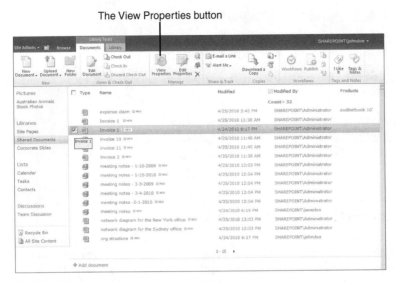

FIGURE 3.5
Selecting a single file by using the check box to the left of the file.

Click the arrow to open the drop-down menu.

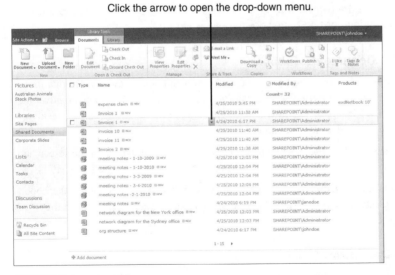

FIGURE 3.6
Hovering over the file's name uncovers the arrow for the drop-down menu for a file.

If you click on the drop-down arrow, a menu opens (see Figure 3.7). The choices in the menu depend on the permissions you have on the file, on the applications installed on your computer, and on the applications installed in SharePoint. You may see more or fewer options than Figure 3.7 shows—and each file may present you with a different menu.

The View Properties option

FIGURE 3.7
Choose View Properties from the menu to view the file's properties.

Click on View Properties to open the properties page, which shows all the properties the document has.

> **NOTE** When you set properties on a file, the properties are copied into the file itself. When you upload a file to a document library that has properties with the same names as the file's properties, they are copied back. This means that if you download a file and then upload it to a different document library that has the same properties, the data of the properties is retained.

Send a Link to a File by E-mail

> **Scenario/Problem:** When viewing a document library, you may want to select a single file in that library and send a link to someone via e-mail.

Solution: You can e-mail a link to a file by using either the Documents ribbon or the drop-down menu for the file. In the ribbon, click the E-mail a Link button, which appears next to an envelope icon (see Figure 3.8). On the drop-down, select Send To and then E-mail a Link, as shown in Figure 3.9.

The E-mail a Link button

FIGURE 3.8

The E-mail a Link button in the Documents ribbon is enabled when you select a single document.

FIGURE 3.9

The Send To menu has the E-mail a Link option in the drop-down menu.

When you click on the E-mail a Link button or menu option, your default e-mail application opens a new message with a link to the document. You can choose who to send the link to and send the message as you would any other e-mail.

Download a File to Your Computer

Scenario/Problem: When viewing a document library, you might want to select a single file in that library and download it to your local computer.

Solution: You can download a file either by selecting the document and clicking the Download a Copy button in the Documents ribbon (refer to Figure 3.8) or by using the Download a Copy option from the Send To menu in the drop-down menu for that file. To do so, open the drop-down menu for the file you want to save to your computer (refer to Figure 3.6) and in the menu that opens (refer to Figure 3.7), select Send To, and then select Download a Copy option under that menu, as shown in Figure 3.9.

Tag a Document, List Item, or Page

Scenario/Problem: You find that a specific document, list item, or page is very useful to you, and you want to be able to mark it so that you can easily find it in the future. You also might want to share this mark with other people.

Solution: As mentioned in Chapter 1, "About Microsoft SharePoint 2010," tagging is a useful mechanism that helps you more quickly find content. This mechanism is available only in SharePoint 2010 Server, not in SPF.

TIP Tagging is not just for highlighting something as useful. There are many different uses for tagging! For example, you might want to tag some documents and items as "unhelpful," or "redundant," or maybe "not relevant." Doing so will allow you to compile a list of documents that you think should be removed, and you can then report them to the site manager.

When tagging an item, you can write basically anything that you want that will help you find that item later on. Then, when you go to your personal site, you can see the phrases that you used and the documents you tagged with those phrases. You also will be able to use the tags when searching for documents, items, and pages. (For more information, see Chapter 4, "Searching in SharePoint.") Tagging can target a document, a list item, a page, or even sites—including external sites.

For example, if you tag two documents in different sites with the phrase "my important presentations," and another document with the phrase "a template for invoices," when you go to your personal site, you will have a page showing you the two phrases, and when you click on one of them, you see links to the documents you tagged with that phrase.

For more information about how to use the tags in personal sites, see Chapter 5, "Social Networking, Personal Sites, and Personal Details in SharePoint Server."

By default, in SharePoint Server there is a shortcut button that allows you to quickly tag a document with the phrase I Like It (see Figure 3.10). This shortcut is available on the Documents ribbon. If you select a document or an item and click on the I Like It button, the document or item is automatically tagged with the phrase "I Like It."

The Tags & Notes button

The I Like It tag button

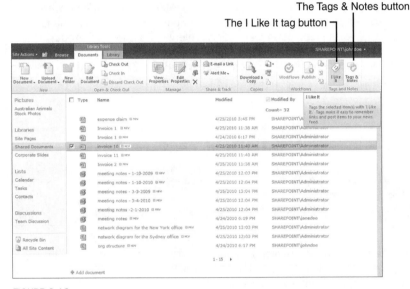

FIGURE 3.10

After Selecting a single document, you can click on either the I Like It or the Tags & Notes buttons.

> **TIP** You can tag multiple documents or list items with the I Like It button by selecting those documents and clicking the button. However, the Tags & Notes button works on a single selection at a time.

> **NOTE** Some views do not allow you to select an item or a file (that is, no check boxes are available). In those views, to tag a file or an item, open the properties page for that file or item and tag that page instead. See "View Properties of a Document," earlier in this chapter, and "View Properties of a List Item," later in this chapter, for detailed instructions on how to get to that page.

To tag an item or a file with a different phrase, select the row for that document or item (see "Using the Documents Ribbon," earlier in this chapter, for a detailed description of how to do that) to show the Documents ribbon for that document or item. When it is open, you see the two tagging buttons on the right side of the ribbon, as shown in Figure 3.10.

If you click the Tags & Notes button, a window appears, showing the tags that you and other users have attached to the document or item (see Figure 3.11).

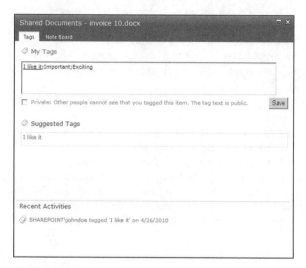

FIGURE 3.11
The tagging dialog, showing the Tags tab.

To write a tag, type the tag's text in the text box and click Save. Alternatively, you can click on a tag from the Suggested Tags list at the bottom of the dialog to quickly add tags that you or others have used in the site most frequently. You can add separate tags by using the semicolon character to separate them. For example, writing "Important; Exciting" tags the item with the two separate words "Important" and "Exciting." The My Tags box at the top shows the tags that are already set on the file or item. (In Figure 3.11, for example, you can see the "I Like It" tag underlined, which means the document was tagged with that tag by the current user.) You can choose to make a tag private so other people will not see it.

When you click Save, the tags you added become underlined to signify that they have been added. You can close the dialog by clicking the X button in the top-right corner. When you open the dialog again, you see the same tags, and the Recent Activities list on the bottom of the dialog shows the date you added the tags.

> **TIP** It is possible to tag a page in SharePoint, but not all pages show the buttons that allow you to tag it. Pages that do allow this usually have the buttons as part of the navigation ribbon. If you cannot find the link, you can still tag the page by using the instructions in the following section.

Tag an External Site

Scenario/Problem: You find a site that is very useful; however, this site is not hosted in SharePoint, and it's not even part of your corporate site. You want to be able to find it again using the tagging mechanism. For example, say that you are tagging documents that are important for your day-to-day work as "Useful for my project," so that you can access them quickly from one location in your personal site. You also might want to add an Internet site to the list of useful items for the project.

Solution: In SharePoint Server 2010, you can tag any link from any site, whether it is hosted in SharePoint or not. To be able to tag external sites, you need to open the tagging dialog by using the Tags & Notes button on the Browse ribbon. SharePoint opens the tagging dialog in page tagging mode, and it provides a link that says "Right click or drag and drop this link to your browser's favorites or bookmarks toolbar to tag external sites," as shown in Figure 3.12. Follow the instructions in the dialog to add the sites to your browser's favorites, and then you are ready to tag external sites.

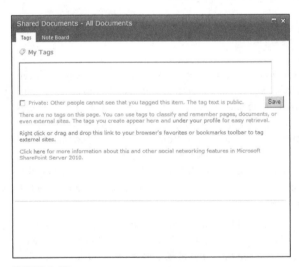

FIGURE 3.12
The tagging dialog, when opened from the Browse ribbon, shows the option to add a special link to your browser's favorites for tagging external sites.

When you want to tag an external site's page with a tag, browse to that page, open your browser's favorites, and click on the link you added. SharePoint directs you to the same tagging dialog you saw earlier in this chapter that allows you to tag the page or site. You also can view or add notes to it, as described in the following section.

View/Add Notes to a Document or List Item

Scenario/Problem: You want to see whether there are any notes about a document or a list item, and you want to add notes about a document or list item.

Solution: In SharePoint Server 2010, you can add notes to a document. These notes are available for other people to read. You can use this feature, for example, to provide feedback on a document without actually changing the document and without having to check out the document or even have editing permissions to the document.

To add notes to a document, select the document in the web part or list view that displays the document to switch to the Documents ribbon. In the ribbon, find and click the Tags & Notes button to open the tagging dialog. In the dialog, select the Note Board tab. This tab allows you to type notes about the document or view notes that other users wrote for that document, as shown in Figure 3.13.

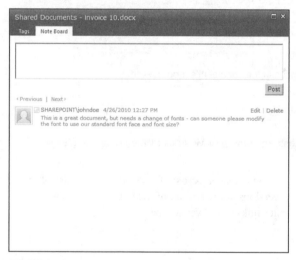

FIGURE 3.13
The Note Board tab of the tagging dialog. Existing notes are shown, with options to edit or delete them.

View Past Versions of Documents

Scenario/Problem: Some document libraries support versioning, which means that every time a file in the library changes, the old version is stored. Sometimes you might want to view an old version of a document without restoring it to be the current version.

Solution: To view the past versions of a specific document, select the document to switch to the Documents ribbon, and then click on the Version History button. Alternatively, you can open the drop-down menu for the file and choose Version History from the menu (see Figure 3.14).

The Version History button in the Documents ribbon

The Version History option in the document's drop-down menu

FIGURE 3.14
The two options to view the versions of a file.

The version history dialog opens, showing past versions of the document (see Figure 3.15).

By default, the Version History dialog displays the list of versions in the order of the version number, with the earlier versions at the bottom of the list. You can change the sort order by clicking on the header links of the version table.

The third (and last) version of the file

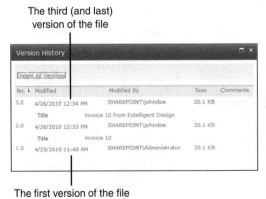

The first version of the file

FIGURE 3.15
The Version History dialog, showing the three versions of a file.

The versions are shown as dates, representing the date the version was created. If you hover the mouse over one of these dates, you can open a menu for the document that allows you to view the version (see Figure 3.16).

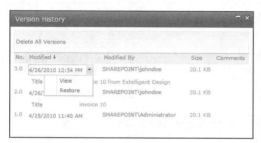

FIGURE 3.16

The drop-down menu for a version appears if you hover over the date for that version and click the arrow. In the menu you can choose to view the selected version.

View Properties of a List Item

Scenario/Problem: The list views or web parts might not show all the columns defined in a list. When you're viewing a list in either a web part on the home page or in one of the list views of that list, you may want to see more details about a list item. For example, a web part or a list view showing a contact list item may show only the contact's first and last names, and you might want to see more details about the contact, such as the address and phone number.

Solution: When viewing in a list view or a web part, you can click on the title of the list item to see its details. Alternatively, use the View Item button in the Items ribbon or select View Item from the item's drop-down (similarly to viewing a document's properties).

The View Item button in the Items ribbon
(available only when you select an item)

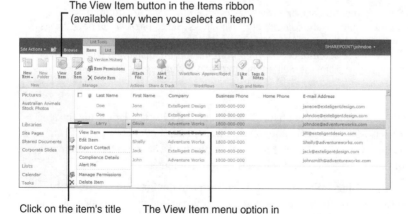

Click on the item's title   The View Item menu option in
to open the properties   the item's dropdown menu
page for that item.

FIGURE 3.17

The drop-down menu for a list item, showing actions that readers can perform, including View Item and the Items ribbon.

Either method opens a properties page showing the metadata of the list item, with all its properties.

View a Microsoft InfoPath Form

Scenario/Problem: As explained in Chapter 1, form libraries are used to host Microsoft InfoPath forms. In many cases, you will want to open one of the forms in a form library to view its contents.

Solution: The form libraries behave much the same as document libraries. Viewing a Microsoft InfoPath form that is in a form library is very much like opening a document for reading: You just click on the link that is the form name (see Figure 3.18).

FIGURE 3.18
A form library with two forms. Click on the name of the form to open it.

NOTE Some forms are configured to allow the data that is in the form to be displayed as a column in the form library. This allows you to preview the data that is in the form without opening it. It can also help you more easily find a specific form. In Figure 3.18, you can see that certain data from the form is displayed, such as the total of the expense claim, as well as the start and end dates for the expense claims.

If the site you are using does not have SharePoint Server installed, or if the form or form library has not been configured to make forms open in the browser, clicking on a form opens it on your computer in Microsoft InfoPath. If you don't have Microsoft InfoPath installed, the form just downloads to your computer.

If the site is using SharePoint Server, and the form and the form library are both configured to show the form in the browser, then clicking on the form opens it using the browser interface.

To close the form and go back to the form library, either close the Microsoft InfoPath application (if the form was opened with the application) or click on the Close link on the top of the form if it was opened in the browser.

Change Sorting and Filtering of a List or Library

Scenario/Problem: In a large document library or a list, finding the piece of information you are looking for can be tricky. To help you find what you are after, you might want to sort a specific column differently from its default sorting order or filter a column on a specific value. For example, in a document library, you might want to sort the documents based on the date they were changed so you can easily see the last one that was changed. Or in a contacts list you might want to filter the Last Name column to display only people with the last name Doe.

Solution: When viewing a list or a document library, there are several ways to change the view to find the specific item or document you want. The following sections discuss the possibilities.

NOTE The changes you make are not permanent. Only you see them, and when you close the browser and navigate to the list again, the default sort order and filters that the list manager has defined are applied again.

To learn how to save a sort order or filter, see Chapter 8, "Creating List Views."

Sort

To sort a list view on a specific field, click on the heading for that field. Clicking on the field header causes the list to be sorted based on that field, either in ascending or descending order. A small arrow appears to signify the sort order. Using this mechanism, you can only sort based on one field at a time.

Another way to define the sort order is to open the column's drop-down menu and click on the sort order you want.

Filter

To filter on a column, move your mouse over the heading for that column. This causes a drop-down menu to appear. Click on the drop-down menu and choose the filter value from the list (see Figure 3.19).

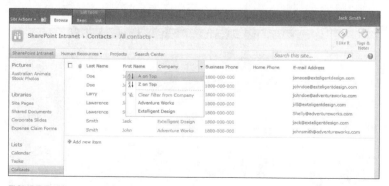

FIGURE 3.19
Choosing the sort order for the Company column in a contacts list.

NOTE When there are many items to display in the filter options drop-down, SharePoint does not automatically display them in the menu. Instead, you see a button that allows you to load the items. This prevents you from waiting for the long list of items to load if you just want to sort the list and not filter it.

Switch List Views in Lists and Libraries

Scenario/Problem: Most lists and libraries have different list views that show different columns and apply different sort orders, filters, and styles. Switching to a different list view may help you more easily find information in the list or library.

Solution: There are two ways to switch views. First, in the regular navigation ribbon, you can click on the name of the view in the breadcrumbs to see the options of other views for that list (see Figure 3.20).

FIGURE 3.20
Click on the name of the view in the breadcrumbs to show other views you can switch to.

Alternatively, in most lists you can switch to the List or Library ribbon. In the ribbon, locate the Current View drop-down, which is usually to the left of the E-mail a Link button. When you open this drop-down, you see the names of all the views that are available for you in the list (see Figure 3.21).

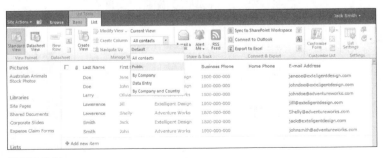

FIGURE 3.21
The view selector drop-down in the List ribbon.

NOTE The ribbon name may change depending on the type of list or library. For example, in calendar lists, the name of the ribbon is Calendar, while in most other lists, the name of the ribbon is List.

These views are either public views (that everyone sees on that list) or a private view that you have created for yourself. For more information on list views, see Chapter 1 and Chapter 8. To switch to the view you want, click on the view name that you want, and the view changes.

TIP Investigate the different views. Some views may be more efficient and helpful for you to quickly find data. There are some things you can do beyond filtering and sorting that you can do only by creating views, so take a look at your options.

Some special instances of views have subviews, which offer other ways to see the same view. For example, in calendar views you can switch between the daily subview, the weekly subview (see Figure 3.22), and the monthly subview by using buttons on the ribbon. These subviews show the information that is defined in the view itself (filtering the items, ordering the items) but in a different manner.

To switch between the subviews of a calendar view, you use the Day, Week, and Month links in the Calendar ribbon when in a calendar view.

The available subviews of a calendar view

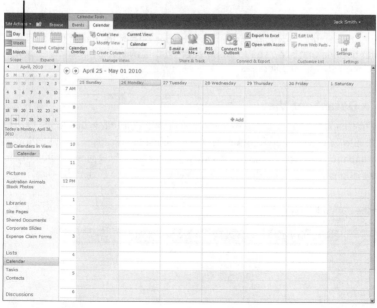

FIGURE 3.22
The weekly subview of a calendar.

Picture libraries also have subviews, but to access them you have to open the view selector, as shown in Figure 3.23. The Details, Thumbnails, and Filmstrip views show the same data in different ways.

FIGURE 3.23
Picture libraries offer subviews for each view.

> **NOTE** Both picture libraries and surveys are unique in that they do not offer ribbons (at the time of this writing). Instead, these two list types offer a toolbar at the top of the page with buttons that allow you to do most of what is available in the corresponding ribbons in other lists and libraries.

Switch to a Datasheet View

As explained in Chapter 1, the datasheet view is a special type of view that looks like a spreadsheet. It allows you to copy information from the list to spreadsheet applications or do some calculations on data in the list. To switch to the datasheet view, switch to the List or Library ribbon and click on the Datasheet View button (see Figure 3.24).

The Datasheet View button

FIGURE 3.24
The Datasheet View button in the List ribbon.

The New Row button
The Show Task Pane button

The Show Totals button
The Refresh Data button

FIGURE 3.25

The datasheet view, showing the list in a spreadsheet format with additional special buttons available in the view.

As shown in Figure 3.25, the datasheet view displays all the columns from the standard view.

Add Totals Calculations to the Datasheet View

If you want to calculate data in the datasheet view, you can add totals to the view by switching to the List or Library ribbon and clicking the Show Totals button (refer to Figure 3.25). This way, you can add a totals row to the view, with options to perform mathematical calculations on the items in the view.

After you add the totals row, any numeric column is automatically calculated with a sum, so that the sum of the values in that column is displayed in the totals row (see Figure 3.26).

FIGURE 3.26

The Sale Price column showing a total for the values of all items in the view.

You can choose the type of mathematical calculation for each column by clicking on the cell at the bottom of the column (see Figure 3.27). For numeric columns, this includes the sum (which is displayed by default), the average (which shows the average of all the values in the view), the maximum (largest value in the view), the minimum (smallest value in the view), and more.

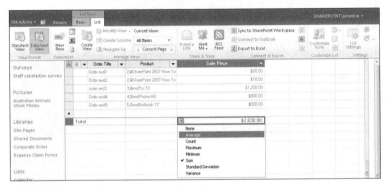

FIGURE 3.27
Numeric columns can do many different calculations.

For non-numeric columns, you can choose the Count calculation to see how many values there are (see Figures 3.28 and 3.29). If you have 20 list items in the view, the count shows 20 as the total.

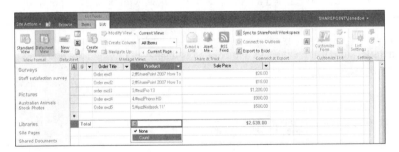

FIGURE 3.28
Non-numeric columns can only have the Count total.

FIGURE 3.29
The Count total shows the number of items.

Use Alerts

Scenario/Problem: Information in sites changes often. Lists and libraries get updated with new items or files, and existing items and files get updated or deleted. Often, you need to know whether something important to you is changed or updated. For example, if a document containing a policy that heavily impacts your work is updated, you want to know immediately. Or if a new list item is entered into a contacts list used to track potential customers, you want to know about it so you can call the customer.

Solution: You can set up alerts that notify you when some changes are made in SharePoint document libraries or lists or on single items. When you create an alert, you are asking the system to send you an e-mail or send a text message (SMS) to your mobile phone when a specific change occurs. The following sections explain how you can create alerts on different kinds of data and how to manage your alerts.

NOTE Alerts by text messages (SMS) to mobile phones requires special configuration by the administrator, so that option might not be available to you.

Create an Alert

You can create an alert on a file or a list item and also on a library or list. The following sections provide the details of how to perform each task.

Create an Alert on a File or List Item

When you set up an alert on a document or list item, SharePoint e-mails you when changes are made to that document or item. To set this type of alert, select the document or list item to switch to the Documents or Items ribbon. On the ribbon, click the Alert Me button and select Set Alert on This Document or Set Alert on This Item (see Figure 3.30).

The Alert Me button

FIGURE 3.30
The Alert Me button in the Documents ribbon when a document is selected.

Alternatively, if you are unable to select a file or a list item because the view does not allow it, open the drop-down dialog for that file or list item and select Alert Me from the menu (see Figure 3.31).

FIGURE 3.31
The Alert Me option in the drop-down menu for a file.

When you select this option, the New Alert dialog appears, and in it you can define what sort of alert you want to get on the item (see Figure 3.32). If your site supports sending text messages, you can select to have the alert sent using a text message to a phone number in the Delivery Method section of the dialog.

FIGURE 3.32
The New Alert dialog for a file, showing options for a new alert.

Under the Send Alert for These Changes section, you have multiple options to choose from. For example, you can choose to be notified just when someone else changes the item or whenever the item is changed (even when you're the one who changes it). The other options in this section are not relevant for alerts on documents and items.

NOTE Different list types have different options in the Send Alert for These Changes section. For example, a calendar list has an option to get an alert when the time or location for an event is changed.

In the When to Send Alerts section, you can define when the e-mail for a change will be sent. If you choose Immediately, an e-mail is sent to you whenever someone changes the document—one e-mail per change. Selecting a daily or weekly summary reduces the number of e-mails you get; you receive only a summary e-mail of all the changes.

After selecting the options that you want, a confirmation e-mail is sent to you to tell you that the alert has been set up. Receiving this message may take a few minutes.

Create an Alert on a Library or List

When you set up an alert on a list or library, SharePoint sends you an e-mail or a text message when changes are made to the list or library (that is, when items are added, removed, or changed).

To set up this type of alert, switch to the List or Library ribbon, click on the Alert Me button, and choose Set Alert on This List or Set Alert on This Library (see Figure 3.33).

FIGURE 3.33
The Alert Me button in the Library ribbon opens a menu with Set Alert on This Library option.

When you select this option, the settings dialog for the alert appears, and in it you can define what sort of alert you want to get. If your site supports sending text messages, you can select to have the alert sent using a text message to a phone number in the Delivery Method section of the dialog.

In the Change Type section, you can choose what kind of change you want to be alerted on. For example, you can select to be alerted only when new items are added, only when items are deleted, or when anything happens (that is, for all changes).

Similarly to setting up an alert on a list item, you can choose when the alert will be sent—either immediately or as a daily or weekly summary.

> **NOTE** Different list types can have different options in the Send Alert for These Changes section. For example, a task list has an option to send an alert when a high-priority task changes or when someone changes a task in a specific view. This allows you to create more complex alerts for different list types.

After you create an alert, you get a confirmation e-mail. Alert e-mails for lists look exactly the same as alerts on list items.

> **TIP** Don't forget that alerts can be annoying if you get too many e-mails. Creating an alert on a "busy" document library and setting it to e-mail you immediately on every change can overload your mailbox. Consider the daily or weekly e-mail options unless you really need to know about new documents or changes as they happen.

Modify or Remove an Alert

To modify or remove an alert, click on the Modify My Alert Settings link that the alert sends to you. Doing so opens the site where that alert was created, in the alert management screen. In this screen you can either click on an alert to change its settings (for example, when it should send the e-mail, what changes it should alert on), or you can select the alert and delete it by using the Delete Selected Alerts button.

Alternatively, you can browse to the list or library on which the alert is set, switch to the List or Library ribbon, click the Alert Me button, and select Manage My Alerts. This opens the same dialog, allowing you to edit or delete any of the alerts you have set in that site.

Manage My Alerts in a Site

To see what alerts you have in a site and manage them without going through a list, as you've done up to this point, you can navigate to the site and click on the [*your name*] button at the top of the page. Then select the My Settings option from the drop-down menu (see Figure 3.34).

FIGURE 3.34
Select My Settings from the [*your name*] menu.

The page that opens shows you your user information. Click on My Alerts in the toolbar to open the alert management screen for the site (see Figure 3.35).

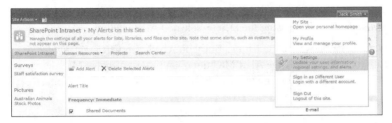

FIGURE 3.35
The alert management page allows you to click on an alert to edit it or select an alert to delete it.

> **TIP** A quick way to get to the alert management page is to add _layouts/ mysubs.aspx to the path to the site where the alerts are set. For example, if the site containing your alert is at http://sharepoint/sample, type http://sharepoint/ sample/_layouts/mysubs.aspx to get to the alerts page.

Export the Contents of a List to Microsoft Excel

> **Scenario/Problem:** You might want to take a snapshot of a SharePoint list and copy its contents to a Microsoft Excel spreadsheet, either to analyze the data or to print it using Excel.

Solution: You can export the contents of a list or a document library to an Excel Spreadsheet by clicking the Export to Excel button under the List or Library ribbons, as shown in Figure 3.36. The export opens a new Excel spreadsheet with the meta-data of the list or library. In the case of document libraries this does not export the files themselves, just the columns of data about the files.

The Export to Excel button

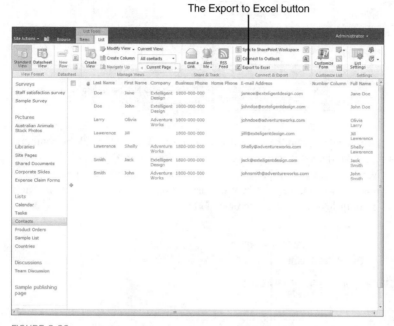

FIGURE 3.36
The Export to Excel button in the List ribbon for a contacts list.

When you click the button, a File Download dialog appears asking you whether you want to save or open the file, as shown in Figure 3.37. The file that is being downloaded is a query file that has instructions for Microsoft Excel. These instructions tell Excel where the list is and what columns to get from the list. Click Open to open the query file in Excel and view the results.

FIGURE 3.37
The File Download dialog when exporting a list to Excel.

After clicking Open, Excel might show you a security notice prompt letting you know that the information Excel is trying to open is from a nonsecure location (a website). Click Enable in that dialog if it shows up, as shown in Figure 3.38.

FIGURE 3.38
The Security Notice dialog when opening the exported list.

After it's opened, the data from the list is available in Excel, including all the columns that were available in the list view you started from, as shown in Figure 3.39. (See "Switch List Views in Lists and Libraries," earlier in this chapter to learn how to switch to different views, or see Chapter 8, "Creating List Views," if you want to create a view that displays more or less information to be exported.)

The Unlink button
The Refresh button

FIGURE 3.39
The contacts list open in Microsoft Excel.

The list in Excel is now connected to the list in SharePoint. If someone makes a change to the list in SharePoint, the change will be reflected in your Excel document if you reopen the file or click the Refresh button in the External Table Data section of the ribbon (refer to Figure 3.39). You can use the Unlink button in the same section to disconnect the spreadsheet from the SharePoint list and continue working on it separately.

CHAPTER 4

Searching in SharePoint

SharePoint has a built-in search engine that allows you to search for files or pages that are in SharePoint or even in other sites or file storage applications. However, the different SharePoint interfaces—SharePoint Server and SPF—have different ways to search and display the search results. This chapter explains how to search using SharePoint's different interfaces.

Search for Documents and List Items

Scenario/Problem: You want to find a piece of content that exists in your corporate network, but you're not sure where in the network it is. It might be a document stored in SharePoint or in a file share, or it might be a list item in SharePoint or in an application database.

Solution: SharePoint has a built-in search facility that enables you to find content in SharePoint (and sometimes also content that is not in SharePoint, depending on the configuration the search administrator set up). The search user interface can be customized, so the search screen in your SharePoint site may look different from what's shown in this chapter. Such customization doesn't change how you search, however.

It is important to note that searching in SPF is different from searching in SharePoint Server, which itself can have different options if FAST technology is installed. Indeed, one of the main reasons corporations buy and install SharePoint Server and the FAST search technology is that the search options that come with these two products offer much more for the administrator and for you, the end user, to use.

The basic search in both SharePoint Server and SPF is the same: You type the search keywords in the search box and click Go. However, SharePoint Server has an additional Advanced option that allows you to search for items using their properties, and a Preferences option that allows you to set the languages you are using to search, the default language, and whether you want to see search suggestions in the search box. SharePoint Server also allows you to search all the SharePoint sites (unlike SPF, which allows you to search only the site you are currently in) as well as content that exists outside SharePoint.

To search for anything, you usually just type in the search box a keyword that represents the item you want to search for and click the Search button, which usually looks like a magnifying glass. The location of the search box can vary, and if you are using SharePoint Server, you may have other options for how to search, including the Advanced link (for advanced searching), a Preferences link (for setting preferences, as mentioned earlier), and dedicated search pages. These options are covered later in this chapter.

The simplest form of searching in SharePoint—the method just described—is known as a *search*. The keyword can be a word that appears in the document (part of the document's contents) or in the document or list items properties (for example, a document name, a contact's company name, or anything else the search administrator decided should be included in the search scope). Figure 4.1 shows an example of a keyword search.

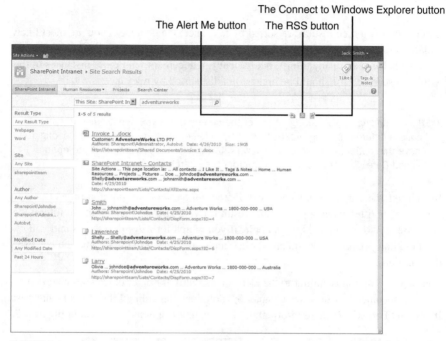

FIGURE 4.1
Searching for the word AdventureWorks produces results that include a document that has the word in its contents, a contact, and a list view that has the same word.

> **TIP** Because search results can sometimes be documents and sometimes list items and sometimes web pages or list views, what you get when you click on a search result will vary.
>
> When opening search results, you might want to open the result in a new window (or a new tab in some browsers) so you don't lose the search results page you are viewing. To do so, right-click the link and choose Open in New Window. Or Shift+click the link to open it in a new window; Ctrl+click opens it in a new tab in some browsers.

You can search for more than one word. The search results contain everything that includes any of those words.

> **TIP** Searching for the words *mountain bikes* results in all the documents that have either the word *mountain* or the word *bikes* as well as *mountains* and *bike* and other forms of the two words. If you want to search only for an exact match for a phrase, surround it with quotation marks (for example, "mountain bikes"). Alternatively, you can use the advanced search (described later in this chapter) to accomplish the same effect.

By default, the search results are sorted by relevance; the document you are most likely looking for should be the first in the list. SharePoint calculates the relevance of the documents based on many things, but basically, a document with more instances of the word you searched for should be highest in a list sorted by relevance.

> **TIP** Depending on the configuration of the search page, you might have an option to choose a different sorting order—to sort by modified date. If the page was configured to have this option, you see a drop-down with the title Sort By and in it the option Modified Date. Select this option to reorder the search results.

In addition, the search results page in a SharePoint Server configuration offers two ways to be notified when a new search result for your search is added in the future: the Alert Me and RSS options. For example, if you search for *AdventureWorks* and you want to know when new documents or list items are created in the future, you can use these options.

The Alert Me option is similar to the alert functionality for other objects in SharePoint (such as documents or lists; see Chapter 3, "Solutions Regarding Files, Documents, List Items, and Forms," for more information) but has fewer options, as shown in Figure 4.2.

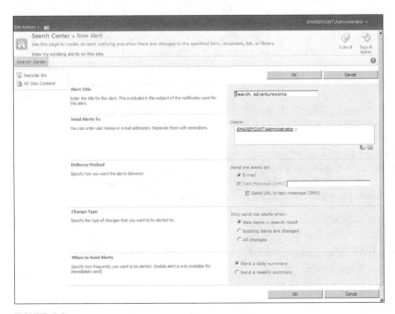

FIGURE 4.2
The search alert settings page.

In the Change Type section, select whether you want to be alerted only on new items, on changed items, or on both. In the When to Send Alerts section, select whether you want daily alerts or immediate alerts when there is something to be alerted on.

> **NOTE** Alerts from searches are never immediate. An e-mail is sent to you only when the change has been picked up by the search engine. Depending on the search configuration that the administrator set up, that can take a while.

Search in SPF

> **Scenario/Problem:** When you are using a SharePoint site that is hosted on a server that has only SPF installed, the search options are different than if you have SharePoint Server installed. (See "How to Tell if a Site Is Based on SPF or SharePoint Server" in Chapter 1, "About Microsoft SharePoint 2010," for more information.)

Solution: Searching in SPF is very simple and doesn't have many options. An SPF site usually has a search box that allows you to search on documents and list items in that site (see Figure 4.3).

The search box in the top navigation bar

FIGURE 4.3
Most sites have a search box in the top navigation bar.

Using the search box in a document library by default searches only on that document library. However, in the search results page after you have searched, you see a Scopes drop-down with an option to revert to searching the entire site instead, as shown in Figure 4.4. This allows you to search only within the document library and not other document libraries.

The Scopes drop-down allows you to revert to searching the entire site.

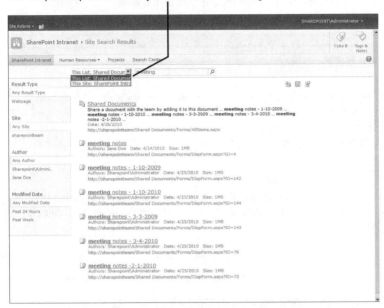

FIGURE 4.4
The search function when you're in a document library searches only in that document library by default, with an option to switch to searching the entire site.

Search Options in SharePoint Server

Scenario/Problem: When you are using a SharePoint site that is hosted on a server that has SharePoint Server installed, the search options are different and more versatile than if you have just SPF installed. (See "How to Tell if a Site Is Based on SPF or SharePoint Server" in Chapter 1 for more information.)

Solution: A variety of options exist in SharePoint Server sites for executing different types of search queries. You can search in SharePoint Server in many ways. The simplest is exactly like in SPF: You use a search box at the top of the page that allows you to type and search. Depending on the site administrator's configuration of the search settings, you may have a Scopes of Search drop-down box. Scopes allow you to specify what you want to search. Site administrators can configure and add scopes, but a few default scopes are available: All Sites, People, and a This Site scope in each site (see Figure 4.5).

FIGURE 4.5

The Scopes drop-down in a SharePoint Server site allows you to select a scope to search on.

The All Sites scope by default searches on everything excluding people. Search results might not come only from SharePoint sites. SharePoint Server has the ability to search on other sources of data outside SharePoint, and the All Sites scope, by default, searches on that content.

NOTE Depending on the scope you choose and on how the search administrator set it up, you may be directed to a different search results page.

Use the Search Center

A search option available in SharePoint Server is to use the Search Center. This site is dedicated to searching and is designed to give you a better searching experience.

If your organization is using the Search Center, you can usually get to it by either finding it on the navigation bar, usually under the name Search. You can also get to the Search Center by performing a simple search from any site; by default, in SharePoint Server you are directed to the Search Center when you do that.

The Search Center has an option to display several search tabs, or search pages (see Figure 4.6). Each of these tabs can be configured to display search results from different sources of content. The site administrator can create other tabs, and these tabs can be configured to show different search results.

FIGURE 4.6
The default Search Center has a search page for people and a search page for other content.

To switch between tabs, just click on the tab name. The term you were searching for is automatically transferred to the new tab, and a search is performed on it.

> **TIP** By default, the Search Center site template is configured not to display any ribbons. To see the ribbons in the Search Center, open the Site Actions menu and select Show Ribbon.

> **TIP** By default, the search the Search Center template is configured not to display any navigational aids, including the Navigate Up button (refer to Figure 4.6, where the button is clearly missing from the top of the page). This makes it difficult to go back to the site you started from. To do that, you can either click the Back button in your browser or manually change the address of your browser to the site you want to navigate to.

Conduct a Federated Search

Federated searching is an optional ability of SharePoint Server that may or may not be available in the site you are using. The idea of federated searching is that the search results display results from more than just what SharePoint is indexing. For example, you can search the Internet. If you are researching a certain term, such as *bicycle*, and would like to see everything related to bicycles from the SharePoint site and also from Bing search or maybe Google or Yahoo!, you should use the federated search option (see Figure 4.7).

TIP If the federated search results come from the Internet, you might want to open them in a new window or a separate tab so that you don't lose the search results page.

A result from an Internet search

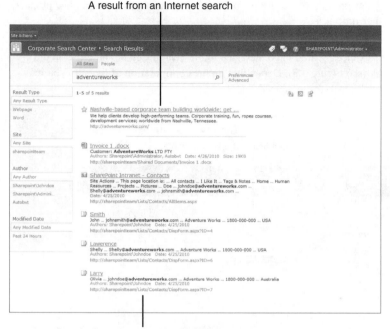

Results from the search in SharePoint

FIGURE 4.7
The federated search results from the Internet are shown on the top of the page.

A site administrator can configure federated searching to show results from many sources outside SharePoint.

TIP Remember that federated search results may be results from the Internet, and many sites contain unreliable data.

Use the Advanced Search (in SharePoint Server)

Scenario/Problem: Sometimes when you want to search for a document or a list item, you don't want to use free text to search on the content of the document or the list item. Instead, you might want to restrict the search to the metadata—the information stored about the document or list item in the columns of the list or library. For example, if you want to search for documents written by John Doe, performing a simple search for the words "John Doe" returns documents that were not written by that person. Instead, it returns any document that has the words "John Doe" in the body of the document, as well as in other columns, such as the column showing who modified the document last.

Solution: Advanced searching allows you to search for documents or list items in a more organized manner than just typing keywords. It lets you focus your search on a particular property of the documents or list items. For example, you can search for documents that person X wrote or documents that were created after the date 1/1/2008 or list items that have the word *AdventureWorks* in the company property but not in other properties.

To get to the advanced search page, navigate to the Search Center and click on the Advanced link (see Figure 4.8). Depending on the configuration of the site, you may also have other links to the advanced search page.

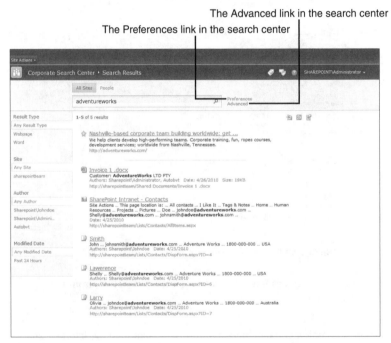

FIGURE 4.8
The Advanced link in the Search Center.

The advanced search page allows you to search more specifically and in a more exact manner on parts of the document or list item (see Figure 4.9).

FIGURE 4.9
The advanced search page.

In this page, you can specify to look for words, exactly as you do with the simple search option. When you type words in the Any of These Words box, the search results contain only documents or list items that have all the words you type, but not necessarily in the same order. You can use the other options to refine your search. For example, if you select The Exact Phase, you can type a few words, and items will be returned in the results only if they contain the exact phrase. And you can specify words that you don't want in the documents and select the None of These Words box.

Another way to narrow a search is to specify a language. This option is usually used for web pages and not for documents, unless the documents have a property called Language.

You can specify the result type to search; for example, for Microsoft Word documents, Microsoft Excel documents, or Microsoft PowerPoint documents. Or you can just select Documents to make sure your search returns only documents—and not list items (see Figure 4.10). The site administrator can customize this box to include more types.

FIGURE 4.10
Selecting the result type.

Finally, you can specify a search on specific properties that the site administrator configured for you to search on. You can add up to five conditions, such as Property X Equals/Does Not Equal Y, as shown in Figure 4.11.

FIGURE 4.11
Searching on properties.

As shown in Figure 4.11, you can chain a few conditions together and choose whether they should be chained by using an Or operator or an And operator. For example, if you specify Author Equals John and Title Equals Example, the only results will be the ones whose author is John and whose title is exactly Example. But if you search for Author Equals John *or* Title Equals Example, the results will include documents that have been authored by John and documents whose title is Example—not just the documents where both conditions are true.

> **NOTE** It is very common for site administrators to customize this interface. It is possible that your search experience will be very different from what is shown here. You may, for example, be able to choose different operators such as Contains.

Search for People (in SharePoint Server)

> **Scenario/Problem:** You may want to find the contact details of people who work with you in the organization. You might need to know someone's phone number, department, manager, and so on.

Solution: SharePoint Server has a user profile database that stores information about users. For more information about this feature, see Chapter 5, "Social Networking, Personal Sites, and Personal Details." If this feature has been set up, you have the ability to search for people and view their details. Also, if someone has created a personal site, you will be able to view the public view of that personal site. (For more information about personal sites and how to create them, see Chapter 5.)

You can perform a people search from most SharePoint Server sites by choosing People from the Scopes drop-down if this drop-down appears next to the site's search box. Or you can navigate to the Search Center and choose the People tab.

As with documents and list items, you can conduct a people search by using either keywords or advanced searching methods. The advanced search when searching for people behaves slightly differently than the advanced search for documents and list items. To view the advanced search options, click on the Search Options link in the People search tab in the Search Center. You then see more search options. You can still search by keyword using the same box, and you can also specify values for specific people properties (see Figure 4.12).

FIGURE 4.12
The advanced search options in the People search tab in the Search Center.

For example, to look for someone whose first name is John and whose job title is Human Resources Manager, type John in the First Name box and Human Resources Manager in the Job Title box. Then click the Search button (the one that looks like a magnifying glass). The search results page that appears shows you the people search results.

Unlike the results for documents and list items, these results are ordered by social distance. This is something special for the people search that shows you the people you work with first, and people they work with second, and then anyone else. SharePoint knows who you work with only if you tell it by using the Colleagues mechanism. This mechanism allows you to specify who you work with either from the search results (by using the Add to Colleagues link) or from your personal site (see Chapter 5). SharePoint automatically recognizes some colleagues, such as your manager, people you manage, and other people who have the same manager. Another thing that is unique to people search results is the Browse in Organizational Chart link that may appear for each result. Clicking this link redirects you to a page that shows an organizational chart and the selected user's location in it. For more information about the organization chart, see Chapter 5.

If you want to change the sort order, open the Sort By drop-down (shown in Figure 4.13) and select either Default, Social Distance, or Name options.

People search results have another distinguishing feature that the results of documents and list items search results do not have by default: The results are grouped showing people who are your colleagues who were returned as part of your search under one group, people who are colleagues to your colleagues as another group, and so on. If your search results include yourself (for example, if you search for people with the same first name as you), the search result for your profile will show up in a group by itself—a group called Me.

In Figure 4.13 you can see that John Doe is labeled My Colleague under the picture. That is because John was marked as someone who is important to the user who searched for him.

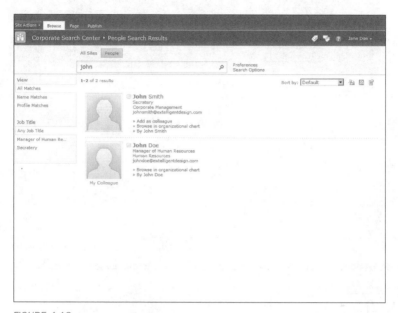

FIGURE 4.13
The people search results page.

To help you find people more accurately, you also have an option to filter the search results further by choosing from different groups of results. For example, if you searched for John Doe, you might want to see only users with those words in the name of the user, and not people who have those words in their description or some other place. To do this, click on the Name Matches link on the left to filter the list of results to show only people whose user name has the terms you searched for. Also, if SharePoint detects that there are other user properties that can help you filter, it automatically adds them as filters to the pane. As shown in Figure 4.13, the Job Title property filter is shown on the site, allowing you to view the results for all job titles (default) or filter on Manager of IT Services or on Secretary.

In the search results shown in Figure 4.13, you can see a blank square to the left of each person's name. If you hover over the square with your mouse, you see a dialog with options to contact the person, such as e-mail, chat, phone, and scheduling a meeting (see Figure 4.14). Click on the square to expand the dialog to show the person's contact details (see Figure 4.15). You can then switch to the Organization tab to see where that person is in the organization's hierarchy, as shown in Figure 4.16.

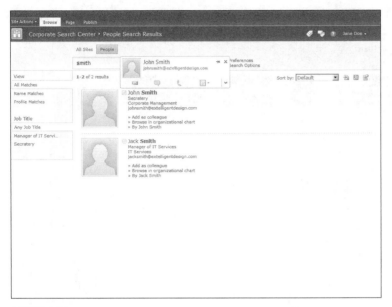

FIGURE 4.14
The person dialog appears when you hover over the square next to the person's name.

FIGURE 4.15
Clicking on the square shows the person's properties.

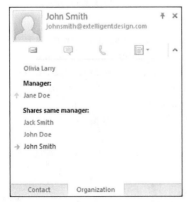

FIGURE 4.16
The Organization tab shows the position of the person in the organization structure.

Search SharePoint from Your Desktop

Scenario/Problem: You want to search for documents from your desktop and not from a site. You want the search results to include documents that are on your own computer as well as in SharePoint.

Solution: Some desktop operating systems (such as Microsoft Windows 7) support federated searching. This allows you to add sources that the desktop will search on, and SharePoint can be such a source. If you add to your desktop a SharePoint site as a federated search source, you can use the built-in search application of your operating system and get results from the SharePoint site, as well as results from your desktop, network, and other sources your desktop might be configured to search on.

To add a SharePoint site as a source for your federated search on the desktop, open the site's search results page (which you can do by simply performing a random search). On that page, click the icon that looks like a folder with a magnifying glass on the top of the search results; this is the Allow Search with Windows Explorer button.

The Allow Search with Windows Explorer button

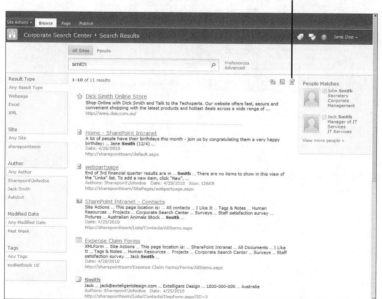

FIGURE 4.17
The Allow Search with Windows Explorer button in the search results page.

After you click this icon, if you are using an operating system that supports it, a dialog appears, asking you to confirm that you want to add the search connector to your desktop (see Figure 4.18).

FIGURE 4.18
A dialog asking you to confirm the addition of the SharePoint search to Windows.

Click Add, and you can search the site from your desktop (see Figure 4.19).

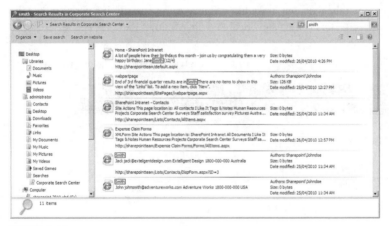

FIGURE 4.19
Searching SharePoint from the desktop.

CHAPTER 5

Social Networking, Personal Sites, and Personal Details in SharePoint Server

Microsoft SharePoint Server 2010 offers social networking features that allow employees of a company to stay connected and update each other on what they are doing. Using these features, you can track newsfeeds about subjects that interest you (for example, items you tagged, colleagues whose status changed, new blog posts) and comments about items that you want to track.

On top of that, in some Microsoft SharePoint Server 2010 implementations, the option to create personal sites is enabled. In this case, you can create a SharePoint site that is totally under your control. You can upload documents to be stored in the site instead of on your desktop and manage your private lists, such as lists of favorite links or lists of friends.

In addition, with SharePoint Server you get a user profile that stores information about you, such as your phone number, e-mail, and other details that would be useful for people in your organization. This chapter explains how to use the social features, how you can view personal details of yourself or of others, and how you can edit your own details, as well as how to create and navigate around a personal site.

Get Started with Social Features

> **Scenario/Problem:** You want to use SharePoint Server's social features to manage your colleagues, set your status, and see the organization hierarchy.

Solution: To open the social networking home page, click the [*your name*] button at the top-right corner of a SharePoint site's page. From the menu that opens, choose either the My Profile option or the My Site option, as shown in Figure 5.1.

FIGURE 5.1
Selecting My Profile or My Site from the menu.

If the My Site link does not appear, it could be one of two reasons: Either you are working on a site that has SPF only (and not SharePoint Server) or the site manager disabled the option to have a personal site. However, the My Profile link should appear if your user account has a profile associated with it. If it doesn't, you must either click on the My Site link (to create a profile) if it is available or contact the administrator to find out why you don't have a profile.

Clicking the My Profile link opens your profile page. By default, clicking the My Site option *does not* create a personal site for you but instead opens the social networking home page, shown in Figure 5.2. This page allows you to navigate to your personal site and to other social networking pages.

The links to navigate through your personal site

The Stay Connected advice

FIGURE 5.2
The social networking home page.

The following sections describe how to perform some of the most common social networking tasks.

Set Your Status to Let Others Know What You Are Doing

You use your status to tell other people what you are doing. This is similar to status updates in social networking Internet sites such as Facebook and Twitter. You can write a small description of what is on your mind or what you are doing, and people in your social network who are tracking your status can see on their newsfeed that you have a new status.

> **TIP** Remember that everyone can see your status!

To set your status, navigate to the My Profile page by either clicking the My Profile link from the [*your name*] drop-down menu (refer to Figure 5.1) or by clicking the My Profile link at the top of the social networking home page (refer to Figure 5.2). You then see a page with your picture (or a generic picture, if you haven't yet uploaded a picture into your profile; see "Edit Your Details," later in this chapter) and a speech bubble with What's Happening? coming out of the picture, as shown in Figure 5.3.

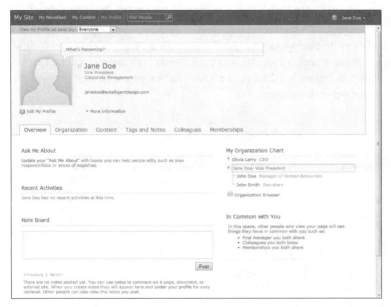

FIGURE 5.3
Setting your status in the My Profile area.

Click on the What's Happening text and type the status you want to change to. Press Enter.

> **NOTE** The text What's Happening is displayed only if you do not have a status set. If you do have a status set, the speech bubble has that status as the text.

Specify Your Colleagues

You might want to specify with whom you are working. This information helps SharePoint track for you what they are doing and helps you share information with them.

To specify your colleagues, open the My Profile page as explained earlier in this chapter, and then click the Colleagues tab. In this tab you can add, modify, or remove your colleagues, as well as group them in different ways (see Figure 5.4).

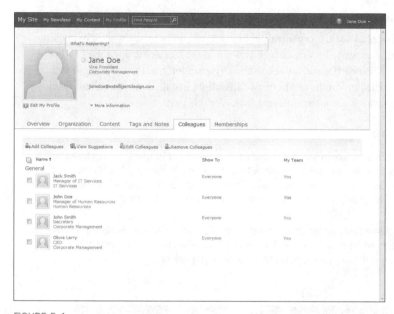

FIGURE 5.4
The Colleagues tab enables you to add, modify, remove, and group colleagues.

Clicking Add Colleagues opens a dialog that allows you to manually select people from the company address book and mark them as colleagues in the Add Colleagues dialog (see Figure 5.5).

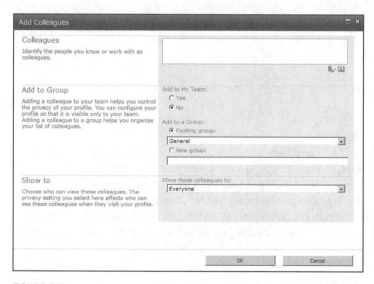

FIGURE 5.5
Adding coworkers to your social network by using the Add Colleagues dialog.

View Where You Are in the Organization Hierarchy

You might want to see the organization hierarchy in order to see who is managing whom in the company. To view where you are in the hierarchy, open the My Profile page as described earlier and switch to the Organization tab. How this tab looks depends on whether you have Microsoft Silverlight installed on your client machine. Figures 5.6 and 5.7 show the different looks for this page.

> **NOTE**   Microsoft Silverlight is a browser extension that is used to display richer interfaces than are usually possible with web pages. Some pages in SharePoint 2010 use Silverlight to show an easier-to-use interface. However, if you have not installed Silverlight, you get an alternative, more simplistic view that doesn't require it.
>
> To install Silverlight, either download it from Microsoft (a link is available on the My Profile page, as shown in Figure 5.6) or ask your administrator to install it if you are not allowed to install software on the machine you are using.

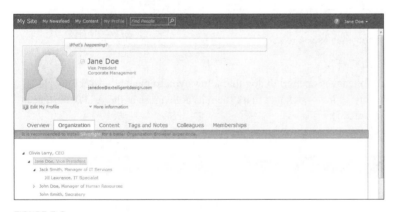

FIGURE 5.6
The Organization tab, showing the people in the hierarchy as a collapsible tree, without Silverlight.

Both Figures 5.6 and 5.7 show the organization hierarchy. In Figure 5.6, without Microsoft Silverlight, you can see the hierarchy with Jane Doe (the current user) highlighted. You can see that Jane reports to Olivia and has three people (Jake Smith, John Doe, and John Smith) reporting to her. Two of them in turn have other people reporting to them; for example, Jill reports to Jack Smith. To see who reports to John Doe, you must expand the view by clicking on the arrow next to his name. Clicking on a name in the view selects the person and exposes a button to open the profile page for that user, as shown in Figure 5.8.

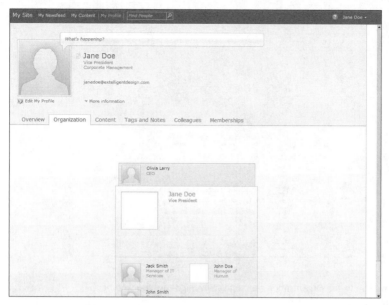

FIGURE 5.7
The Organization tab, showing the people in the hierarchy as a collapsible tree, using Silverlight.

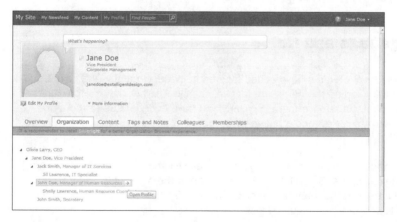

FIGURE 5.8
Selecting a person in the Organization tab to see his profile.

The Silverlight version of this window shows the same structure but with a richer interface. It shows people's pictures (or blank pictures, if those people haven't updates their profiles to have pictures) and in boxes showing who reports to whom. You can see in Figure 5.7 that Jane reports to Olivia and manages Jack Smith, John Smith, and John Doe. If you click Jack Smith, Silverlight moves the two Johns to the side and shows that Jack manages Jill (see Figure 5.9).

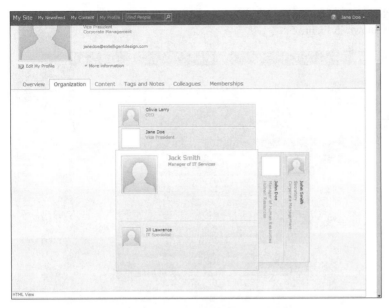

FIGURE 5.9
Selecting a person in the Organization tab, using Silverlight, to see who he is managing.

To view a person's profile, simply click that person's name.

Manage Tags and Notes

Scenario/Problem: You have added tags on items, documents, and pages. Now you want to find the items you tagged, change whether they are private or public, and maybe remove them. Similarly, you have added notes to the items, and you want to review and manage those notes.

Solution: Your personal site has a page that allows you to review your tagged items and your notes. To switch to this page, open the My Profile page as explained earlier in this chapter (refer to Figure 5.3). In that page, click on the Tags and Notes tab (see Figure 5.10).

On the right side of the page you can see all the items for which you have set tags or notes. These are grouped by the month the tags or comments were created, and you can browse the months by using the arrow icons on the top of that list.

On the left side of the page is an option to filter the items to see only items that have tags, only items that have notes, only items that were tagged or noted as private, or only items that were tagged or noted as public. The left side shows a list of all the tag terms you have used, and you can click on a tag to filter the items on the right to display all the items that were tagged with that term (see Figure 5.11).

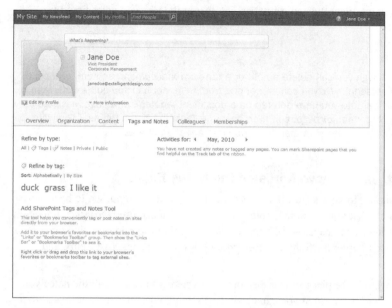

FIGURE 5.10
The Tags and Notes tab.

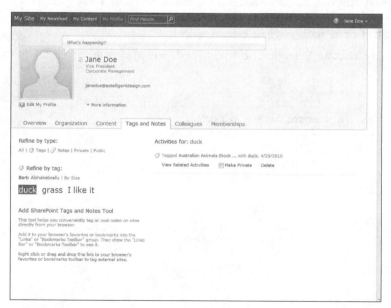

FIGURE 5.11
Selecting a specific tag.

When you find an item that is tagged or noted, you can click on the link to the item to open the item, you can remove the note or the tag (by clicking the Delete link), and you can change whether the tag or note is supposed to be private or public. You can also click the View Related Activities link to edit the tags and notes board for that item.

> **NOTE** Although you can delete a note or a tag from a document, an item, or a page from your personal site, you cannot set one from here, nor can you edit a note from here. To edit a note you have entered on a document, an item, or a page, navigate to that document, item, or page, and then open the Tags and Notes tab as if you were going to add a new note. In that dialog you can edit the old note.

Add, Edit, and Remove Notes on the Notes Board

Notes are similar to your status, but unlike the status, which is supposed to be a short description of what you are doing, notes can be long. You can use notes to comment on documents, items, and pages—even on external sites. (For more information on how to add notes, see Chapter 3, "Solutions Regarding Files, Documents, List Items, and Forms.")

The notes board is the place in your personal site where you can see all the notes you have written and from which you can easily create more notes that are not related to a specific item, file, or page.

To view the notes board, click on the My Profile link, and you see the notes board under the Overview tab. It includes a text box where you can create a new general note by just typing in the box and clicking the Post button to add a new general note. It also includes a list of all the notes you have created under it.

To delete a note, click the Delete link next to it. To edit a note, click the Edit link next to it.

> **TIP** Remember that everyone can see your notes.

View Newsfeed Updates for Your Social Network

Scenario/Problem: You want to use the social networking features to see what other people you are working with are doing.

Solution: Navigate to the social networking site and click on the My Newsfeed button at the top of the page. If one of your colleagues has changed his or her status or profile, you see a line showing that information (see Figure 5.12).

FIGURE 5.12
Viewing the newsfeed updates for your social network.

Configure Newsfeed Updates for Your Social Network

Scenario/problem: You want your newsfeed page to show when someone else in the organization has changed his or her interests to match yours or when a colleague has tagged a document or rated or commented on a document.

Solution: In the newsfeed page (refer to Figure 5.12), click the Newsfeed Settings link. The Edit Profile page for your profile appears. (See "Edit Your Details," later in this chapter, for more information.) SharePoint automatically scrolls down to the Newsfeed Settings section, as shown in Figure 5.13. In this section you can configure what you are interested in seeing in your newsfeed.

To select what you want to follow, simply check and uncheck the appropriate boxes in the list of activities. When SharePoint Server identifies that an update is required (for example, when someone's birthday is today), it adds that to your My Newsfeed page.

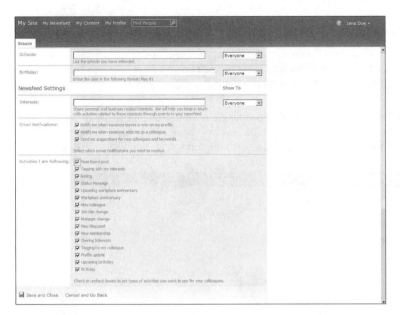

FIGURE 5.13
Selecting what activities you want in your newsfeed.

Create a Personal Site

Scenario/Problem: You want to store files and collaborate with your coworkers online, but you also want to keep some information to yourself. Maybe the SharePoint administrators have not created a specific site for the purpose you require, and you want to be able to work in the SharePoint environment but do not have the facility to do so.

Solution: My Site is a feature of SharePoint Server through which every user can have his or her own personal site. The personal site can hold private document libraries and lists that are shown and available only to the site owner (unless the owner chooses to share them with other people; see Chapter 10, "Managing Security," for more information). The site can also hold public document libraries and lists where the user can collaborate with other users.

To create a personal site, click the [*your name*] button at the top-right corner of a SharePoint site's page. From the menu that opens, choose the My Site option (refer to Figure 5.1).

If the link to My Site doesn't appear, it could be for one of two reasons: Either you are working on a site that has SPF only (and not SharePoint Server) or the site manager disabled the option to create a personal site. If the link is not shown and you are sure that the site is using SharePoint Server, contact your administrator and ask for the link to My Site.

By default, clicking on the My Site option *does not* automatically create a personal site for you. Instead, doing so shows you the newsfeed page. To create your personal site, click on the My Content option in the top navigation bar. If you don't yet have a personal site, and the administrator allows personal sites to be created, a personal site is created for you.

After the site is created, a dialog might appear (depending on the browser you are using), asking if you want to configure My Site for Microsoft Office so that Microsoft Office remembers your My Site for opening and saving files. This is a useful feature that adds a link to the personal site in Microsoft Office applications so you can get to it easily when you are saving or opening a file. This makes it easier for you to save documents to your personal site from Microsoft Office applications. If you select not to configure it, a Set as Default My Site link appears in the top of the site to enable you to configure it in the future.

Your personal site is then created and ready for you (see Figure 5.14).

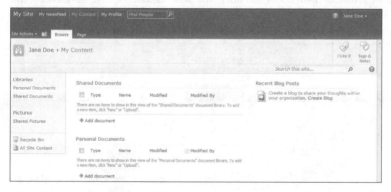

FIGURE 5.14
A personal site created for Jane Doe.

Get Started with Your Personal Site

Scenario/Problem: You have a personal site, and you want to learn your way around it and customize it to show your personal data when you view it.

Solution: There are many things you can do with your personal site, including create lists and libraries, modify how different pages look, and change the way the site itself looks. Some of these tasks are covered later in this chapter, and some are covered in other chapters, specifically, Chapter 7, "Creating Lists and Document Libraries," and Chapter 9, "Authoring Pages."

Learn Your Way Around a Personal Site

As explained earlier in this chapter, the My Content link at the top of the page opens your personal site, which you control and which has content that you uploaded and created. Other users can browse your site, but they can't see all the content there unless you allow them to do so. (To learn how to assign permissions, see Chapter 10.) However, by default you already have two different document libraries configured with different permissions: one for personal documents, which only you can see, and one for shared documents, which other users can read as well. In this page you can create new content, such as new pages, new sites (for example, a blog), new document libraries, new lists, and so on.

Upload a Document to Your Personal Site

To upload a document to your personal site, first open the personal site by clicking the My Content tab in the top navigation bar.

When your site is open, you need to choose where to upload the document. By default, personal sites have two document libraries: a personal one, where only you can see the documents you upload, and a shared one, where documents you upload can be viewed by other users in your company. To select which document library you want to upload to, simply click the Add Document link under one of the document libraries web parts in the page (either Shared Documents if you want other people to have access to the file, or Personal Documents if you want to keep the file private), as shown in Figure 5.14. A dialog appears, allowing you to choose the file you want to upload, as shown in Figure 5.15.

FIGURE 5.15

Adding a document to the Shared Documents library.

For more information on how to add documents to document libraries, see Chapter 6, "Creating and Managing Files, List Items, and Forms in SharePoint."

Edit Your Details

Scenario/Problem: The details that other users see about you are no longer up to date, and you want to update them to reflect recent changes. For example, you might have been promoted, and your job title changed, or maybe you have a new manager. Editing your details is very important because it allows other people in your company to find you quickly using the people search.

Solution: This section explains how you can change the details that appear to other users or are searched in the people search. The details that you can edit are different in every company, so the details you can fill in when you open your details page may differ from what's shown in this chapter.

To edit your details, open the My Profile page as explained earlier in this chapter. There you see your picture (or a generic picture) with the Edit My Profile link under it (refer to Figure 5.3). Clicking this link redirects you to a page where you can edit your details. As mentioned previously, these details vary, depending on your company's configuration. Figure 5.16 shows how to enter text in an About Me section. You can upload a picture by clicking the Choose Picture button (see Figure 5.17 for the dialog that comes up). You can set your mobile phone number, fax number, and home phone. You can see more profile details by scrolling down.

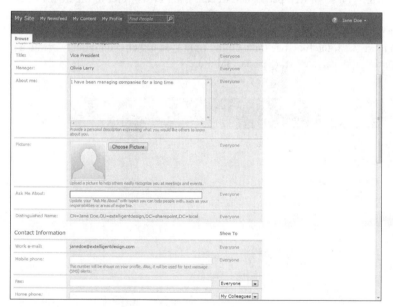

FIGURE 5.16
The Edit Details page enables you to edit some details about yourself.

FIGURE 5.17
The Upload Picture dialog allows you to choose a picture of yourself for your profile.

Create a Blog

Scenario/Problem: You want to create a site where you can write articles on topics related to your work and share them with your coworkers.

Solution: A blog is the most appropriate type of site for this kind of requirement. You can usually create a blog under your personal site if the SharePoint administrator has allowed it.

To create a blog, navigate to your personal site and click on the My Content tab. On the right of the page you see a web part called Recent Blog Posts (refer to Figure 5.14). If you haven't yet created a blog, the web part shows a link for creating a new blog. Clicking that link automatically creates a blog for you under your personal site. As shown in Figure 5.18, the blog has links on the right side to help you quickly create a new post (article), manage existing posts, and more.

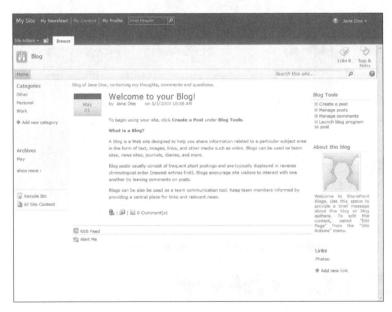

FIGURE 5.18
A personal blog.

By default, the new blog has a post called Welcome to Your Blog, with an explanation about what a blog is and how to use one. You might want to delete that post to begin with (by using the Manage Posts link on the right). To create a new post, click the Create a Post link on the right side of the page. A dialog for the blog post's text appears, as shown in Figure 5.19.

FIGURE 5.19
Creating a new blog post.

Later chapters in this book talk more about managing sites, including blogs. You'll learn how to delete posts (which are items in a list; see "Delete a File or List Item" in Chapter 6), manage permissions on the site (covered in Chapter 14, "Managing Site Security"), and edit pages (see Chapter 9).

CHAPTER 6

Creating and Managing Files, List Items, and Forms in SharePoint

SharePoint is most commonly used to store files, list items, and forms. This chapter covers tasks for the authors of files or list items, such as how to upload a file, create a new list item, edit the properties of list items, and publish the results to share them with other users.

Upload a File

Scenario/Problem: You want to upload a file to a document library in a SharePoint site.

Solution: Uploading a file to SharePoint is an easy process. There are three ways to do so. If you are writing a document in a Microsoft Office application, an easy way is to upload the document straight from the application by saving it directly into SharePoint.

If the file you want to upload is not an Office file, or if you prefer to upload the file without opening it in an Office application, you can upload the file using the web interface with your Internet browser.

The third option, which is a bit more advanced, enables you to upload the file to a library as if that library were a folder on your computer. This method is known as using *web folders*, and it requires that some components be installed on your machine. When these components are installed, web folders are easy and efficient to use.

Upload a File from the Web Interface

To upload a file from the Web interface using your web browser, browse to the library to which you want to upload the file, and then go to the folder where you want to put the file. If you have the required permissions to add files to the folder, the Documents ribbon shows an Upload Document button. Some document libraries also have an Add Document link at the bottom of the list of documents.

You can use the Upload Document button in the ribbon as a regular button (just click the button) or as a drop-down menu to show more options for uploading, such as the option to upload multiple files, as shown in Figure 6.1. This option, available only for users of Microsoft Internet Explorer, will open a different dialog window, which is explained at the end of this section.

The Upload Multiple Documents option

The Upload Document button

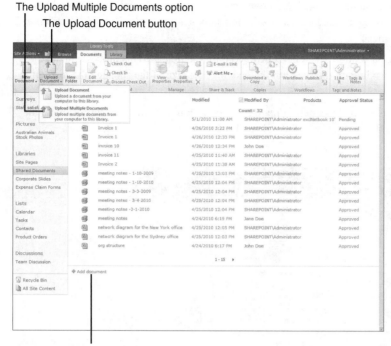

The Add Document link

FIGURE 6.1
The Documents ribbon with the Upload Document button and the Add Document link.

Clicking the Upload Document button or the Add Document link opens the Upload Document dialog, where you can choose a single file by using the Browse button (see Figure 6.2).

FIGURE 6.2
The File Upload dialog, with the Upload Multiple Files link that enables you to upload many files at once if you have the right Microsoft Office components installed on your machine.

If you are using a compatible browser and have the required components, the option in the Upload Document dialog to upload multiple files using the Upload Multiple Files link becomes available. This button redirects you to the same dialog you would have opened if you had clicked Upload Multiple Documents from the Upload Document drop-down menu.

If you selected a single file, click OK to commit the upload. This process can take a while, depending on the speed of the network, the size of the file, and the load on the server.

When the upload is done, depending on the setup of the document library, you might be prompted for properties for the file and see a Save button (see Figure 6.3).

FIGURE 6.3
After the file is uploaded, you might be prompted for more information about the file. In this example, you are asked for information for the Title and Products columns.

NOTE If you change your mind about uploading the document at this stage, you have two choices available in the dialog's ribbon: Cancel and Delete. If you cancel, the document is still in the document library, but it stays checked out to you as a draft document. If you choose Delete, the document is removed from the document library.

If the library supports multiple content types for files, you might have to select what content type this file belongs to, and that may change the properties that you are asked for (see Figure 6.4).

FIGURE 6.4
The properties entry screen when the Presentation content type is selected.

If you selected to upload multiple files, you have two options for the interface.
The default dialog that comes up allows you to drag and drop files and folders to the
dialog window. After you drag the files, the dialog shows the list of files that are to be
uploaded (see Figure 6.5). To add more files, you can continue to drag and drop into
the dialog until you have all the files you want in the page. To remove a file, click the
Remove link in that file's row. Click OK to finish uploading the files. The dialog then
uploads each file and updates the status in that file's row to Done when the file has
completed uploading. Finally, the dialog shows that it has completed uploading all
the files (see Figure 6.6).

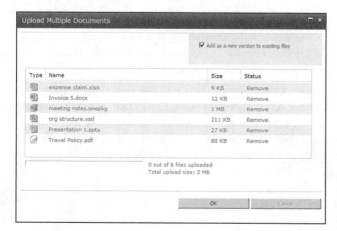

FIGURE 6.5
Uploading multiple docu-
ments by dragging and
dropping.

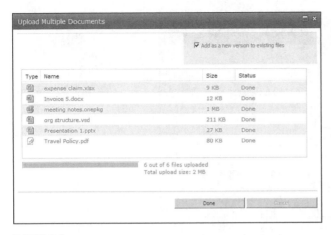

FIGURE 6.6
The Upload Multiple Documents dialog after it has finished uploading.

The second option you have is to browse for the files you want to upload. To use this option, click the Browse for Files Instead link in the Upload Multiple Documents dialog. A dialog appears, in which you can browse for files and select them. When you use this method, you are not asked for properties for the files, and the files are all uploaded but not checked in to the document library. You still need to check in each file that you uploaded and set the properties for each one separately.

Of course, if check-in is not required on the document library in question, you don't need to check in the files, but setting the properties (for example, the titles for the files) might be a good idea. See "Edit the Properties of a File or List Item" and "Check In and Check Out a File or List Item," later in this chapter, for more details on how to do this after you upload the files.

Upload a File from an Office Application

Office 2003 and later versions have built-in functionality that enables you to save files straight into SharePoint. Different versions may present different user interfaces for doing this, but the principle is the same in all versions.

To save a document from an Office application such as Word, PowerPoint, or Excel, you use the Save or Save As functionality of the application. When the Save As dialog appears, in the File Name box type the path to the SharePoint site into which you want to save the file, and then click Save or press Enter (see Figure 6.7). (This step does not save the document yet because you have not given it a name.)

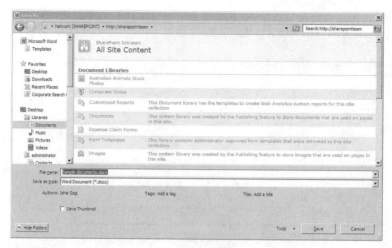

FIGURE 6.7
Clicking Save after typing the path to a SharePoint site displays the document libraries in the site inside the Save As dialog.

This action opens the site's structure in the dialog box and shows you the document libraries in that site, as well as the subsites under that site (see Figure 6.8).

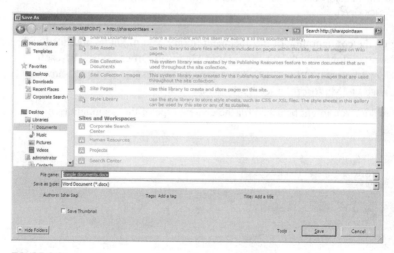

FIGURE 6.8
To see the subsites, scroll down the window.

You can now navigate to the document library that you want by double-clicking its name (see Figure 6.9), or you can browse the subsites by double-clicking them and selecting a document library from there.

Alternatively, if you know the path to the document library or folder you want to save to, type that in the File Name box and click Save to open the folder directly. When you have browsed to the folder to which you want to save, give the file a name in the File Name box and click Save to save it to the folder.

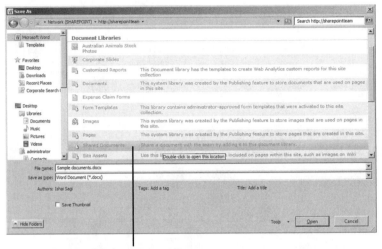

Double-click the document library, or
click it once and click the Open button.

FIGURE 6.9
To open a document library and browse its folders, either double-click it or single-click it to select it and click Open.

Depending on the configuration of the document library, you might be presented with several different dialogs, which look different in Microsoft Office 2003, Microsoft Office 2007, or Microsoft Office 2010. The following figures, for example, show the dialogs presented to Microsoft Office 2007 users.

In the first dialog, you might be asked for the content type of the document (see Figure 6.10).

FIGURE 6.10
A dialog that asks for the content type of the document.

Finally, when you are done with all the dialogs, your document is in SharePoint but still checked out. You can check it in from the web interface (see "Check In and Check Out a File or List Item," later in this chapter) or from the Office application. In some versions of Microsoft Office, to help you check in the document you just saved, the Microsoft Office application displays a bar at the top to remind you that the document is still checked out and not visible to other users, as shown in Figure 6.11. Click the Check In button to see the Check In dialog, shown in Figure 6.12.

FIGURE 6.11
A bar to remind you to check in the document.

FIGURE 6.12
The Check In dialog.

To check in the document without using the bar, click the Check In option, which appears in different places depending on the version of Microsoft Office you are using. In Microsoft Office 2003, it appears just under the File menu as the Check In menu option. In Microsoft Office 2007, it appears under the Microsoft Office button and then under the Server menu option. In Microsoft Office 2010, it appears under the File menu and then under the Info option (see Figure 6.13).

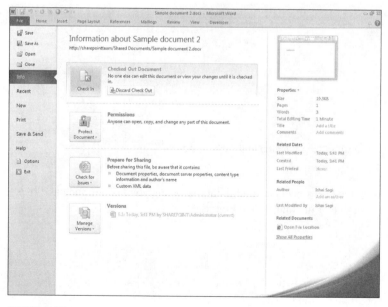

FIGURE 6.13
The Check In option under the Info menu in Microsoft Office 2010.

Selecting Check In prompts you to make sure you want to check in and prompts for check-in comments.

Upload a File Using Web Folders

Web folders is an interface in SharePoint that is usually installed as part of Microsoft Office but may be distributed by other applications. This interface enables you to browse a SharePoint site as if it were a folder on the network. This capability can be useful for copying and pasting a large number of files to or from SharePoint and even for deleting files.

The easiest way to open a document library as a web folder is to switch to the Library ribbon, and then click the Open with Explorer button option in the Connect & Export group, as shown in Figure 6.14.

FIGURE 6.14
Selecting the Open with Explorer button in the Library ribbon.

Selecting this option opens the document library, allowing you to copy and paste files into the library or one of the folders (see Figure 6.15).

FIGURE 6.15
In this view of the document library, you can copy or paste the files you want to use.

> **NOTE** Note that uploading files through web folders does not provide you with an interface for specifying the files' properties, and you still need to edit the properties of the files through the web interface. (See "Edit the Properties of a File or List Item," later in this chapter, for information.)

Upload a Picture to a Picture Library

Scenario/Problem: You want to upload a picture to a picture library.

Solution: Because picture libraries do not have a ribbon, the way to upload pictures is slightly different from the way you upload to document libraries.

To upload a single picture to a picture library, click the Upload Picture button on the toolbar above the picture library, as shown in Figure 6.16. The File Upload dialog appears; it is the same dialog that appears when you upload a single file to a document library (refer to Figure 6.2).

The Upload Picture button   The Upload Multiple Pictures option

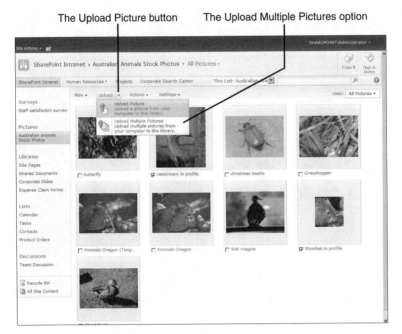

FIGURE 6.16
The Upload Picture button in the picture library toolbar.

You can also upload multiple pictures at one time. To do so, either click the Upload
Multiple Files link in the dialog (refer to Figure 6.2) or open the drop-down of the
Upload button in the toolbar by clicking the arrow next to the button text, as shown in
Figure 6.16. However, unlike with document libraries, doing this opens a different
interface if you have Microsoft Office installed. Choosing to upload multiple pictures
opens the Microsoft Office Picture Editor application, which shows the pictures you
have on your computer (see Figure 6.17). You can upload these pictures as the original
pictures or convert the pictures to smaller images, optimized for viewing on the web.

Create a New Document

Scenario/Problem: You want to create a new Microsoft Office document (for
example, a Microsoft Word document, a Microsoft Excel workbook).

Solution: To create documents in document libraries, you use the New Document
button in the Documents ribbon. This opens the Office application and the template
that was specified by the manager of that document library. For example, if the
manager specified that the default template for a document library is a Microsoft
Excel template, Excel opens and creates a new file using that template.

When you are done authoring the document, click Save in the application, and the
document is automatically saved in the folder where you started. For more information
about saving files into SharePoint, see "Upload a File from an Office Application,"
earlier in this chapter.

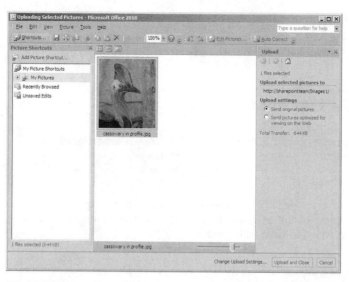

FIGURE 6.17
The Microsoft Office Picture Editor is used to upload multiple pictures.

The New Document button offers more choices of templates if the manager configured additional content types for the document library. If that is the case, clicking the New Document button creates a new document based on the template of the default content type. Using the drop-down menu for the New Document button enables you to select other content types that may use different templates and different applications (see Figure 6.18).

FIGURE 6.18
Using the New Document drop-down menu to select a content type for a new file.

For example, the content type Presentation uses a Microsoft PowerPoint template, the content type Financial Report uses a Microsoft Excel template, and the content type Product Whitepaper uses a Microsoft Word template.

Create a New List Item

Scenario/Problem: You want to create a new list item (for example, add a contact to a contacts list or a new event to a calendar list).

Solution: When you're working in a list, you create a new list item by using the New Item button in the Items ribbon or using the link Add New Item that may be shown under the view displaying the existing list items.

However, unlike with documents, using the New Item button does not open another application but rather opens a dialog that enables you to fill in the properties or columns for the new list item (see Figure 6.19).

FIGURE 6.19
A sample properties page for creating a new task.

Because each list can have different properties (or columns) in different orders, the screen can look totally different in each list. For example, the announcements list has properties such as Title and Body (see Figure 6.20), whereas the contacts list has properties such as First Name, Last Name, and Business Phone (see Figure 6.21).

FIGURE 6.20
A sample properties page for creating a new announcement.

FIGURE 6.21
A sample properties page for creating a new contact.

Like document libraries, lists can support multiple content types. This means that the New Item button in the Items ribbon might also offer a drop-down of options for you to choose the sort of list item you want to create (see Figure 6.22). Depending on the content type you select, the properties fields may change.

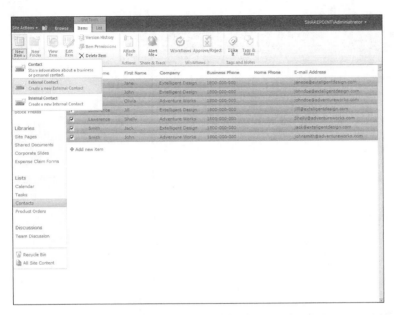

FIGURE 6.22
Choosing content types for creating different types of contacts.

For example, a contacts list might give you the option of creating an item of type
External Contact, which would be used for contacts outside the company. This
content type asks you to fill in the property for Company (see Figure 6.23).

FIGURE 6.23
A sample properties page for
creating a new external contact has
the Company column.

An item of type Internal Contact, on the other hand, does not ask for that property because it assumes that the contact belongs to your company. Instead, it has the property Department (see Figure 6.24).

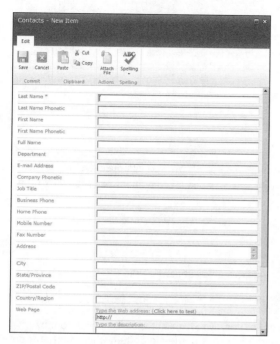

FIGURE 6.24

A sample properties page for creating a new internal contact has the Department column.

Another way to create new list items is to use the datasheet view. This is described later in this chapter, in the section "Use the Datasheet View to Add, Edit, or Delete Items and Files."

Fill a Form

Scenario/Problem: You want to fill a form in a SharePoint form library.

Solution: In a form library, you can fill a form by clicking the New Document button in the Documents ribbon. Clicking this button opens the form either in the browser or in Microsoft InfoPath, depending on the configuration of the form and on whether you have Microsoft InfoPath installed (see Figures 6.25 and 6.26).

Form template's location: http://sharepointteam

FIGURE 6.25

A form open for editing in Microsoft InfoPath Filler.

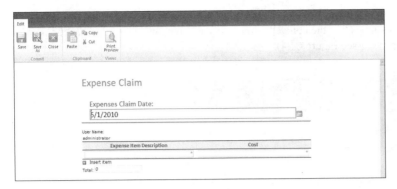

FIGURE 6.26
A form open for editing in the browser.

If the library is configured to have more than one form, you can open the drop-down menu for the new form, the same way you do when creating items or documents from different content types.

Delete a File or List Item

Scenario/Problem: You want to delete an existing file from a document library or delete a list item from a list.

Solution: To delete a single file or list item, you highlight that file or list item by checking the check box that appears to the left of the file or item when you hover on the row for that file or list item. This causes the row to be highlighted and the ribbon to switch to the Documents ribbon or the Items ribbon. In the ribbon, click the Delete Document button, shown in Figure 6.27. You are prompted to confirm the deletion.

FIGURE 6.27
Selecting Delete Document from the Documents ribbon when a specific document is highlighted.

NOTE Deleting files requires a different set of permissions than editing, so you might not see the Delete option in the menu. In that case, you should ask the manager of that list to delete the item.

An alternative way to delete a single item or file is to hover over the item's title or the file's file name and then open the drop-down menu that becomes available (see Figure 6.28). From this menu, you choose Delete Item or Delete.

FIGURE 6.28
Deleting a single file by opening the drop-down menu for that file.

You can also delete several files or items at once by selecting those files or items using the check boxes that are shown on the left of the view displaying those items or files (see Figure 6.29). The check boxes become visible if you hover your mouse's cursor over the row for an item or file. After you select several files or items, you use the Delete Document button on the Documents ribbon or the Delete Item button on the Items ribbons to delete them all at the same time.

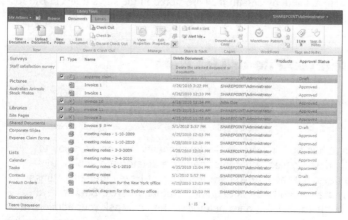

FIGURE 6.29
Selecting multiple files by using the check boxes.

Another method for deleting multiple files or list items is to use the datasheet view. For more information, see "Use the Datasheet View to Add, Edit, or Delete Items and Files," later in this chapter.

Finally, in document libraries, you can also use the Open with Explorer option in the Library ribbon. This opens the document library in Windows Explorer, just as it would any folder on your computer, and it allows you to select the files you want to delete and either press the Delete key on the keyboard or right-click the files and choose Delete from the context menu (see Figure 6.30).

FIGURE 6.30
Selecting multiple files using Windows Explorer.

When items or files are deleted, by default they are stored in the site's Recycle Bin for 30 days, and you can restore them during that time. See the following section.

Recover a Deleted File or List Item

Scenario/Problem: You have accidentally deleted a file or a list item that you need.

Solution: SharePoint has built-in Recycle Bin functionality that enables you to retract deletions. By default, files and items that were deleted are kept in this Recycle Bin for 30 days, but the site you are using might have different settings. After this time, they are moved to the site administrator's Recycle Bin. So if you don't see a file or list item that you have deleted in the past, ask your administrator to recover it for you.

To restore a file, click the Recycle Bin link in the left navigation bar. Clicking this link opens the Recycle Bin page, which shows all the files and list items you have deleted in that specific site (see Figure 6.31).

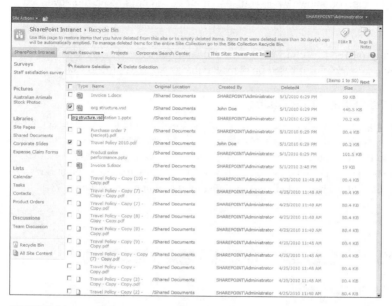

FIGURE 6.31
The Recycle Bin page.

In the deleted items list, you can see the name of the deleted item or file, the original location (site and document library or list and folder), and other data about the file or item, such as who created it in the first place, when it was deleted, and, for files, what size it was.

To restore one or more files and items, select the check box next to each item you want to restore and click Restore Selection. The item or file is restored with all its versions and properties.

You can also permanently delete an item or file from the Recycle Bin by selecting Delete Selection.

Edit the Properties of a File or List Item

Scenario/Problem: You want to change some of the values that have been entered into the columns for a specific file or list item. For example, you might want to change the details for an event in a calendar list or the name or title of a document in a document library.

Solution: Lists and document libraries in SharePoint might be configured to ask you for properties for files and list items. This data appears when you view the properties of a file or list item (see Chapter 3, "Solutions Regarding Files, Documents, List Items, and Forms") or as columns when you view the document libraries or lists. This data may also be shown when you search for documents using the advanced search (see Chapter 4, "Searching in SharePoint").

Properties information is useful when you are looking for a file or a list item. You might be able to search for it based on the value that is set in its properties.

Use the Edit Properties Dialog

To edit the properties of a file, locate the file in the folder where it was saved and highlight that file by checking the check box that appears to the left of the file or item when you hover on the row for that file or list item. When you select the file this way, the ribbon switches to the Documents ribbon. If you have permissions to edit that file's properties, the Edit Properties button is available in the ribbon (see Figure 6.32).

The Edit Properties button

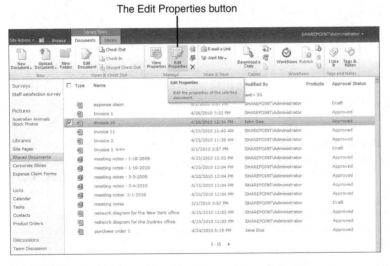

FIGURE 6.32
The Edit Properties button in the Documents ribbon.

> **NOTE** It is easy to confuse the Edit Document button with the Edit Properties button. The Edit Document button opens a document for editing, whereas the Edit Properties button opens the document's properties page.

Alternatively, you can hover the mouse over the link to the file and then open the dropdown menu of actions for that file. If you have permissions to edit that file's properties, you see the Edit Properties option in this menu (see Figure 6.33).

FIGURE 6.33

The Edit Properties menu option appears when you have permissions to edit a document or a list item's properties.

With list items, the procedure is slightly easier than with files. Although you can go through the same process as for files (described in the preceding paragraph), you can also simply click the title of the list item to open the dialog that shows the item's properties and then choose Edit Item from the available ribbon. Clicking this button switches the dialog to one where you can modify the current properties of the file or list item.

When you're editing the properties of a file or a list item, properties that are mandatory are marked with a red asterisk (*), and you must fill in those properties before you can save your changes (see Figure 6.34). If you don't fill in those properties, SharePoint does not let you click OK and tells you which properties are not filled in.

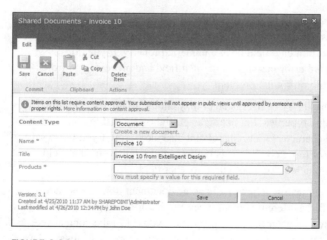

FIGURE 6.34

When you do not fill in a required property, SharePoint prompts you to do so when you try to save.

File and list item properties can be of different types, and each type has a different way of capturing data (see Figure 6.35). For example, a text property displays a text box for you to enter data. A date property can appear as a text box (for the date) with a button next to it that looks like a calendar that enables you to choose a date, and it might even have two drop-downs for selecting a time. A yes/no field appears as a check box.

FIGURE 6.35
For different property types, you enter or select data in different ways. In this task form, you can see six different types.

SharePoint also validates the properties based on the types. This means, for example, that you cannot write text in a date field or in a numeric property. If you do so, SharePoint shows you a red error message under that field and prevents you from saving the properties until you fix the problem.

In addition, the document library or list manager may choose to impose additional conditions on some of the properties. For example, it might state that the title of a file should be fewer than 43 characters long. SharePoint also alerts you if you try to save the properties when one of those conditions is not met, and it tells you what field is not set correctly and what limitations are configured for that field.

An important action when creating a new file in some document libraries is choosing the content type for the file. Different content types require different properties, so it is recommended that before you enter the other properties, you select the content type first. This should not be a problem because the Content Type property is always the first one to appear in the list of properties if the document library was configured to use more than one content type, as you can see in Figure 6.36.

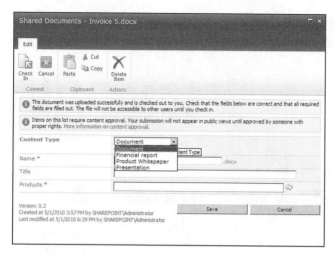

FIGURE 6.36
The content type is the first thing you need to choose when uploading a file.

Changing the content type causes the properties page to refresh and load the properties that are required for the selected content type. However, if the new content type has some of the same properties as the old one, the values in those properties are not lost. You can therefore switch between content types without worrying about losing the information.

After you have filled in all the properties you want, click Save at the bottom or the top of the page to save the changes.

If the document library is set up to require you to check in and check out files, you must check in the file after changing its properties. See "Check In and Check Out a File or List Item," later in this chapter, for more information on how to do so.

To edit the properties of multiple list items or files, you can also use the datasheet view. For more information on this, see the next section.

Use the Inline Editing Interface

Some views support an option called *inline editing*. When this option is turned on, you can edit the properties for a file or a list item without opening the properties page. When this option is available, a new button appears next to the check box of each row (see Figure 6.37). This icon, when clicked, switches the row to editing mode, where you can change which columns are visible in the view. In the editing mode you can also cancel by clicking the Cancel button or save the changes by using the Save button, as shown in Figure 6.38.

FIGURE 6.37
Hovering over a row when inline editing is enabled.

FIGURE 6.38
Editing the properties of a list item in inline editing mode.

Use the Datasheet View to Add, Edit, or Delete Items and Files

Scenario/Problem: You want to add, edit, or delete multiple items in a list or library in an easy way. The details that you want to modify are similar, and you don't want to have to click each one to edit or delete it separately. You also don't want to click the New button many times.

Solution: The datasheet view, as explained earlier, is similar to a Microsoft Excel datasheet and allows copying and pasting of data into the list or library (see Figure 6.39).

FIGURE 6.39
A datasheet view showing a contacts list.

This interface makes adding, editing, and deleting multiple list items or files a lot easier. You can create list items by copying data from Microsoft Excel or another spreadsheet application. You can edit the properties of many list items or files by copying cells, and you can delete many files in one action.

If you want to see the datasheet view, there are certain requirements for your computer. First, the datasheet component must be installed on your machine. This component is part of the Microsoft Office installation for Microsoft Office Professional 2003, 2007, or 2010. Second, the browser you are using to view the site must be compatible with the datasheet view and allow showing ActiveX controls. If you are getting error messages (see Figure 6.40), contact your administrator for assistance.

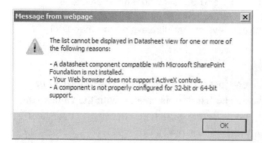

FIGURE 6.40

An error message that appears when you're trying to switch to a datasheet view and Microsoft Office Datasheet Component is not installed on the local machine.

Switch to Datasheet View

Some views are built to be datasheet views by default. In this case, just switching to the view displays the datasheet interface. For more information about how to switch between views, see "Switch List Views in Lists and Libraries" in Chapter 3.

However, you can also switch to a datasheet view version of any standard view even if the view creator did not create it as a datasheet view. To switch to the datasheet view from a standard view, you switch to the List ribbon or Library ribbon and click the Datasheet View button in the View Format section of the ribbon (see Figure 6.41). To switch back to the standard view, click the Standard View button in the same ribbon (see Figure 6.41).

FIGURE 6.41

The Standard View and the Datasheet View buttons.

NOTE If you are trying to switch to datasheet view with a browser that is not supported (for example, Mozilla Firefox, Google Chrome), the option to switch to datasheet view is displayed but not enabled.

Add a List Item Using Datasheet View

You can use datasheet view to add list items. This approach doesn't work with document libraries because they require you to upload a file for each row, and the datasheet view doesn't have an interface to upload a file. Because list items are made strictly of data in columns, you can create new ones from datasheet view.

NOTE When some columns are mandatory and the view doesn't show these columns, datasheet view doesn't let you create new items. To be able to create new list items in datasheet view, you must use a view that displays all the mandatory columns.

To create a new list item in datasheet view, just type values in the last row (the one marked with an asterisk) in the datasheet. The list item is created with the values you typed in. To finish adding the list item, press Enter or click another row in datasheet view. The datasheet creates the list item (see Figure 6.42).

FIGURE 6.42
Creating a new list item using datasheet view.

If there are many rows in a datasheet and you want to avoid scrolling down to the bottom to add a new list item, you can quickly get to the last row by clicking the New Row button in the List ribbon (which is available only when in datasheet view). Clicking this button scrolls down to the new row at the bottom.

Add Multiple List Items from Microsoft Excel by Using Datasheet View

A useful way to use datasheet view is to populate a list with the data from an existing spreadsheet. If you have a spreadsheet with many items, instead of typing them one by one using the method described in "Create a New List Item," earlier in this chapter, you can use datasheet view to paste in the values.

For example, if you have a Microsoft Excel spreadsheet that contains information about products, and you want to copy that information to a SharePoint list, you can use datasheet view to copy the information to the list, even if the columns are not the same. To do this, open the spreadsheet and select the information you want to copy (see Figure 6.43), and then select Copy from the Edit menu.

FIGURE 6.43
Select the Microsoft Excel information that you want to copy to the SharePoint list. Then copy it.

Next, switch the SharePoint list to datasheet view, which shows the columns you want to paste into. Remember that the view must be showing all mandatory columns for that list.

If the columns in datasheet view are not in the same order as in the Microsoft Excel spreadsheet, you must reorder them in datasheet view. To do this, simply drag and drop the column headers until the order is correct so that when you paste the information, it goes in the correct columns.

When the datasheet view is ready for the data, right-click the first cell and choose Paste to paste the data from Microsoft Excel (see Figure 6.44).

The information from the Microsoft Excel spreadsheet is pasted into the list. Because this can be a lot of information, SharePoint might take a while to create the list items. You can see the progress on the left side of the screen in datasheet view. If an item has not been added yet, it has an icon showing that it still needs to be synchronized with SharePoint. You must wait until all the items have been synchronized before you close the window or navigate to a different page.

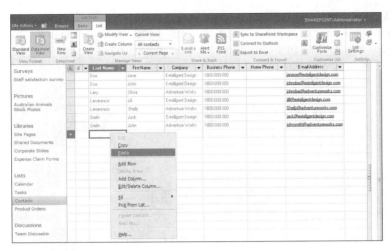

FIGURE 6.44
Right-clicking the first cell in the first data column and choosing Paste.

Check In and Check Out a File or List Item

Scenario/Problem: Some document libraries and lists require you to check out a file or list item before changing it. (*Changing* includes changing the properties of a file or list item and editing a file's contents as well.) You want to make changes to the file or list item and then share the changes with other people working on that site.

Solution: Checking in documents from the Office interface is mentioned earlier in this chapter, in the section "Upload a File from an Office Application." You can use the method described there, and you can also use the same process to check out a document: Just open the document using the Microsoft Office application and select the Check Out option from the menu. If you choose Edit from the document's or list item's drop-down menu, usually the document or list item automatically checks itself out for you. However, check-out and check-in are also offered on the web interface because not all files are Microsoft Office documents, and sometimes you do not want to open a Microsoft Office application just to check out a document (for example, just to make sure no one else is modifying it). When you are finished making changes and want other people to see your changes, you should check the document back in.

To check out a document, select the file or list item by using the check box that becomes available when you hover your mouse's cursor over the row for that document or list item. If the check-out mechanism is enabled, the Documents ribbon or Items ribbon shows the Check Out and Check In buttons under the Open & Check Out section of the ribbon (see Figure 6.45).

FIGURE 6.45
The Check Out and Check In buttons in the Documents ribbon.

The Check Out button might be grayed out if the document or item is already checked out to another user, and the Check In button is be clickable only if the document or list item is currently checked out to you.

TIP The Check Out and Check In options are also available from the drop-down menu for files and list items. This is similar to the Edit Properties and Delete actions. Figure 6.33, earlier in this chapter, shows those options in the menu and how to get to the drop-down menu of a file or a list item.

When checking out files (as opposed to list items), if you are using Microsoft Internet Explorer, you are asked whether you want to check out the file to a local drafts folder. (Other browsers may support this option in the future as well.) If you select OK, a copy of the file is placed in a special folder, usually called SharePoint Drafts, under the My Documents folder on your computer. (You can change this location from your Office applications.) If you do not choose this option, the file is just marked as checked out to you, but no copy of the file is made. The SharePoint drafts folder allows you to work on the document on your machine, even when the machine is not connected to the SharePoint site. When you connect again, you can go back to the document library to check in the document; doing this uploads it from the SharePoint drafts folder.

Checking in a file increases the version number of the file. The amount of increase depends on the settings for the list or document library. With the simplest setting, every time you check in a file or list item, its version is increased by 1. However, settings can change this. The next section provides more information on how different settings can affect the check-in process.

Publish a File or List Item

Scenario/Problem: A document library or list requires you to publish a file or list item that you have created or modified before it shows the new file or item to other users.

Solution: Some document libraries and lists require you to publish files and list items before other people can see them. This is similar to checking in a file or list item, as described in "Check In and Check Out a File or List Item," earlier in this chapter. The big difference is that the list or library manager can choose to set it up so that checking in a file or list item does not make it visible to everyone. It will be visible just to other people who have editing permissions on the library, and readers will be able to see only the last published version. However, the list or library manager may choose to allow everyone to see unpublished versions, in which case the publishing of an item or file is just a way to track version numbers. For example, a regular check-in increments the version number of a file or list item by 0.1, and publishing increments it by 1.

If the document library or list you are working on has the publishing requirement, the Documents ribbon or Items ribbon has a Publish button available in the Workflows section. If the selected file or item is checked in but not published or if it is checked out to you, you can click the Publish button (see Figure 6.46). Clicking this button checks in the file again, changes the version number of the item or file, and enables readers to view this version.

FIGURE 6.46
When publishing is required, you must click the Publish button to publish a major version.

If the list or library you are working on is set up to require approval, the file is not published until someone who has the appropriate permissions approves it (see Figure 6.47). This means that despite your publishing the file, readers may still see only the previously published version until someone approves your version. Of course, this also depends on the configuration.

A file that has been published but not approved ⌐
A file that has been checked in but not published ⌐

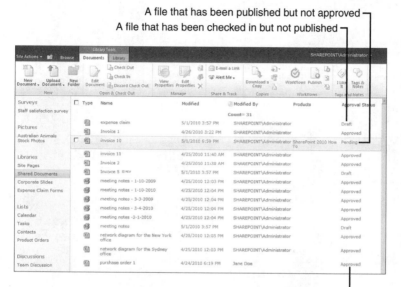

A file that has been published and approved ⌐

FIGURE 6.47
When publishing and approval are required, checked-in files are still considered to be drafts, and published documents that haven't been approved are considered to be pending approval.

To see how to approve a file that was published, see "Approve or Reject a File or List Item," later in this chapter.

See What Files or List Items Are Checked Out to You

Scenario/Problem: You have checked out some files or list items, and you want to find them to continue editing them, discard the check-out (deleting the changes you have done and reverting to the version before you checked out), or check them in again.

Solution: The option to see a report on all files or list items that are checked out to you in a site does not appear on all sites. Its inclusion depends on the features that the site manager enabled on the site you are using or on the site collection you are using.

To access a report, you need to use the Site Actions menu that appears at the upper-right corner of the page (if you have the required permissions and if the site uses the right features). From this menu, select Manage Content and Structure. This redirects you to a page designed for quicker management of a site, as shown in Figure 6.48.

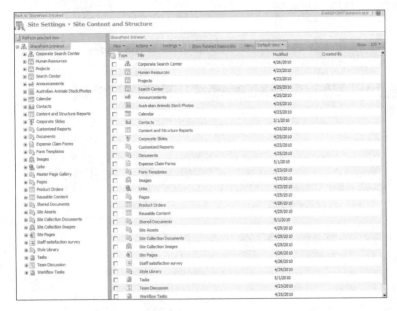

FIGURE 6.48
The Site Content and Structure page.

One option this page offers you is a way to locate the files that are currently checked out to you. This option is available under the Default View drop-down in the right section of the page. You open that drop-down and select the Checked Out to Me option (see Figure 6.49).

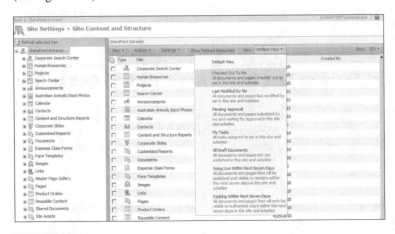

FIGURE 6.49
Selecting the Checked Out to Me option shows the files checked out to you in the site.

You can then use the drop-down menus for each of the files to check them in, or you can select multiple files with the check boxes and check them all in by using the Actions menu (see Figure 6.50).

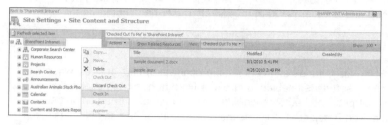

FIGURE 6.50
Selecting Check In from the Actions menu enables you to check in the selected files.

Restore an Earlier Version of a File or List Item

Scenario/Problem: You want to restore a file or list item to an earlier version and make it the current version.

Solution: Chapter 3 explains how to view the earlier versions of files and list items. To restore one of those versions, hover the mouse cursor over the date and time for that version, and then open the drop-down menu that appears. From the drop-down menu, select Restore (see Figure 6.51).

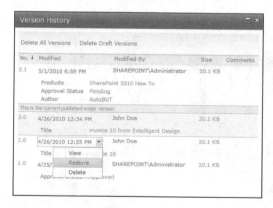

FIGURE 6.51
Selecting Restore brings back an earlier version of a file or list item.

Selecting the Restore option creates a new version for the file or list item and increases its version number. If the list or library requires check-in or publishing, the new version still must be checked in after the restoration. See "Check In and Check Out a File or List Item," earlier in this chapter.

NOTE A version can be restored only if the file is not checked out by someone else.

Approve or Reject a File or List Item

Scenario/Problem: You are the approver on a list or library, and you need to approve or reject a file or list item that another user has submitted for approval.

Solution: Some file libraries and lists require approval of files or lists. When this content approval setting is enabled, an item or file that has been checked in or published is not published automatically but instead remains in a pending state until it is approved or rejected. This means that the file or item is still considered a draft and is given the Draft status.

To be able to approve or reject files or items, you need specific permissions on the library or list. When a file or an item is approved, it is assigned Approved status in the list or library, and it is displayed to anyone who has permission to view the list or library.

When a file or an item is rejected, it remains in a pending state and is visible only to the people who have permission to view drafts (refer to Figure 6.47).

To approve or reject a file or an item, select the row for that item and click the Approve or Reject button in the Workflows section of the Documents ribbon or Items ribbon (see Figure 6.52). In addition, you can use the Approve/Reject option from the file or list item's drop-down context menu.

The Approve and Reject buttons in the ribbon ⌐

The Approve/Reject option in the file's drop-down menu

FIGURE 6.52
Selecting Approve/Reject from the context menu or from the ribbon.

Clicking this option or either of the buttons from the ribbon opens a dialog where you can choose to approve, reject, or keep the file or item in a pending state (see Figure 6.53). You can also add comments about your decision.

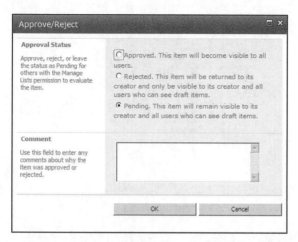

FIGURE 6.53
The Approve/Reject screen enables you to change the status of a file or an item.

See What Files or List Items Are Waiting for Your Approval

Scenario/Problem: You are the approver on a list or library, and you need to see what files or list items other users have submitted for your approval.

Solution: When a list or library is set to require content approval, views are added to the regular list views to help you manage the approval of files or list items. You see those views only if you have approval permissions on the list or library.

To see what files are waiting for your approval, select Approve/Reject Items, as shown in Figure 6.54. The Approve/Reject Items view shows you all the items, grouped by their status. To see the ones that are awaiting approval, look under the Pending group (see Figure 6.55).

For more information on how to approve or reject a file or list item, see "Approve or Reject a File or List Item," earlier in this chapter.

FIGURE 6.54
Selecting Approve/Reject Items.

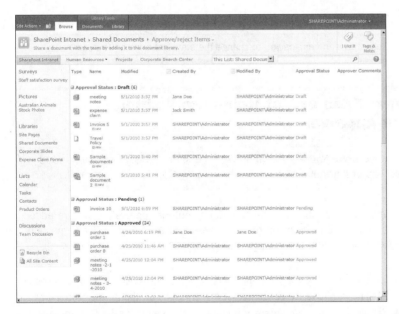

FIGURE 6.55
The Pending group shows files or items awaiting approval.

Use a Slide Library

Scenario/Problem: You want to use a slide library to share slides with other people or use slides that other people have shared with you.

Solution: The following sections explain how to use the unique interface of a slide library with Microsoft PowerPoint 2010.

Upload Slides to a Slide Library

To share slides that you have created, navigate to the slide library to which you want to publish them and click the Upload button in the library's toolbar, as shown in Figure 6.56.

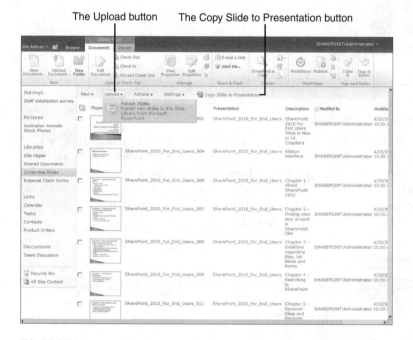

FIGURE 6.56
The Upload button in a slide library toolbar.

Clicking this button opens Microsoft PowerPoint on your computer. It also opens a dialog that asks you to browse to a presentation that has the slides you want to share. After you select the file you want, click Open. The next dialog shows the slides in the presentation you selected. It allows you to select one or more slides and publish them to the slide library (see Figure 6.57).

FIGURE 6.57
Choosing slides to be
published to the slide library.

Use Slides in a Slide Library

To use slides that have been published to a slide library, navigate to that library and
select the slides you want. Then click the Copy Slide to Presentation button on the
library's toolbar (refer to Figure 6.56). Microsoft PowerPoint opens on your computer
and displays a dialog that enables you to choose whether you want to add the slides to
a new presentation or to one that is already open in PowerPoint. Additional formatting
options are available, as shown in Figure 6.58.

FIGURE 6.58
The Copy Slides to PowerPoint dialog.

Click OK to add the slides to the presentation with the selected options.

CHAPTER 7

Creating Lists and Document Libraries

IN THIS CHAPTER

- ▶ Open the Create Dialog for Lists and Libraries
- ▶ Create a New Document Library
- ▶ Create a New Folder in a Document Library
- ▶ Create a New List
- ▶ Create a New Survey
- ▶ Add a Column to a List or Document Library
- ▶ Add a Site Column to a List or Document Library
- ▶ Choose a Default Value for a Column
- ▶ Enforce Unique Values on a Column
- ▶ Enforce Custom Validation on a Column
- ▶ Choose a Column Type
- ▶ Enforce Custom Validation on a List or Library
- ▶ Change or Remove a Column in a List or Document Library
- ▶ Change the Order of Columns in a List or Document Library
- ▶ Branching in Surveys
- ▶ Rename a List or Document Library or Change Its Description
- ▶ Change the Versioning Settings for a List or Document Library
- ▶ Change the Document Template for the New Button in a Document Library
- ▶ Add a Content Type to a List or Document Library
- ▶ Remove a Content Type from a List or Document Library
- ▶ Enable or Disable Folders in a List or Document Library

You use lists and document libraries throughout SharePoint to store any information that users need. This chapter explains how to perform basic tasks related to creating and customizing lists and document libraries, including creating columns (metadata), setting the document templates for document libraries, and more.

Open the Create Dialog for Lists and Libraries

Scenario/Problem: You want to create a list or a library.

Solution: There are different ways to get to the list or document/picture/form library creation page, and the choices depend on the configuration of the site.

The first step is to open the site where you want the document library to be created. In most sites, you see a Site Actions menu option, and you can create a new document library directly from this menu. However, this option only creates a library based on the default template, and you might want to create more advanced document libraries (such as a special document library for pages, pictures, assets, or slides), or you might want to create a list instead. To do this, choose the More Options option in the menu to open the Create dialog (see Figure 7.1).

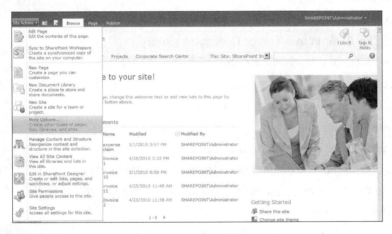

FIGURE 7.1
Open the Site Actions menu and choose More Options.

In sites where the More Options option is missing from the menu, you must use the View All Site Content link either on the Site Actions menu or the link in the left navigation bar (see Figure 7.2). Selecting this option opens the All Site Content page, where you can then click the Create button to get to the Create dialog.

The Create dialog allows you to create lists and libraries, showing all the different kinds of lists and libraries you can create in that site (see Figure 7.3). Different sites may show different kinds of list and library templates.

View All Site Content in the Site Actions menu

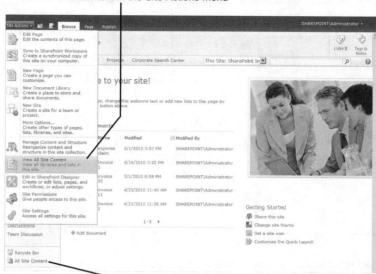

View All Site Content in the left navigation bar

FIGURE 7.2

Use either option to get to the All Site Content page.

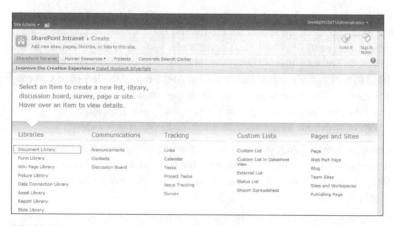

FIGURE 7.3

The Create dialog if you don't have Microsoft Silverlight.

This dialog can have two different appearances: one that uses Microsoft Silverlight and one that doesn't. If your machine doesn't have Microsoft Silverlight installed, you are directed to a Create dialog that looks like the one shown in Figure 7.3 (with a link to install Microsoft Silverlight in the yellow bar at the top of the page). If you have Microsoft Silverlight, you see the much more user-friendly Create dialog shown in Figure 7.4.

FIGURE 7.4
The Create dialog with Microsoft Silverlight installed.

The Create dialog shown in Figure 7.3 shows the available lists and library templates under categories. For example, the templates for document libraries (including the form library, picture library, and slide library) are all under the Libraries category.

The Create dialog shown in Figure 7.4 has three sections. The first section, on the left, lets you filter what templates are shown for the list and libraries you can create. For example, you can choose to filter by type. For example, you can select to display only library templates, or you can filter by category, showing only templates that offer functionality related to a category such as collaboration. At the top of the left pane you can also select the source of the templates shown. By default, you have two options there, Installed Items (showing templates available on the servers you are using) and Office.com, both of which are templates published on the Microsoft website.

The second section of this dialog, in the middle, shows the templates available for creating a list or library in the site. This list may change from site to site depending on the choices you made in the first section. Figure 7.5 shows several library templates available by default in SharePoint.

The last section, on the right, is where you specify the options for the new document library or list. (For more details, see "Create a New Document Library" and "Create a New List," later in this chapter.)

The top of this dialog provides more options to find the template you are looking for—including filtering the templates by language and searching for a specific template by its name or description. For example, you can type the word *Task* in the search box to search the templates. Figure 7.6 shows search results of two list templates that deal with tasks: Project Tasks and Tasks.

FIGURE 7.5
The list and library Create dialog, showing only library templates.

FIGURE 7.6
Searching the list templates.

NOTE You can also use the Create dialog to create other types of information. You can use it to create sites and pages as well as libraries and lists. To be sure you are creating what you are expecting to create, you should use the filter option on the left to select the type of structure you want to create.

Create a New Document Library

Scenario/Problem: You want to create a new document library.

Solution: To create a document library, you need to use the Create dialog as explained in the preceding section. The way you create the library depends on which Create dialog you are using (which depends on whether you have Microsoft Silverlight installed).

Using the Create Dialog with Silverlight Installed

In the Create dialog, click the Library filter on the left so that you only see library templates in the templates selection of the dialog (refer to Figure 7.5). From these templates, click on the Document Library one, and then give the document library a name on the right section of the dialog (see Figure 7.7). The name for the document library determines not just the title that the users will see but also the link that will be created document library. For example, if you call the document library Presentations, the link to the document library is the link to the site and then /Presentations. This is important because although you can change the title of the document library later, you cannot change its link.

FIGURE 7.7
Selecting the Document Library template and naming the new document library.

TIP If you want to avoid creating complicated links, choose a short name for the document library when you are creating it and then later change the title for the document library. For example, if you want to create a document library for human resources policies, you can name it HRP when creating it and then change the title to Human Resources Policies after it has been created. That way, the link is short and easy to type or view (when sending it in e-mail, for example), and the title explains to all users what should be in that document library.

Using this approach can also help you avoid unreadable links. For example, if your document library's name has spaces in it, the link to the document library will have the special character combination %20 instead of the spaces, which will make the link look long and complex. You can create the document library with a short name without spaces and then rename the title to have the spaces. The simpler link will remain.

Although you can have two document libraries with the same title, you cannot have two document libraries with the same link. This means that the link to the document library must be unique, and in this initial screen, you choose the unique name. If that name is already in use, SharePoint prevents you from creating the document library and asks for another name. Remember that you can always change the title later.

After selecting a name for the document library, you can either click Create to create the new document library with the name you chose and the default settings for that kind of library, or click More Options to switch to a dialog with more settings for the new document library (refer to Figure 7.7). This dialog, when shown for a document library, shows the same options you would see if you were creating the document library using the Create dialog without Silverlight installed. The following section explains the details.

Using the Create Dialog Without Silverlight Installed

When you don't have Silverlight installed, the Create dialog shows the Document Library link as an option under the Libraries category. If you click the link, you are directed to the new document library settings page, which is almost always the same as the More Options dialog that is shown when you choose More Options from the Create dialog.

This dialog might show different options for the document library, depending on the server configuration. For example, some SharePoint servers can allow a document library to have an associated e-mail address and receive e-mails sent to that library directly into the document library itself. If that option is enabled in the server, the settings page asks you for additional information, such as the e-mail address that should be associated with the document library. If the option is not enabled, the setting isn't displayed on the page (see Figure 7.8).

In this page, you can set the description for the library. This description is usually displayed to users in the All Site Content page next to the library's name. In most cases, it also appears in all the views for the library, just above the view. You can change the description later, in the library's settings.

For more information about how to change the title or description for a list or a document library, see "Rename a List or Document Library or Change Its Description," later in this chapter.

The next option you can set is whether a link to the document library should be added to the quick launch navigation bar (the left navigation bar for the site). You can change this option later also.

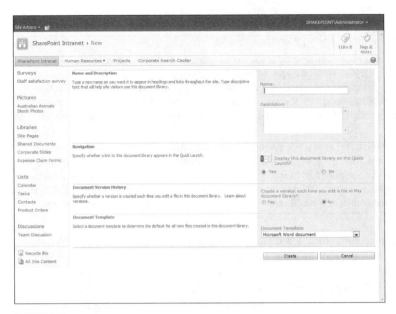

FIGURE 7.8
The new document library settings page shows the same settings as the More Options dialog.

The next choice to make is whether SharePoint should manage versions for documents in the document library. If you choose Yes, all changes in documents will create new versions of the documents. Although you can change this option later, if you choose No, all changes made in documents until you change the setting will not be stored in separate versions. However, if your site has a size quota and you are worried about consuming a lot of space, leaving this setting turned off can save quite a bit of space.

For more information about changing the versioning information for a list or document library, as well as setting some more advanced versioning options, see "Change the Versioning Settings for a List or Document Library," later in this chapter.

The last option, Document Template, enables you to choose the application or type of file that will be used when the user clicks the New button in the document library. For example, you can choose Microsoft Word to have SharePoint open an empty Microsoft Word document when the user clicks the New button, or you can choose any of the other Microsoft Office applications. For web pages, you can choose Basic Page to create an empty page that you can type text on. Or you can choose Web Part Page to create a page that allows the user to add web parts.

By default, the new document library has only the Document content type associated with it, so the New button does not show any options for different kinds of file types. However, here you can set a specific file type that the users can use with the New button. You can change this later also, as explained in the section "Change the Document Template for the New Button in a Document Library," later in this chapter.

When you are finished selecting the options, click Create to create the document library. A new, empty library is created with the settings you chose.

Create a New Folder in a Document Library

Scenario/Problem: You want to create a new folder in a document library.

Solution: To create a new folder, you navigate to the document library where you want to create the folder and then to the folder in the document library where you want the new folder to be (if you don't want it under the root of the document library). Then switch to the Documents ribbon and click on the New Folder button in the New section. A New Folder dialog appears, asking for the name for the new folder. Enter the name and click Save to create the folder.

NOTE The New Folder button is unavailable if any of the following conditions are true:

▶ The document library is configured not to allow creating folders.

▶ You do not have permissions to create items in the document library.

▶ The current view is configured to display as a flat view.

(See the section "Specify How Folders Will Be Used in a View" in Chapter 8, "Creating List Views," for more information.)

NOTE Folders are handled as list items in the document library. This means that if a library requires approval, the folder is not visible to other users until it is published and approved. For more information about publishing and approving files and list items, see Chapter 6, "Creating and Managing Files, List Items, and Forms in SharePoint."

Create a New List

Scenario/Problem: You want to create a new list.

Solution: As with the process of creating document libraries, there are two interfaces to create lists: one that uses Microsoft Silverlight if it is installed on your machine and one that doesn't. The section "Create a New Document Library," earlier in this chapter, describes the general differences between them, so this section focuses on the rich interface that uses Microsoft Silverlight only. If you do not have it installed, remember that clicking the link for the type of list you are creating opens a page that is similar to (but not always the same as) the More Options dialog explained here.

To create a list in a site, open the Create dialog as explained earlier in this chapter, filter the types of templates shown to show only list templates, and click the link for the type of list you want to create.

For example, you can create a list of events by choosing the Calendar type or a discussion board list by choosing Discussion Board. If you want a list that does not have any specific columns like those lists, you can choose the Custom List type to create a list that has only one column (Title). You can later add additional columns, as explained in "Add a Column to a List or Document Library," later in this chapter.

After you select the template, type a name for the new list in the name box on the right side of the dialog and either click Create to create the list with that name or click the More Options button to switch to the More Options dialog, which allows you to set more advanced options for the list before you create it.

Unlike with document libraries, the link to the list (or any other lists) is the site link, then /Lists/, and then the name you choose for the list.

> **TIP** As with document libraries, it is recommended that you choose a short name for a list when you are creating it and after that change the title.
>
> As with document libraries, the name you choose here must be unique in the site. If you choose a name that is already in use in the site, SharePoint does not let you create the list and asks you for a different name. Remember that you can change the title to anything you want after the list has been created.

In the More Options dialog you can set the description for the list that will show up in the All Site Content page of the site next to the list's name and in the views of the list. You can modify this later, in the list settings. For more information about how to modify the title or description of a list, see "Rename a List or Document Library or Change Its Description," later in this chapter.

Some lists, such as the survey list, have additional special settings, which are covered later in this chapter, but most lists have exactly the same initial settings.

Finally, you can choose whether a link to the list should be added to the quick launch navigation bar of the site. This, too, can be modified later, either through the list settings or through the site navigation settings. (Read more about changing site navigation in Chapter 13, "Customizing SharePoint Sites.")

When you are done selecting options, click Create to create the list. A new, empty instance of the list type that you selected is created, with the settings you chose.

Create a New Survey

> **Scenario/Problem:** You want to create a new survey.

> **Solution:** You create a survey the same way you create a new list, using the process explained in the section "Create a New List," earlier in this chapter.

However, the new list settings page that is shown if you have created the survey from a machine that doesn't have Microsoft Silverlight installed or if you clicked the More Options button has a very different settings dialog for the new survey you are creating.

Although most of the settings are exactly like the ones for a regular list, the survey list has two more settings that you need to set before creating the list. These options appear in the Survey Options section of the page.

The first option to configure—Show User Names in Survey Results?—enables you to decide whether the survey will be anonymous. If you choose No, the person viewing the results of the survey can't tell who answered what in the survey in any way. This setting is useful if you want to get honest feedback from people who might be concerned about revealing their true opinions (for example, using an employee satisfaction survey).

Choosing Yes tells SharePoint to show the name of the person who answered next to his or her answer in the reports. This setting is useful when you want to track who answered what (for example, in a survey that collects data from employees about what hotel they like to stay in when they are traveling).

The next option is whether to allow multiple responses. By default, a survey allows each person to answer the survey only once—like a voting system. However, you might want to create surveys that allow people to respond multiple times (for example, a survey that asks employees for suggestions for improving the company, where every employee might want to answer several times, every time they think of a new suggestion).

After you finish with the settings for the survey, click the Create button. Unlike with other list types, when you create a survey, you are immediately redirected to create questions for the survey.

The questions are almost identical to list columns, and creating them is almost the same as the process described in the following section. However, surveys also have additional options for column types that are not available in regular lists: the Rating Scale question type and a Page Separator. The section "Choose a Column Type," later in this chapter, describes these options in more detail.

When you are finished configuring the first question of the survey, you can either click the Next Question button to create another question or click the Finish button to finalize the survey. You can add, modify, or remove questions in the future (see "Change or Remove a Column in a List or a Document Library," later in this chapter).

When you create questions for surveys, the questions support another unique option called *branching*. This enables you to display different questions to users based on the answers they answered previously. For more information about branching, see "Branching in Surveys," later in this chapter.

Add a Column to a List or Document Library

> **Scenario/Problem:** You want to create a new column and add it to an existing list or document library. For example, you might want to add a date column called Birthday for a contacts list or a choice or lookup column called Client to a document library so that users can choose which client the document is about. (For more information about choice and lookup columns, see "Choose a Column Type," later in this chapter.)

Solution: To add a column to a list or document library, switch to the List ribbon or the Library ribbon and click the Create Column button in the Manage Views section of the ribbon, as shown in Figure 7.9.

NOTE The Create Column option creates a new column in the list or library but does not let you select from the site columns that are already set up in the site. To learn how to add an existing site column to the list or library, see "Add a Site Column to a List or Document Library," later in this chapter.

FIGURE 7.9
The Create Column button in the List ribbon.

Choosing the Create Column option opens a dialog where you can define the type of column you want to add, as well as choose the settings on that column (see Figure 7.10).

FIGURE 7.10
Creating a new column.

The first choice to make is the name of the column. Column names must be unique in the list; that is, you can't have two columns with the exact same name.

After choosing the name for the column, you must choose the type of the column, as shown in Figure 7.10. There are numerous types of columns, and developers can add to those types, so you might see more than the built-in types shown in the figures in this book. Also, as mentioned earlier in "Create a New Survey," creating a new column in that type of list (also known as creating a new *question*) shows more options than are available for standard list types.

All column types require you to choose a name for the column. They also allow you to specify the description for the column and whether the column is required (making the column mandatory in the list, forcing the user to fill it in when creating or editing an item) and whether the column should be added to the default view of the list or library. Except for the column type, all options can be modified in the future. Changing the column type for a column is possible but is limited to certain column types. For more information about modifying a column see "Change or Remove a Column in a List or Document Library," later in this chapter.

However, each column type can offer different configuration options for that column. For example, a Single Line of Text column type has a Maximum Number of Characters setting, whereas a Multiple Lines of Text column type has a Configuration option for how many lines it should allow.

Some column types also have an option for more complex validation settings, under the heading Column Validation, as shown a little later in Figure 7.12. Other columns do not support this type of complex validation.

For more information about choosing a column type and the different configuration options that each type may have, see "Choose a Column Type," later in this chapter.

Add a Site Column to a List or Document Library

Scenario/Problem: You want to add to an existing list or document library an existing site column that has been defined in the site.

Solution: As explained in Chapter 1, "About Microsoft SharePoint 2010," a site column is a column that is defined at the site level rather than at the list or library level. Reusing those columns in lists and libraries makes a lot of sense. If a change to the column setting is required in many lists and libraries, it is possible to change the column at the site level once to update all the lists and libraries using that column.

If you want to use an existing site column instead of create a new column, you can open the list's or library's settings page by switching to the List ribbon or Library ribbon and clicking the List Settings or Library Settings button.

In the list's or library's settings page that opens, scroll down to the Columns section of the page. Here, you see the list of all the columns that have been added to the list or library. In this section, click the Add from Existing Site Columns link. This selection opens a page that enables you to choose one or more site columns to be added to the document library or list (see Figure 7.11).

To choose a column, you locate it in the Available Site Columns box, select it, and click the Add button to add it to the Columns to Add box. If you regret your choice and want to undo it, select the column in the Columns to Add box and click the Remove button.

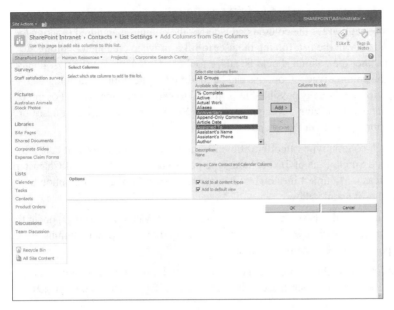

FIGURE 7.11
Choosing site columns for a list or library.

To more easily find a column, you can filter the columns that are in the Available Site Columns box by choosing the group for the column. Site columns are grouped in logical groups. For example, the Core Document Columns group holds columns that are commonly used by most documents: Author, Comments, Date Created, and so on. By default, you see the site columns from all groups available to you. To choose a different group, open the Select Site Columns From drop-down box and select a different group.

> **NOTE** When adding a site column, you cannot specify any settings on it because any column settings are defined at the site level. However, after adding the column, you can modify it as you would any other column. (See the instructions in the section "Change or Remove a Column in a List or Document Library," later in this chapter.)

Choose a Default Value for a Column

> **Scenario/Problem:** You want to define a default value for an existing or new column in a library or list. For example, in some instances, you want date columns to default to the current day's date or text columns to default to the current user's name; or for choice columns, where the user can choose from multiple choices, you may want to select one of the choices as the default.

Solution: Some types of columns can have default values. Default values appear in the column when a user is creating a new list item or is uploading a new file, but the user can choose to change the value.

Some column types allow more advanced settings for default values than others. The specifics for those column types are covered in the section "Choose a Column Type," later in this chapter.

Enforce Unique Values on a Column

Scenario/Problem: You want to make sure no two list items in a list or library have the same value in a column. For example, you want to make sure no two files have the same title or no two tasks have the same title.

Solution: The option to enforce unique values is available for some column types (refer to Figure 7.10), including the single line of text, number, choice, and lookup. Selecting Yes in this option tells SharePoint to make sure that users do not enter the same value in two different list items.

Enforce Custom Validation on a Column

Scenario/Problem: You want to set more complex validation rules on a column. For example, in a single text column, you might want to prevent users from entering certain words such as the word *test*. Or you might want to make sure the user filling in the form types *I agree* before submitting the form to make the user think twice before submitting it.

Solution: Most column types support a rudimentary type of validation, allowing you to select whether the column must have a value (in most cases). Some columns are even more specific, requiring you to, for example, specify a minimum and a maximum for a Number column. (For more details, see "Number (1, 1.0, 100)," later in this chapter.) However, sometimes you need more validation options than are available.

Some SharePoint columns support a formula-based validation mechanism similar to Microsoft Excel formulas. This mechanism is available for columns under the Column Validation heading, and this heading is collapsed by default. Expanding this section reveals two additional settings that you can set for the column.

The first option is the formula. Here you can type a formula that is evaluated when the user tries to save the value for that column. For example, you can add a formula to prevent the word *test* from being used as a value:

```
=[column_name]<>"test"
```

In this example, you replace `column_name` with the name of the actual column you are validating, as shown in Figure 7.12.

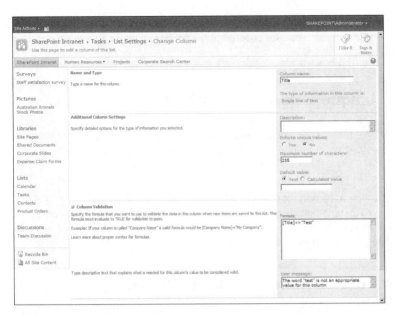

FIGURE 7.12
Setting custom column validation on a text field.

The second option you can set in this section is the message that is displayed to the user when validation fails. For example, you can write **The word "test" is not an appropriate value for this column**. This message is displayed to the user below the column in red text, as shown in Figure 7.13.

FIGURE 7.13
The column validation prevents a user from submitting a task with the title test.

You can also enforce validation based on comparison between two columns. This is covered later in this chapter, in the section "Enforce Custom Validation on a List or Library."

Choose a Column Type

Scenario/Problem: You are creating a new column in a library, list, or site, and you have to select a column type for the new column.

Solution: When you're creating a new column, the first thing you need to decide in addition to the name for the column is its type. The type of the column defines what kind of data can go into it, and SharePoint has a lot of different built-in column types for you to choose from. The following sections explain each built-in column type and the different settings you can define for each one.

Single Line of Text

You use the Single Line of Text column type when you want the user to enter simple text in a single line (that is, no line breaks), as shown in Figure 7.14.

FIGURE 7.14
The First Name column in a contacts list is an example of a Single Line of Text column.

Aside from the regular settings, such as the description for the column and whether the column is mandatory, you can also define the maximum number of characters allowed in the field (up to 255 characters) and the default value for the column (see Figure 7.15).

FIGURE 7.15
Defining the settings for a Single Line of Text column type.

The default value for a Single Line of Text column can be either a static piece of text that you type if you select the option Text or a calculated value showing the current user's account name by using the token [Me]. For example, you might want to create a calculated default that will have text (that the user can change) saying who purchased an item. The default is the name of the current user filling the form, but if the user is filling in the form for someone else, the text might need to be changed. Figure 7.16 shows how to configure this, and Figure 7.17 shows how it looks to users.

FIGURE 7.16
Defining a calculated default value.

FIGURE 7.17
The calculated default value when a user creates a new item.

Multiple Lines of Text

The Multiple Lines of Text column type allows users to enter text with more than one line (that is, line breaks are allowed). It can be configured to allow different editing options for the user, as shown in Figure 7.18.

A Multiple Lines of Text column configured to show two lines of plain text

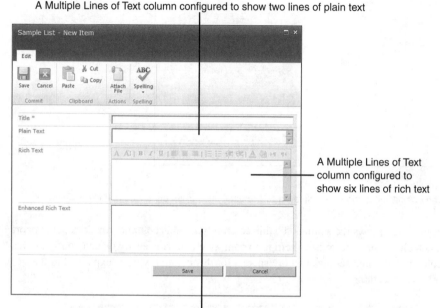

A Multiple Lines of Text column configured to show six lines of rich text

A Multiple Lines of Text column configured to show six lines of enhanced rich text

FIGURE 7.18
Different configurations of the Multiple Lines of Text column.

As shown in Figure 7.18, the column type can be configured to allow rich formatting of the text: You can make parts of the text bold, underlined, or a different font or color, and you can even include pictures, tables, and links. This configuration is not available in document libraries, and you see it only when adding a site column or a column in a list.

The enhanced rich text option shows as an empty text box, but when the user switches to that text box, the Editing Tools ribbon appears, enabling the user to edit the text using the enhanced text-editing options available through that ribbon, as shown in Figure 7.19.

FIGURE 7.19
The Editing Tools ribbon is displayed to the user when in an enhanced rich textbox control.

Figure 7.20 shows the settings for this column type. This column type does not support a default value, so there is no setting to configure one. However, you can configure the column with three settings that are special for this column type, as explained in the following sections.

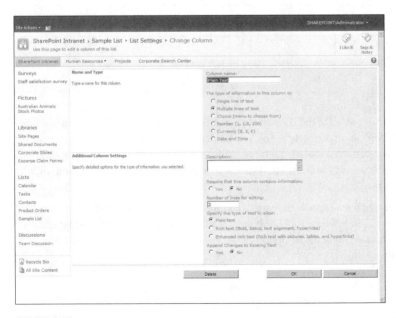

FIGURE 7.20
Defining the settings for a Multiple Lines of Text column type.

Number of Lines for Editing

The Number of Lines for Editing setting determines how many lines are displayed in the editing box for the text. This can be any number from 1 (where only one line will be displayed, but users can scroll down or up in the box) to 1,000. This setting does not affect the length of the text that can go into the column, just the appearance of the editing box (refer to Figure 7.18).

> **TIP** It is recommended to keep the number small in the Number of Lines for Editing setting so that the column editing box doesn't take a huge amount of space in the editing form.

Specify the Type of Text to Allow

In the Specify the Type of Text to Allow setting, you can specify the type of text that can be entered in the editing box. The simplest option is Plain Text, which allows just simple, unformatted text (refer to Figure 7.18). The users do not have options to make any part of the text bold or a different font.

The next option, Rich Text, enables the users to set formatting on parts of the text and set the font, font size, alignment, color, and other kinds of formatting that are common when writing rich text.

The last option, Enhanced Rich Text, allows even more special formatting, such as making parts of the text into hyperlinks, adding images to the text, and creating tables.

Append Changes to Existing Text

The last option, Append Changes to Existing Text, lets you configure what happens when someone edits the value of the column in a list item or a file. The default setting is No, which means that when someone edits the value, it just changes to the new value. Users who then view the properties of the list item or file see the new value, not the old one. If they want to see the old one, they must open the list item's or file's version history if versioning is configured in the document library.

Choosing Yes here changes how the column is displayed when users view the properties of the list item or file. Instead of seeing just the current value, users also see the entire history of what the value was before, including who made changes and when. This option can be turned on only when versioning is enabled on the list or library because SharePoint must track the old versions of the value to show this information. For information about how to configure versioning on the list or library, see "Change the Versioning Settings for a List or Document Library," later in this chapter.

When the Append Changes option is enabled, the old entries and the current one appear under the editing box for the column. If there are no old entries, that is shown also (see Figure 7.21).

Address	No existing entries.

FIGURE 7.21
The Address column shows that there haven't been any old values.

When there are old entries, such as corrections to a value, they are shown to a user viewing the item as a list of values, complete with who wrote the value and when (see Figure 7.22).

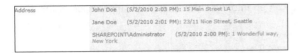

FIGURE 7.22
The Address column shows the history of changes when viewing the properties of a list item.

When you are editing a list item of a file, the list of values appears below the editing box for the column, and the edit box it is empty (see Figure 7.23).

FIGURE 7.23
The Address column shows the history of changes when editing the properties of a list item.

Choice Column

You can use a choice column when you want users to choose from a list of options for the value of the column in different configurations (for example, a list of regions or countries, as shown in Figures 7.24 through 7.26), with different controls appearing to the user.

FIGURE 7.24
A choice column that allows users to select one or more choices from a list.

FIGURE 7.25
A choice column that allows users to select only one choice, using the drop-down menu configuration.

FIGURE 7.26
A choice column that allows users to select only one choice, using the radio buttons configuration.

Choice columns enable you to specify the values you want the users to choose from, and you can configure them to allow the users to either make a single selection or select multiple values from the list (see Figure 7.27).

FIGURE 7.27
The configuration options for a Choice column type.

Specify the Choices

To specify the choices from which users can choose, simply type the choices in the box titled Type Each Choice on a Separate Line (refer to Figure 7.27). Use a line break to separate choices; for example, for a list of countries, type the countries in the box with a line break between each country name.

Choose How the Choices Will Be Displayed

The next configuration setting you can set is how the choices are displayed to the user. The first two options, Drop-down Menu and Radio Buttons, enable users to select only one option from the list of choices, whereas the last option, Checkboxes, allows multiple selections of values.

The Drop-down Menu option is useful when you have a lot of choices and don't want to overwhelm users. The values appear in a drop-down menu, which opens to reveal the list of choices (refer to Figure 7.25).

The Radio Buttons option is useful when the list of choices is small and will not take a lot of space on the page. The advantage of this option is that the user sees all the options on the page without having to open a drop-down menu (refer to Figure 7.26).

The Checkboxes option is useful when you want the users to be able to choose more than one option (refer to Figure 7.24).

Allow Fill-in Choices

When you choose to allow fill-in choices, the column enables users to type a value if the value they are looking for does not exist in the list of choices you chose (see Figure 7.28). The values that users type are not added to the list.

FIGURE 7.28
When the Allow Fill-in Choices option is enabled, users can type a value manually.

Default Value

As with most other column types, you can type a default value that will be selected when the user creates a new item. If you want nothing to be selected by default, clear the Default Value box; otherwise, you need to make sure you type in the Default Value box the exact text of one of the choices.

Number (1, 1.0, 100)

The Number column type is useful when you want to capture a numeric value. With this column type, the user is asked to type a number in a text box. For example, you might ask for a 1-to-10 rating for a document or the number of products in stock. Figure 7.29 shows the settings for this column type.

FIGURE 7.29
The configuration options for the Number column type.

Minimum and Maximum

With this option, you can configure for a Number column the minimum and maximum numbers that the user can choose in the value.

Number of Decimal Places

In the Number of Decimal Places option, you configure how many decimal places the value can have. If you choose the value 0, fractions of numbers are not allowed; only integers are allowed. Choosing the value 1 enables users to specify numbers with one decimal place, such as 15.4. Choosing the value 2 allows a precision of two decimal places, and so on up to five decimal places. The default option for this setting is Automatic, which displays how many decimal points are in the entered number.

Show as Percentage

Choosing the Show as Percentage option causes the value entered in this column to be displayed as a percentage.

Default Value

Like other columns, this column supports a default value that you can enter as a static default value or as a calculated value. This column supports many mathematical formulas using standard arithmetic operators (such as +, -, *, and /) to perform calculations. For example, you can have a calculated default value of =128+10, which results in a default value of 138. Another option is to use special functions in the calculation. Number columns support such functions as Pi(), which returns the number for pi; AVERAGE(), which returns the average of the numbers you give it; and MAX, which returns the biggest number in the list of numbers you give it.

> **NOTE** As you can see, having calculated defaults for the Number column is not extremely useful; essentially, you are typing in a static number. However, these formulas do work in this column type, and you might find a use for them. To take full advantage of these formulas, see the "Calculated (Calculation Based on Other Columns)" section, later in this chapter. For more information about the types of formulas and how to use them, see http://tinyurl.com/SPcalculated2010.

Currency ($, ¥, e)

The Currency column type is almost exactly the same as the Number column type. The only option that is different in the Currency column type from the Number column type is Currency Format. This option determines what symbol will be used next to the value when displaying the value in the item's or file's properties. For example, choosing United States displays values with the dollar sign ($) next to the value, while choosing one of the European currencies displays the euro sign ($) next to the value.

Date and Time

The Date and Time column type lets users specify a date or a date and time as the value for the column. For example, in a calendar list, users can specify the start date and time of a meeting. However, for a list of contacts, if you want a column with the birth date of a contact, for example, you need to configure the column to ask only for the date, not for the time. Figure 7.30 shows the two modes for this column.

FIGURE 7.30
Two date and time columns: one shows only dates and the other shows date and time.

Figure 7.31 shows the configuration options for this column type.

FIGURE 7.31
The configuration options for a Date and Time column type.

Date and Time Format

With the Date and Time Format configuration option, you can choose whether the users can choose just a date or a date and time. This choice changes what the date-choosing control looks like.

Default Value

You have the option to choose a specific date or make the current date the default. Also, you can use the Calculate Value option and set a default that calculates based on the current date using the [Today] token. For example, to set the default to be two weeks from the current date, type [Today] +14 in the Calculated Value box. This capability is useful when you want to use a column as an expiration date, for example, while allowing the users to change the expiration date. You can set the default value to be two weeks in the future from creating the list item or file, but the user can still change the date manually.

> **NOTE** If a user just selects a time and not a date, SharePoint doesn't save anything in the column. To avoid this, you should set a default date value for the column.

Lookup (Information Already on This Site)

Lookup is one of the most useful column types. It is similar to the Choice column type in that the users get to choose from a list of values (refer to Figures 7.24 through 7.26 for examples of how this might appear to users). However, unlike the Choice column type, the Lookup column type does not store the choices in the settings of the column. Instead, the choices are in another list or library.

For example, if you create a SharePoint list in a site and enter a list of countries in that list, you can use the Lookup column type to show values from that list. This feature is helpful when you want other users to be able to manage the list of choices. The other users do not need permissions to change settings on the current list; they just need permissions to change items or files in the list of values (the remote list).

Unlike the Choice column type, though, in the Lookup column, the values that users choose show up as links to the list item or file selected. This can help create a complicated system of lists connected to one another (for example, a list of orders connected to a list of products). When users create a new order, they can choose a product or products, and when they view an order, the product name appears as a link to the product list item.

You can configure a Lookup column to display additional columns from the list it is looking up to. For example, in an orders list, instead of just seeing the name of the product for an order, you can also see the product ID or when the product expires, as if these were separate columns in the list you added the lookup column to.

Finally, the Lookup column can enforce relationship behavior. It can control the relationship between the two lists selected. For example, you might want to restrict deleting products while there are still orders referring to those products. This option allows you to do that, and it is explained in more detail later in this chapter.

Figure 7.32 shows the configuration options for this column type.

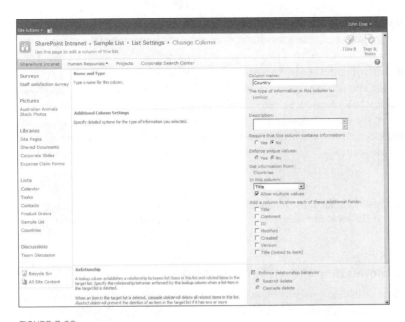

FIGURE 7.32
The configuration options for a Lookup column type.

Get Information From

In the Get Information From field, you specify which list has the information you want
to display to the user. The choices here are the available lists in the current site. It is
not possible to reference a list from another site.

In This Column

In the In This Column configuration option, you specify which column in the list to
which you are connecting will be displayed to the user as the possible values. For
example, the most common choice for this setting is the Title column, which displays
the titles of the list items or files as the options for the user to choose from.

Allow Multiple Values

As you can do with the Choice column, you can have the Lookup column enable users
to choose more than one value. When you select the Allow Multiple Values option, the
user interface for selecting values changes, allowing the users to select multiple values,
as shown in Figure 7.33.

FIGURE 7.33
The user interface for selecting multiple values in a lookup column type.

NOTE Selecting Allow Multiple Values disables the Enforce Unique Values and Enforce Relationship Behavior settings.

Add a Column to Show Each of These Additional Fields

As mentioned earlier, you can configure a Lookup column to display more than just one column (the one selected in the "In This Column" section, mentioned earlier). The additional columns are displayed to users in list views and when viewing the properties of the list items or files, but they are not displayed to users who are editing the properties because they are part of the Lookup column.

The additional columns are displayed with the name of the Lookup column before them, as shown in Figure 7.34.

FIGURE 7.34
The user interface displaying additional columns from a Lookup column.

NOTE Not all columns from the looked-up list are available to display under this section. This feature supports only columns from certain column types (for example date, Number and Single Line of Text column types).

Yes/No (Check Box)

The Yes/No column type is one of the simplest column types available. It enables the user to select either Yes or No by selecting or clearing a check box. The only configuration option you can set for this column type is the default value for it: Choose either Yes or No.

NOTE A common problem that a lot of people have when creating forms in SharePoint is how to add a check box for the user to agree to conditions before saving the form (or a similar requirement). This requirement can be answered with a Yes/No column, combined with list validation (see "Enforce Custom Validation on a List or Library," later in this chapter), or it can be achieved with the Choice column type: You simply specify just one choice (I Agree, for example) and make the column mandatory.

Person or Group

The Person or Group column type enables users to choose a value from a list of users or groups (see Figure 7.35).

FIGURE 7.35
The user interface for entering data in the Person or Group column type.

You can see an example of this column type in the tasks list, where users who want to assign a task to other users choose from the list of users to whom they want to assign the task. The selected values appear as the names of the users chosen when a user views a list item or a file's properties, and the name is a link to the chosen user's properties page. As you can do with Lookup columns, you can configure whether this column type allows multiple selections (see Figure 7.36).

FIGURE 7.36
The configuration options for the Person or Group column type.

Allow Multiple Selections

The Allow Multiple Selections configuration option lets you define whether the column will allow users to choose more than one user in this column.

Allow Selection Of

The Allow Selection Of configuration option defines whether the user will be able to choose only people (other users) or also groups. If you want groups to be selectable, you must change this option.

Choose From

In the Choose From configuration option, you specify what users and groups appear to the user to pick from. By default, this option is set to All Users, which enables the user to choose from the list of all the users that SharePoint recognizes, even users who do not have access to the current site or list. The second option, SharePoint Group, limits the selection to users in a specific security group in the current site or site collection. This option is useful if you want to let users select from a restricted list of users, in which case you should create a security group and set the column to show only users from that group.

Show Field

In the Show Field configuration setting, you define what will be displayed as the selected value when a user views the list item or file properties. The default is the name of the user who was selected, together with that user's presence information (whether that user is online or busy, for example; this requires that special instant messaging software be installed and configured on the user's machine). You can change this option to display other information about the selected user.

Hyperlink or Picture

The Hyperlink or Picture column type enables users to enter data that will be displayed as either a link or a picture when the value is viewed (see Figure 7.37). You should choose this column type when you want users to freely type a link to a web page (in SharePoint or otherwise) or to a picture.

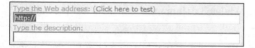

FIGURE 7.37
The user interface for entering data into a Hyperlink or Picture column type.

The only setting to set on a Hyperlink or Picture column type, Format URL As, determines how to format the link that the user types when viewing the list item's or file's properties. The first option is to format it as a hyperlink, which displays the title that the user chose as a link to the page the user chose. The second option is to format as a picture, which shows the picture to which the user typed the link instead of showing the link itself.

Regardless of what settings you choose, the user interface looks the same: The user is asked to enter a URL path and a title (refer to Figure 7.37). However, when you're looking at list views and viewing the properties of a list item or file, the difference is apparent. As Figure 7.38 shows, the same information is shown in two columns of type Hyperlink or Picture, one formatting the information as a link and the other formatting the information as a picture.

FIGURE 7.38
A view showing one column configured to show the data the user typed as a picture and another column configured to show the data the user typed as a hyperlink.

Calculated (Calculation Based on Other Columns)

A Calculated column type does not allow the user to enter data in it; it is used only to show data based on a calculation of other columns. For example, if you want a Full Name column that displays information automatically based on the First Name and Last Name columns, you can create a Calculated column that concatenates the values in those two columns.

As another example, say that you have a list of orders that has a column for the number of products ordered and another column for the price for a single product. The Calculated column can display the total revenue for the order by multiplying the numbers in the two columns.

The configuration options for this column type include a special formula builder control that enables you to specify the calculation required for the column, as shown in Figure 7.39.

FIGURE 7.39
The configuration options for a Calculated column type. The formula in this figure concatenates two columns and a piece of text.

Formula

In the Formula text box, you can define the calculation that will be performed (refer to Figure 7.39). You can select the columns on which you want to perform a calculation from the list on the right and click Add to Formula to add a reference to that column in the formula.

For example, to concatenate two text columns, add the two columns from the list and use the ampersand (&) character to connect them. You can also add a piece of text in quotation marks. The value is automatically displayed everywhere, including in list views and views showing the list item's or file's details.

For a complete list of formulas that you can use, see http://tinyurl.com/SPcalculated2010.

The Data Type

The second option you need to configure for the Calculated column type is the data type that will be used for the calculation. Select the appropriate data type that matches the data type of the columns for which you are performing an operation. It is possible to perform an operation on columns of different types. For example, you can multiply the value in a Number column by the value in a Currency column, but you must decide how the result of the operation will be displayed—either as a number or as currency.

Rating Scale

The Rating Scale column type is available only in surveys. You use it when you want the user to rate several items in a Likert scale control. It's like asking many questions in one column, where the answer for each question is a number. These questions are referred to as the sub-questions of the column.

For example, you might want to gather input on user satisfaction on several aspects of a service, or you might want to know how strongly users agree with certain statements about different aspects of a book (see Figure 7.40).

FIGURE 7.40
The Rating Scale column data entry user interface.

The Rating Scale column type is useful in surveys where you want to assess how users feel about multiple subjects. It gives the user an interface for quickly and easily answering several questions. You can configure this column to specify what questions will be included, what ratings the user can choose, and what the values mean. Figure 7.41 shows the configuration page for this column type.

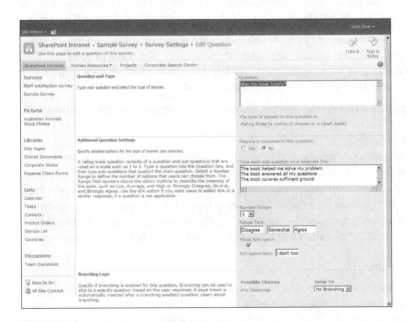

FIGURE 7.41
The configuration page for the Rating Scale column type.

Type Each Sub-question on a Separate Line

The Type Each Sub-question on a Separate Line setting is where you specify the sub-questions that appear to the user to rate. You type each one in a separate line, as shown in Figure 7.41.

Number Range

In the Number Range setting, you specify the range of numbers the users can choose from when rating your sub-questions. You can choose any number from 3 to 20.

Range Text

In the Range Text setting, you specify the text that will be displayed above the low, medium, and high rating options. This helps the user understand what the numbers mean. For example, in Figure 7.40, number 1 means Disagree, while number 3 means Somewhat Agree and number 5 is Agree.

Show N/A Option and N/A Option Text

Show N/A Option and N/A Option Text enable you to specify whether you want to allow the user to not rate some of the sub-questions. This is useful if the user might not have an answer for one of the sub-questions. If you select that you want the option to be available, you can also change the text shown for the option. For example, in Figure 7.41 the text was modified to I don't know. Figure 7.40 shows how the user sees this.

Page Separator

The Page Separator column type is unique to surveys. It enables you to add a page break between questions, so if you have a very long survey, a user is not presented with a single page with all the questions on it, but instead sees a subset of the questions and has a Next button to go to the next page.

A page separator does not have any settings that you need to set. You can't even give it a name.

External Data

The External Data column type is available only when you have SharePoint Server installed. It is used in a similar fashion to the Lookup column type, but instead of allowing the user to select a value from a list in the current site, it shows the user values from a business application that the administrator or developer has set up.

A common example for this is a company that has a database with information about customers. Instead of migrating that information into a SharePoint list, the administrator configures a business data application integration. Then you can create columns that allow the users to choose from the list of customers who exist in that database. By default, no external data applications are configured, so this column type is used only after developers and administrators have configured it. Figure 7.42 shows the configuration options for this column type when an external content type and field are selected.

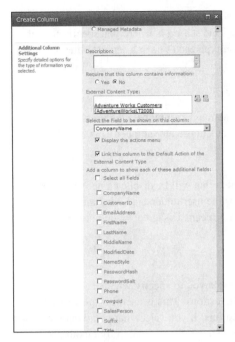

The configuration options for an External Data column type, with External Content Type and Field settings selected.

External Content Type

In the External Content Type selection box, you select which external content type the column will connect to. If you click the database icon, a dialog box appears, showing all the content types that you can select from and to which external data source they belong. If no application is configured in your system, the dialog tells you so.

In the dialog you can search for the entity you want to allow the users to select (for example, Product) and select it. After you select an entity, more options you can set on the column become available, the same as in a column of type Lookup (refer to Figure 7.42).

Select the Field to be Shown on This Column

The Select the Field to be Shown on This Column option enables you to select which field from the database should be used as the title field for the selection that the user made. For example, in the Product entity, choosing the Product Name field makes a lot of sense. However, you might want to choose the Product Serial Number field instead.

Display the Actions Menu

The Display the Actions Menu option enables you to select whether an Actions menu should be displayed when a user moves the mouse cursor over a value in the column. Some entities can have actions that the developer has developed for them, such as Show Product or Delete Product. To see the list of actions available for an entity, select this option and then see what actions show up.

Link This Column to the Default Action of the External Content Type

The Link This Column to the Default Action of the External Content Type option determines whether the values appear as links. When this option is selected, the user is redirected to a profile page for the entity. For example, when showing the name of a product, the name appears as a link that, when clicked, opens a page with more information about the product and actions to perform on the product.

Add a Column to Show Each of These Additional Fields

You might want to display more information than just the name of the selected entity when users are viewing the list item's or file's properties. The Add a Column to Show Each of These Additional Fields option enables you to select more properties of the entity that will be displayed as if they are separate columns when viewing the properties of the list item or file, even though, when editing the properties, the column is shown as only one. This is displayed in the same way as the Lookup column with the same option selected (refer to Figure 7.34).

This option is visible only after you select a content type and a field.

Managed Metadata

The Managed Metadata column type is available only when you have SharePoint Server installed (not SPF). It is similar to the Lookup column type in the fact that it, too, displays options to the user from a predefined list of options that is not part of the column itself. However, the Managed Metadata column type is more advanced both in the way it is displayed to the end users and in the options administrators have to manage the items available for the users to choose from.

Unlike with a Lookup column, the items the users choose from in a Managed Metadata column type do not come from another list. Instead, the values come either from an enterprise term repository (managed by the administrator) or from a custom term set that you can create in the site collection.

The terms in the term sets can be hierarchical. For example, instead of having a flat list of products for the user to choose from (as in the example in the "Lookup (Information Already on This Site)" section earlier in this chapter), the administrator of the Managed Metadata service can create a term set that has product categories with products in each category. This can evolve to more levels of hierarchy if required. For instance, you might have a category for Mobile Phones and under it the names of the manufacturers, and under each manufacturer the model numbers of the phones, as shown in Figure 7.43.

The user interface for this type of column is a textbox with an icon next to it. The user can either write the term in the text box or click the icon to open the dialog that shows the terms that are available, as shown in Figure 7.43.

FIGURE 7.43
The user interface for selecting a value from a Managed Metadata column.

Figure 7.44 shows the configuration options for the Managed Metadata Column type.

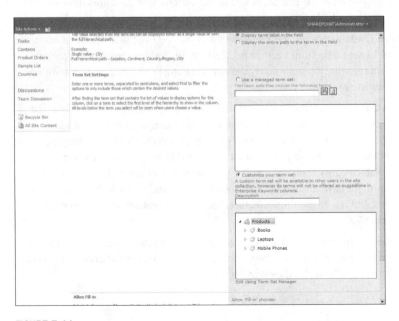

FIGURE 7.44
The configuration options for a Managed Metadata column.

Allow Multiple Values

For the Allow Multiple Values option, you set whether the users can choose multiple terms. You should not select this option if you want the users to be able to select just a single term.

Display Value

The Display Value option sets how the terms will be displayed to a user viewing the properties of the file or list item. Because the terms may be hierarchical, showing just the value of the term (the term label) can lead to confusion if there are two terms with the same label but under different hierarchies.

For example, if you have a term set that has mobile phones under the manufacturers, and if two different manufacturers have the same name for a mobile phone, you will not know by looking at the label which mobile phone it is unless you select Display the Entire Path to the Term in the Field, which displays the entire hierarchy as the value of the column.

Term Set Settings

As mentioned earlier, you can connect a column to an existing term set by using the Use a Managed Term Set option. This option allows you to select the existing term set from the box under it, as shown in Figure 7.45.

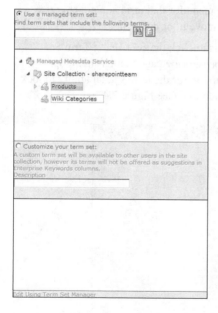

FIGURE 7.45
Selecting an existing term set.

If you want to create your own new term set instead, select the Customize Your Term Set option. This enables you to create the term set in the box under that option. By default, when you select the Customize Your Term Set option, a new term set is added with the label Untitled. You can rename the term set by clicking on it once and typing the new name. To create terms in the term set, open the drop-down menu for the term set (hover with the mouse over the name of the term set, and then open the menu that appears) and click Create Term, as shown in Figure 7.46.

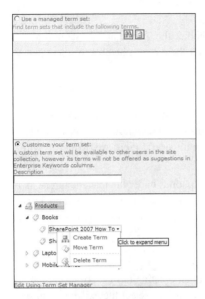

FIGURE 7.46
Creating a new term in a custom term set.

Clicking on the Create Term option creates a new term without a label (name), and you can then give it a name. You can then open the menu for that term and either create terms under it (using the Create Term option), move it, or delete it.

A more advanced way to manage the term set is to click the Edit Using Term Set Manager link at the bottom of the box. This opens a new page that has more options for managing the term set, including the description for the term set, an ability to lock down the term set, different sorting options, and more (see Figure 7.47).

FIGURE 7.47
The term set manager.

Enforce Custom Validation on a List or Library

Scenario/Problem: You want to configure more complex validation for columns to prevent users from entering conflicting information in two different fields. For example, if you have two date columns, Starting Time and Due Date, you want to make sure users enter a bigger value in the Due Date column.

Solution: To configure validation at a list or library level, open the list or library settings page by switching to the List ribbon or Library ribbon and clicking the List Settings or Library Settings button. In the list or library settings page, click the Validation Settings link to open the validation settings page shown in Figure 7.48.

FIGURE 7.48
The list validation settings page.

Here you can define a formula that will be evaluated when the user tries to save a new item in the list or library. The formula must evaluate to TRUE for the save to be successful.

For example, if you have two date fields, select the Due Date column from the Insert Column box on the right and click the Add to Formula link to add it to the box, and then do the same with the Starting Time column. In this way, you add the column names (surrounded by square brackets) to the formula. Add a > (greater than) sign between them, as shown in Figure 7.48, and click Save.

Another option in this page is to set the message the user sees if the formula fails to evaluate to TRUE. For example, Figure 7.48 is set to display a message to the users that the Due Date must be after the Starting Time.

You can use AND and OR operators to chain validation conditions in the formula. For example, you can have the formula check that either the State/Province column or the Country/Region column has a value and that either Home Phone or Mobile Phone has a value, as shown in Figure 7.49.

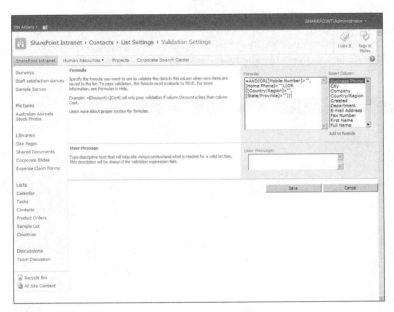

FIGURE 7.49
Chaining conditions by using the AND and OR operators for a complex validation rule.

Change or Remove a Column in a List or Document Library

Scenario/Problem: You want to modify the settings of a column in a list or library. For example, you want to change the default value for the column, change the column's title, or add or remove choices for a choice column.

Solution: To change a column's setting in a list or document library, go into the list or document library's settings page by switching to the List ribbon or Library ribbon and clicking the List Settings or Library Settings button.

In the list or library settings page, scroll down to the Columns section of the page. Here, you see the list of all the columns that have been added to the list or library.

When you click the title of the column you want to modify or remove from the list or library, the settings page for that column appears. In this page, you can either modify the column (rename it, change its settings, or even change its type) or delete the column by using the Delete button at the bottom of the page.

NOTE Some columns cannot be deleted, and the Delete button is not displayed for those columns. These built-in columns are an integral part of SharePoint and cannot be removed from lists and libraries.

CAUTION Changing the type of a column can have significant repercussions. You can lose data if you move from one column type to another. For example, switching from any type of column to a Choice column causes any value that doesn't exist in the choice list to be lost.

Change the Order of Columns in a List or Document Library

Scenario/Problem: You want to change the order in which columns are displayed to the user when either entering the values for the columns or viewing the details for a list item or file. For example, in a contacts list, you might want the users to enter the first name before entering the last name.

Solution: To change the order of columns in the data entry page for a list or library (but not in the views), you go into the list's or document library's settings screen by switching to the List ribbon or Library ribbon and clicking the List Settings or Library Settings button.

NOTE For information on changing the order of columns in a view, see "Specify the Order of the Columns in the View" in Chapter 8.

In the list or library settings page, scroll down to the Columns section. Here, you see the list of all the columns that have been added to the list or library. If the list does not use more than one content type, a Column Ordering link is available under the list of columns. If there is more than one content type, you have to change the column order for each content type separately by clicking on the content type name under the Content Types section above the Columns section. This opens the content type settings page, which also has the columns list and a Column Order link beneath it.

Clicking on the Column Order link opens a page that allows you to reorder the columns (see Figure 7.50).

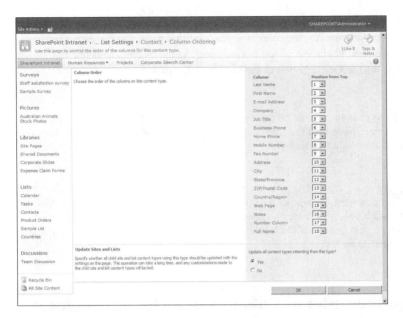

FIGURE 7.50
Reordering the columns in a list or library.

In the Column Order page you can specify for each column the order by using the drop-down boxes to the right of the column names. If you change the order for one column—for example, change mobile phone to be the third column—the column automatically moves to the place you have selected, pushing the other columns down as necessary.

When you are finished ordering the columns to your liking, click OK at the bottom of the page.

Branching in Surveys

Scenario/Problem: You want to make it easier for the user to answer a survey by displaying the questions in the survey in different pages. Additionally, A survey has a lot of questions, and depending on the answer to some of them you may or may not want answers to other questions.

Solution: As mentioned earlier, in the section "Create a New Survey," surveys have a special capability to redirect users to different questions based on the answers to previous questions. This is known as *branching*.

For example, if you create a survey with three questions: Did you read the book? Do you plan to read the book? and Was the book good? you can assign a branching on the first question so that a user who answers Yes is redirected to the third question. A user who answers No is redirected to the second question. The second and third questions are not shown when the survey interface is first shown to the users. They are shown only after the user answers the first question. Users have a Next button that allows them to continue to the next question in the branch. Figure 7.51 shows how branching looks to the user.

FIGURE 7.51
Branching in a survey. The user sees only the first question, with a Next button to go to the next question, depending on the answer.

To define the branching in a survey, you first create all the questions and then edit the columns you want to be conditional so that they have the branching. You don't need to add page separators unless you want to; the survey automatically splits the questions into pages, depending on the branching. Figure 7.52 shows how to define the branching on the first question to redirect the users based on the answer.

FIGURE 7.52
Defining branching in a survey.

Rename a List or Document Library or Change Its Description

Scenario/Problem: You want to rename a list or document library, or you want to change the description shown for that list or library. For example, say that a library was created with the name Documents, and you want to modify it to a name that tells the user more about the types of documents that should be uploaded to that library—Management Presentations, for example.

Solution: To change an existing list's or library's title or description, open the list's or library's settings page by switching to the List ribbon or Library ribbon and clicking the List Settings or Library Settings button. At the top of the page that appears, under the General Settings section, click Title, Description, and Navigation link.

On the page that opens, shown in Figure 7.53, you can set a new title for the list or library, change the description, and choose whether a link to the list or library should appear in the quick launch navigation bar.

FIGURE 7.53
Changing the list or library name, description, and navigation options.

NOTE Changing the name of a list or library does not change the link to that list or library. The link stays the same, but the title that is displayed changes.

Change the Versioning Settings for a List or Document Library

Scenario/Problem: You want to change how a list or library deals with storing versions for documents and list items. For example, say that a document library was created with versioning turned off, and you want to turn it on. Or say that a library was created and configured to have versioning but not to support automatic check-out of a document when a user opens a document for editing, and you want to change that.

Solution: To change the versioning settings for a list or library, open the list's or library's settings page by switching to the List ribbon or Library ribbon and clicking the List Settings or Library Settings button. At the top of the page that appears, under the General Settings section, click the Versioning Settings link.

In the versioning settings page, you can define how the list or library creates versions for list items or files. This page is different for lists than for libraries because documents and list items behave differently.

Set the Versioning Settings for a List

The first setting for versioning in a list is whether content approval is required (see Figure 7.54). This option is not strictly about managing versions of the list item but rather about the publishing process for a modification to a list item. If you select this option, every time a modification is made to a list item (or when one is created), the list item is not displayed to all users automatically. Instead, the list item gets an approval status of Pending, and no one can see it except its author and people who have permissions to view drafts in the list—until a person with the permissions to approve items in the list approves that item, thereby changing its status from Pending to Approved.

FIGURE 7.54
The Versioning settings page for a list.

The next section is Item Version History. Here, you can define whether versions should be tracked for the list and how many versions should be kept. This second option is optional, and you can leave it unlimited if you want to. Finally, if you set the Require Approval option, you can also limit the number of approved versions to keep.

The last option on this page, Draft Item Security, is also valid only if you chose to require approval. It lets you define who can see draft items that have not been approved yet. The options are any user who can read items in the list, only users who can edit items in the list (who might need to be able to see the drafts to edit them), or only the people who can approve items in the list (which is the minimum required because they must be able to view the drafts to approve them).

Set the Versioning Settings for a Document Library

The versioning options for a document library are almost identical to those of a list. The only two differences are explained here.

As shown in Figure 7.55, the first option that is different is that, instead of just selecting that the library should store versions, you can select how versions will be stored: either as major versions (which is how lists behave) or so that any change will result in a new version (changing the version number from 1 to 2 to 3, and so on).

FIGURE 7.55
The Versioning Settings page for a document library.

This setting does not enable you to specify that a certain change is not major enough to warrant an increase of the version number for the document. For example, if you change a document by spell checking it and correcting the spelling or updating the date it was last printed, this change might not be important enough. This is why you might want to choose the option for major and minor versions, which allows users to decide whether the change is major, thereby increasing the version number by 1, or minor, thereby increasing the number after the decimal point for the number.

The second option that you can configure for document libraries only is the Require Check Out option. Selecting this option can help reduce conflicts when several users want to work on the same file. This option forces users to check out a file before editing it by automatically checking out the file for them and preventing others from editing it. This way, users can't forget to check out a file but start to work on it without realizing that another user is also working on the same file.

> **NOTE** It's important to remember that when the Require Checkout option is selected, uploading multiple documents adds those documents as checked out, and they are not visible to other users until you check them in.
>
> There is no automatic check-in of a file because SharePoint cannot know when the editing is done and the user is ready to check in the changes. Users therefore must be aware of this fact and get used to checking in files and not keeping them checked out forever.

Change the Document Template for the New Button in a Document Library

> **Scenario/Problem:** You want to change what kind of document is created when the user clicks the New button in a document library. For example, say that you want to make the New button create a Microsoft PowerPoint presentation out of a specific template in the document library that is specific for presentations. Or say that you want a Microsoft Excel template for expense reports to open in the Expense Reports document library.

Solution: If you want to change the template or application used when a user clicks the New button in a document library, you can specify it in the document library settings. You do so by switching to the Library ribbon and clicking the Library Settings button.

> **NOTE** You might want to show several choices of templates to users as a menu under the New button. That is possible if you use content types. See "Add a Content Type to a List or Document Library," later in this chapter, as well as "Create a Content Type" in Chapter 13 for more information.

At the top of the page that appears, under the General Settings section, click the Advanced Settings link.

On the page that appears, you can either edit the template that is used by clicking the Edit Template link on the right side or link to a Microsoft Office document that you have uploaded to SharePoint (see Figure 7.56). You need to ensure that the link to the document that you entered works by clicking the Edit Template link after adding the link.

FIGURE 7.56
The Advanced Settings page for a document library with options to allow content types, set the template URL, and enable or disable the New Folder command.

NOTE The Template URL box is disabled if there are multiple content types enabled for the document library. If you want to change the template in that scenario, you have to change it for each content type separately by clicking the content type's link in the library settings page and then clicking the Advanced Settings link in that page (see Figure 7.60, later in this chapter).

You should upload to the Forms folder that exists in any document library. That folder is hidden, and users don't see it in list views, which means they don't see your template as a file to be modified and managed. However, you can decide to put the template in another location, not in the current document library. Just remember that this location must be readable by all users and not just you. Therefore, putting the document in another location can be problematic from a security point of view because you must be sure that all the users who are allowed to create documents in the document library are also allowed to read from the location of the template.

> **NOTE** To get to the Forms folder, you type the link to the document library, followed by /forms/. For example, if the link to your document library is http://sharepointlocal/Sample/Shared Documents/, type the link http://sharepointlocal/Sample/Shared Documents/Forms. This link opens the Forms folder (which should look empty). You can upload to this folder a document to be used as a template.

The file type you use as a template determines what application is used when the user clicks the New button. For example, if you choose a Microsoft Excel document as the template, the Microsoft Excel application opens when the user clicks the New button.

> **NOTE** Not all file types can be used as templates. You can use only file types from applications that are compatible with SharePoint, such as Microsoft Office applications.

If you want to add several options for templates under the New button, you must do so by adding multiple content types to the document library. See the next section for details.

Add a Content Type to a List or Document Library

> **Scenario/Problem:** You want to add a content type that is defined in the site to a list or library. As explained in Chapter 1, using content types is a useful way to specify groups of properties for files or list items. Content types can also specify a document template for creation of a new document of that content type. For information about creating new content types, see "Create a Content Type" in Chapter 13.

Solution: To add a content type to a list or library, you first enable management of content types in that list or library. To do so, go to the list or document library settings page by switching to the List ribbon or Library ribbon and clicking the List Settings or Library Settings button.

At the top of the page, in the General Settings section, click the Advanced Settings link. On the Advanced Settings page, shown in Figure 7.56, select Yes under Allow Management of Content Types? Then click OK at the bottom of the page.

You then return to the list or library settings page, which now has a section for content types (see Figure 7.57).

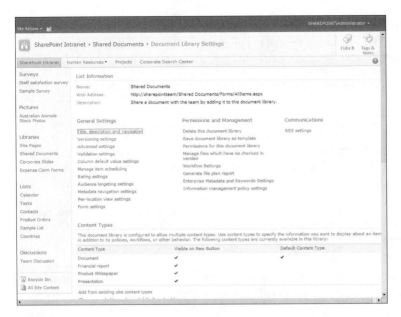

FIGURE 7.57
The Content Types section appears only if content types are enabled for the list or library.

To add a content type, click the Add from Existing Site Content Types link in the Content Types section. The content type selection page appears, enabling you to select one or more content types to add to the list (see Figure 7.58).

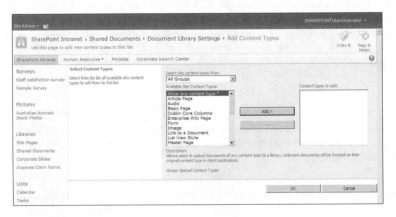

FIGURE 7.58
The Add Content Types page.

On this page, the available content types appear in the box on the left. Select the one you want and click the Add button to move it to the box on the right (which shows the types you selected). If you want to remove a content type you added by mistake, select it from the box on the right and click the Remove button.

When you are finished selecting all the content types you want for the list or document library, click OK. The resulting list or library settings page shows the list of content types available in the list or library.

Remove a Content Type from a List or Document Library

Scenario/Problem: You want to remove a content type from the list or library so that it is not available for the users in that place.

Solution: To remove a content type from a list or document library, go to the settings page for that list or library by switching to the List ribbon or Library ribbon and clicking the List Settings or Library Settings button.

The settings page shows the list of content types available in the list or library (if content types are enabled), as you can see in Figure 7.59. To remove one, click the link to that content type.

FIGURE 7.59

To remove the Financial Report content type, click the Financial Report link in the Content Types section.

The configuration page that opens shows the content type for that specific list or library (see Figure 7.60). Changes that you make in this page affect only the list or document library but not other lists and libraries that use the same content type. You can tell this by the fact that the content type has a parent with exactly the same name—and this is possible only when viewing the settings of a content type in a list or library, and not the settings for the content type that is defined in the site. As long as you see this, changing the content type affects only the list or library from which you started.

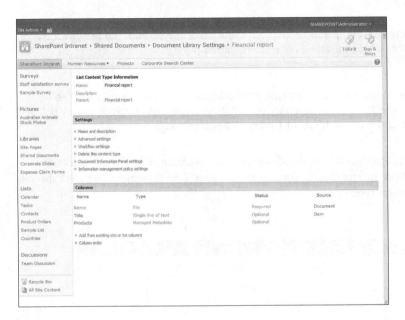

FIGURE 7.60
The content type settings page.

To remove the content type from the list or library, click the Delete This Content Type link. Doing so opens a prompt that asks you to confirm the deletion of the content type. Click OK to remove the content type.

NOTE   The Delete This Content Type link does not actually delete the content type; it just removes the content type from the list or library. An easy way to be sure that you are not deleting the content type from the site is to look in the breadcrumbs at the top of the page. If the breadcrumbs show that you are under the settings for the list or library, you are not deleting the content type but instead just removing it. In any case, SharePoint does not let you delete a content type from a site if it is still in use by a list or library, so you can feel safe to click this link.

Enable or Disable Folders in a List or Document Library

Scenario/Problem: You want to enable or display folders in a list or library. For example, say that you want to prevent users from creating subfolders in a document library, or you want users to create list items in a folder structure inside a list.

Solution: To enable or disable folders in lists and libraries, go to the list or library settings page by switching to the List ribbon or Library ribbon and clicking the List Settings or Library Settings button. On the settings page, click the Advanced Settings link to get to the advanced settings page of the list or library (refer to Figure 7.56). On that page, choose Yes or No for the Make New Folder Command Available option, which is located in the Folders section of the page.

CHAPTER 8

Creating List Views

IN THIS CHAPTER

- ▶ Create a Personal or Public View for a List or Library
- ▶ Specify Columns for a View to Display
- ▶ Specify the Order of the Columns in a View
- ▶ Specify How Items in a View Are Sorted
- ▶ Specify How Items in a View Are Filtered
- ▶ Specify How Items in a View Are Grouped
- ▶ Specify Totals for a View
- ▶ Specify a Different Item Style for a View
- ▶ Specify How Folders Will Be Used in a View
- ▶ Specify the Item Limit for a View
- ▶ Enable or Disable Inline Editing in a View
- ▶ Enable or Disable Selecting Multiple Items in a View
- ▶ Create Mobile Views
- ▶ Modify a View
- ▶ Delete a View

As explained in Chapter 3, "Solutions Regarding Files, Documents, List Items, and Forms," list views are important and help users find the content they are looking for more easily. If you are in charge of a document library or list and want to make it more accessible and more usable to users, you should consider creating list views for the users. Even if managing a particular list is not your responsibility, you will want to learn how to create a personal view that is visible only to you, where you can set the view to display information that is relevant to you specifically and that you often need to find. This view will save you a lot of time.

This chapter covers how to create custom list views, either personal or public ones, and what settings can be set on them.

Create a Personal or Public View for a List or Library

Scenario/Problem: In some lists, you have permissions to create new views—either personal views (that only you are able to see) or public ones (that everyone is able to view). You now want to create a view that will help you or other users find information in the list or library more easily.

Solution: To create new views, either personal or public, go to either the List ribbon or Library ribbon and click the Create View button in the Manage Views section of the ribbon. Or you can click on the current view name in the breadcrumbs shown in the Browse ribbon to open the view selector and choose Create View from the options, as shown in Figure 8.1

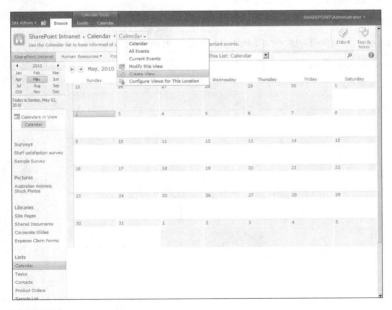

FIGURE 8.1
Clicking the Create View option.

On the page that opens, choose from a list of available view types (see Figure 8.2). Different lists can have different types of views. For example, the events list has a special view type for recurring events; this kind of view shows instances of each recurring event as if it were a single event and not relevant to other types of lists.

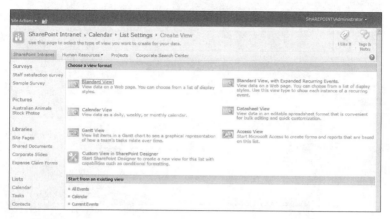

FIGURE 8.2
The view type selection page.

Also, depending on what applications you have installed on your computer, you might get additional view types, such as the Access view that is displayed only if you have Microsoft Access 2007 (or later) installed and configured on your machine.

Create a Standard View

If you want a standard list view, select the Standard View link. The Create View page that appears enables you to name your view if it is going to be the default view for the list (see Figure 8.3). You can also select whether it is going to be a public or personal view and choose the settings for the view.

Select Whether a View Is a Default View

Making a view a default view causes SharePoint to display that view when users navigate to the list or document library. Because that setting affects all users, and not just you, this option is valid only for public views because personal views are visible only to you and not to other users.

Select Whether a View Is a Personal View or Public View

The option to choose between a public view and a personal view is a very important one. If you have the necessary permissions to create public views, consider carefully before creating a view as a public one. After all, creating too many views can confuse the other users of that list or library. If you are creating a view for your own use, it is better to keep the view private.

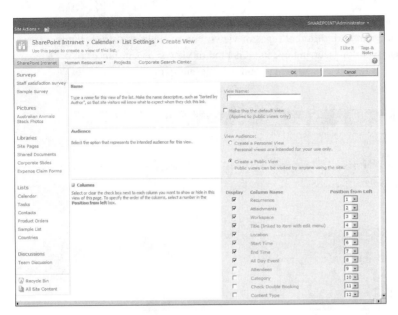

FIGURE 8.3
The Create View page for a standard view.

> **TIP** Naming a view is very important. You will want to know how the view is different when selecting the view from the view picker, and the only thing you see there is the view name. However, you should avoid long names because they are hard to read in the view picker.

If you do not have permissions to create public views, the option to create one is grayed out, and you are able to choose only to create a personal view.

After you fill in the name for the view and select whether it is a personal or public one (and if it is public, whether it should be the default), save the view by clicking OK. The view is created, and you can select it from the view picker. However, you should probably change the view first. The rest of the tasks in this chapter explain what you can change in a view.

Create a Calendar View

Calendar views show information from a list or document library as if this information were events on a calendar. There must be one date column to define as the start date column and one column to define as the end date—the time interval. It is enough to have one column to be both the start and end dates. For example, in a document library, you can create a calendar view that shows the documents based on the day they were created (see Figure 8.4).

To create a calendar view, select the Calendar View type. The first two options in the view setting screen are similar to those of the standard view: naming the view and selecting whether it is going to be a default view and whether it is a personal or public view (refer to Figure 8.3).

FIGURE 8.4
A document library with a calendar view based on the created date.

Next, choose the columns on which the time interval in the calendar will be based. For example, in a document library, to create a calendar view based on the created date of the document, select the Created column for both the beginning and end (see Figure 8.5).

FIGURE 8.5
Configuring a calendar view based on the Created Date for a document library.

As another example, for a tasks list, you can choose the start date of the task as the start column and the due date as the end column to create a view that shows the tasks in a calendar-style view.

Calendar views have three subviews: the daily view, which shows each day separately (see Figure 8.6); the weekly view, which shows week by week (see Figure 8.7); and the monthly view, which shows the entire month (refer to Figure 8.4).

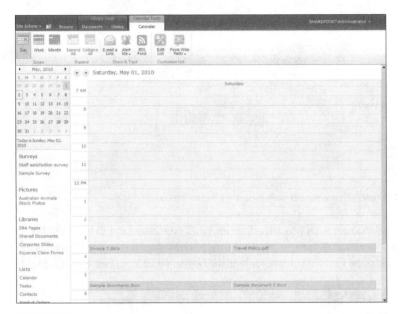

FIGURE 8.6
The daily view for a document library.

These subviews are part of the view itself and are all configured as part of creating the calendar view. For more information about configuring the subviews separately, see "Specify Columns for a Calendar View," later in this chapter.

Create a Gantt View

A Gantt view displays items based on date columns—very much like the calendar view. However, it shows the items in a Gantt chart, where each item is displayed as if it were a task in a project plan. A tabular version of the view appears to the left of the chart, showing more details on the list items (see Figure 8.8).

Creating a Gantt view is similar to creating a standard view. Select the Gantt view type in the view type selection page, and you get the same options to name the view and select whether it should be the default view and whether it should be personal or public.

FIGURE 8.7
The weekly view for a document library.

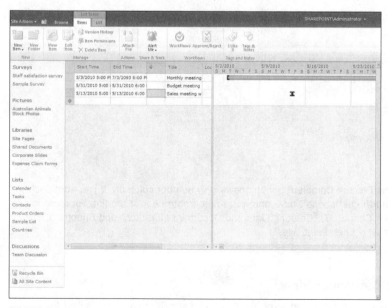

FIGURE 8.8
The Gantt view for an events list.

After configuring those options, scroll down to the Gantt Columns section of the page (see Figure 8.9). In this section, you configure what columns will be used as the title column, starting date column, and due date column. Optionally, you can also specify a percentage column to indicate in the Gantt chart how the item has progressed and the predecessors column. (A predecessors column is a column that specifies for each item which should be completed before it can start. This is most common with tasks that have to be done sequentially.)

The column you select in the Title box is displayed in the Gantt chart as the title of the item. In most cases, this is the title column, but you can also display a different column as the title.

FIGURE 8.9
Creating a Gantt view.

> **NOTE** The Percent Complete option shows only number columns. If you want such a column and the list doesn't have one, you must create one for the list. For more information, see Chapter 7, "Creating Lists and Document Libraries," and Chapter 13, "Customizing a SharePoint Site."

Create a Datasheet View

Creating a datasheet view is exactly like creating a standard view. You select the datasheet view type in the view type selection page, and you get the same options to name the view and select whether it should be the default view and whether it should be personal or public.

However, a datasheet view has fewer advanced options to choose from than standard views. For example, you can't specify a grouping for the view (see "Specify How Items in a View Are Grouped," later in this chapter) or the display style for the items (see "Specify a Different Item Style for a View," later in this chapter). This is because the datasheet view is displaying the items in a sheet—rows and columns. Refer to "Switch to a Datasheet View" in Chapter 3 for more information about the datasheet view.

Specify Columns for a View to Display

Scenario/Problem: When creating or editing a view in a list or library, you want to specify different columns to be displayed to the users in the view. For example, in a contacts list, you want to display the first and last name columns in the view but not the company.

Solution: The following sections explain how you can select which columns are displayed to the users in different types of views.

Specify Columns for a Standard View or a Datasheet View

After filling in the name for a view and selecting whether it is a personal or public one (and if it is public, whether it should be the default), scroll down to see the list of columns (refer to Figure 8.3). Here, you can choose which columns are displayed in the view and in what order they should appear. To select a column, select the check box next to the column name. To hide a column, remove the check from the check box.

TIP In document libraries, the Title column is separate from the Name column. The Name column holds the actual file name, while the title can be blank. When building views for document libraries, remember that the name of the document is more likely what the users are looking for and that, unlike in lists, it is the Name column that can be displayed as the link to the file and not the title column.

Specify Columns for a Calendar View

In calendar views, you can't choose multiple columns to display and order them in the same way that you do for standard views. The reason is that in a calendar, the users see only one column as the heading for the item.

It is possible to set for each subview separately what column will be displayed as the link to the item or file. Normally, you would use the Title column (for lists) or Name column (for document libraries), but you can choose any column you want. That column will be displayed as the heading for the item or document in the view.

Both the daily and weekly subviews support a subheading column, which is displayed beneath the heading. You can either choose a column to be used as a subheading or leave it not configured if you do not want a subheading.

Specify Columns for a Gantt View

In Gantt views, as explained earlier in this chapter, you must choose a column that will be used as the title in the Gantt chart under the Gantt Columns section. However, unlike a calendar view, a Gantt view also shows a tabular view of the items below the chart, which means you can also modify which columns are displayed in that part of the view. To do so, use the Columns section of the page to select which columns will be displayed.

Specify the Order of the Columns in a View

Scenario/Problem: When creating or editing a view in a list or library, you want to specify a different order for the columns that are displayed to the user in the view. For example, in a contacts list, you want the first name to be displayed before the last name or vice versa.

Solution: In standard, datasheet, and Gantt views, you can change the order of the columns you chose to display. For example, you might want to show the title of the item first, followed by the date it was created, and then the date it was modified; or you might want the title to be followed by the modification date and then the creation date.

NOTE In calendar view you don't have the option to reorder columns because only one column appears (two in daily and weekly views).

To rearrange the order of the columns in the view, use the Position from Left drop-down boxes. These drop-down boxes contain numbers that you can choose for the column order. If you want a column to be displayed first, change the number in the drop-down box next to that column to 1. The next column should be 2, and so on. If you change a column that had a higher number to a lower number (say, from 4 to 1), the other columns automatically arrange themselves. For example, changing the Position from Left setting for the Title column that had the value 4 to the value 1 automatically changes the three columns that are before it (Recurrence, Attachments, and Workspace) to be 2, 3, and 4, respectively.

NOTE The Title (or Name, in document libraries) column usually appears three times in this view creation page because there are three different ways to show the title for a list item. The simplest one is just Title, which displays the title of the list item or document as regular text. The second option is Title (Linked to Item), which displays the title as a link to the item. The last option is Title (Linked to Item with Edit Menu), which displays the title as a link but also allows a drop-down menu to open when the mouse cursor hovers over the title. This last one is the default in most views.

Specify How Items in a View Are Sorted

Scenario/Problem: You want to specify how a view should sort the items. For example, in a contacts list, you want it to sort on the Last Name column in ascending order so that Adams is before Brahms. Furthermore, if two people have the same last name, you want them sorted by their first names, so that Anne Adams appears before Brenda Adams.

Solution: SharePoint supports sorting based on up to two columns. To select the sort order, scroll down to the Sort section of the view creation page (see Figure 8.10).

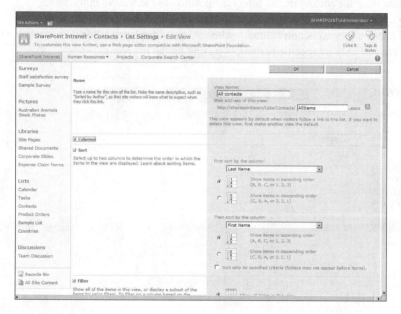

FIGURE 8.10
Changing how items are sorted in a view.

Under First Sort by the Column, choose the column by which the view should sort first and how that sorting should take place (ascending or descending). Then you can optionally select another column to further sort the items, using the second column selection drop-down. This determines how items with the same value in the first column you selected will be sorted.

For example, you might want to sort an event list by Start Date column first and Title column second; that way, if two items have the same start date, the one scheduled to start first will appear first.

A different example would be to sort a document library using the Title column (ascending) first and then the Created column (descending) second. That way, if two files have the same title (not name), the one created later would appear before the older one.

> **NOTE** Some view types do not allow you to pick a sort order. For example, the Calendar view type does not have a sort order because calendars always display the events in them sorted by the start date of the event.

The last option under the Sort section is Sort Only by Specified Criteria. By default, SharePoint views show folders above any files or items, regardless of the name of the folder. If you want the sorting to also affect the position of the folders in the view, select this option, and folders are treated as if they were items when they are sorted. Figure 8.11 shows how a document library with folders is displayed when the view is configured to sort only by specified criteria—sorting on the file name.

FIGURE 8.11
A view configured to sort only by specified criteria. Folders are sorted as if they were documents and do not appear before the documents.

Specify How Items in a View Are Filtered

> **Scenario/Problem:** You want to limit the view so that it shows only items with certain values in certain columns. For example, a common requirement is to display announcements until a certain date, when they then expire.

Solution: Filters determine what items or files are displayed in a view, based on the data that is in the columns. A solution to this problem would be to create a column for the expiration date and add a filter to the view that displays only the announcements whose expiration dates are in the future.

To define filter criteria for a view, scroll in the view creation page to the Filter section (see Figure 8.12). By default, no filter is applied on a new view, so the view displays all items.

FIGURE 8.12
The Filter section in the view creation page.

To define a filter, use the column picker drop-down and select the column based on which you want to filter items. Then choose the operator that you want for the filter and the value you want to use for the comparison. For example, if you want to filter a view to display only items that have a title (excluding the items that do not have a value in the Title column), choose the Title column in the column drop-down, select Is Not Equal To, and leave the value box empty (see Figure 8.12). This forms the condition Title Is Not Equal to Nothing.

> **NOTE** Not all columns can be filtered. The column picker drop-down shows only columns that support filtering. For example, columns of type Hyperlink do not support filtering and are not shown in the column picker drop-down.

Another example for a filter you might want to create on a view would be items that you or another person created. The simplest way to do this is to choose the Created By column in the column drop-down, select the Is Equal To operator, and then enter the name of the person you want (either you or anyone else) in the value box (see Figure 8.13).

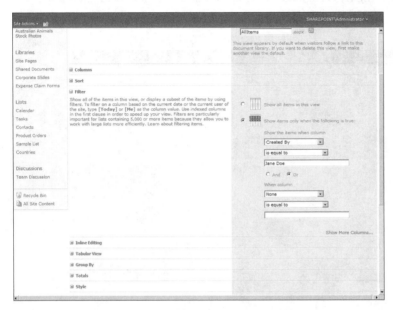

FIGURE 8.13
Setting a filter for the Created By column by typing the name of the person.

When you browse to the new view, the documents (or list items) are displayed only if they were created by a user with exactly the same name that you typed (in this example, Jane Doe).

If you want the filter to be dynamic and change based on the person, you can use a token instead of typing the person's actual name. For example, you can use the [Me] token instead of the value; this is replaced with the name of the user viewing the view and is not limited to a name you chose beforehand (see Figure 8.14).

FIGURE 8.14
Setting a filter for a view that displays for every user his or her documents, using the [Me] token.

This capability is useful when you want to set up a public view (for everyone to use) so that anyone visiting the view can see his or her documents or items without requiring you to create a view for each person separately.

> **NOTE** Another useful token is [Today]. For date fields, it is replaced with the current date. With this token, you could create a view that displays only the documents or items created or modified today, or in a tasks list, you could show all the items that are due today.

You can add, or chain, up to 10 filter conditions in each view. To add an additional filter condition, first decide how the filter will be added—using either the AND or the OR operators. You use the OR operator when you want the items or files to be displayed if they match at least one of the filter conditions.

For example, you can set the first filter column to Created By Is Equal to John Doe and use the OR operator to add the second filter column, Created By Is Equal to Jane Doe (see Figure 8.15). This condition sets the view to display only documents that were created by either John Doe or Jane Doe.

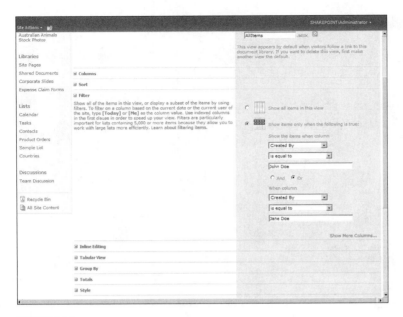

FIGURE 8.15
Setting up two filters, using the OR chaining operator to show documents that were created by either John Doe or Jane Doe.

By using the AND chaining operator, you can create conditions such as Created By Is Equal to John Doe and Created Is Equal to Today. This operator restricts the view to display only documents that match both filters. Another example would be to create the filters Created By Is Not Equal to John Doe and Created By Is Not Equal To Jane Doe (see Figure 8.16). When viewing this view, the users see all files (or items) that have been created by users other than John Doe or Jane Doe.

You can continue and add up to 10 filters, as mentioned earlier. To add additional filters after the first two, use the Show More Columns link below the last filter. Every time you click this link, a new filter criterion section appears.

If you want to remove a condition from the filter, just change the column in the column picker drop-down to None. Even though the condition section still shows, the filter does not have that condition when you save the view.

FIGURE 8.16
Adding another filter criterion and joining the criterion with the AND chaining operator.

> **TIP** Chaining a lot of conditions can be confusing. The most common mistake people make is choosing AND instead of OR or vice versa. Make sure you selected not only the right operator and value but also the right chaining operator.

Specify How Items in a View Are Grouped

Scenario/Problem: You want to group the data shown in a view. Grouping makes it easier to get to the content you want.

Solution: SharePoint list views support a feature called *grouping* that enables you to define a grouping on a column in a list view. For example, grouping contacts by the company to which they belong is a common use of grouping. Grouping documents by the person who created them can be another good idea (see Figure 8.17).

FIGURE 8.17
A view of a document library grouping files by the Created By column.

> **NOTE** Grouping is available only for standard and Gantt view types.

To take advantage of grouping, select the column whose values you want to use as groups. If there are empty values in the selected column for some of the items or files in that view, they are placed under a group without a name (see Figure 8.18).

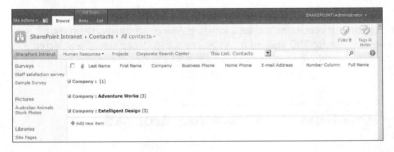

FIGURE 8.18
A view of a contacts list, grouped by the Company column, where one contact doesn't have a value in the Company column.

To define the grouping when creating a view, scroll down to the Group By section in the page and expand it by using the plus (+) sign next to the section title (see Figure 8.19). In addition to choosing the column, you can also select the order in which the groups appear: either ascending or descending.

You can specify up to two columns for grouping. The second column's groups appear under each group only if there are items in that group. For example, grouping contacts by company and then by country makes finding people easier if you know their company and country (see Figure 8.20).

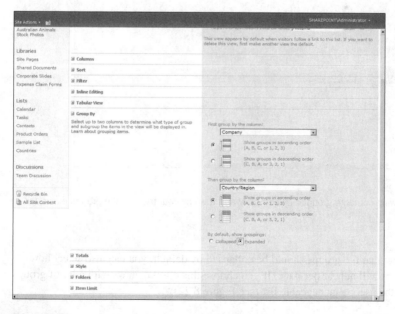

FIGURE 8.19
The Group By section in the view creation page.

FIGURE 8.20
Grouping by company and then by country/region.

> **TIP**   When grouping by a column, it's a good idea not to display that column as part of the view because the values appear as a group. For example, if you are grouping by country, you should remove the Country column from the list of columns displayed in the view.

In addition to specifying the columns for grouping and the order of the groups, you can also specify whether the groups show up expanded or collapsed by default. If you choose that columns should be collapsed by default, you can also choose how many groups to display per page. These settings affect both grouping columns.

If you choose that the groups should be expanded by default, the view displays the groups with the items shown as soon as users open the view (see Figure 8.21).

FIGURE 8.21
A view showing contacts grouped by company and then by country, with the groups expanded by default.

If you select that the groups should be collapsed by default, you can also select how many groups will appear per page. If you choose this option, views with a lot of groups still show the users a manageable list (see Figure 8.22).

FIGURE 8.22
A view showing the items grouped, with a limit of two groups per page.

The paging mechanism enables users to move back and forth between the pages by using the arrow at the bottom of the view.

Specify Totals for a View

Scenario/Problem: You want to include a mathematical calculation on a column in a view. For example, you want the view to show an average of the numbers in a certain column or the total of another. For example, you have a number column called Number of Leave Days that is used to track how many leave days have been requested by a contact, and you want to create a view that displays the average leave requested by everyone in the list.

Solution: A total is a mathematical calculation that you can add to a view. The result of the calculation shows up at the top of the view, just under the header for the column being calculated. If you want to see some calculations of the values in a column, you can specify this under the Totals section of the view creation page.

Different column types can have different kinds of calculations. For example, a date column can show the count of unique date values in that column, and then average of the date values, and then the largest date or smallest one. A text column can show only the count of unique values because it is not possible to do mathematical calculations on pieces of text. A number column can have more functions, such as sum (the sum of all the values in that column), standard deviation, and variance.

For example, if you have a number column called Number of Leave Days that is used to track how many leave days have been requested by a contact, you can create a view that displays the average leave requested by everyone in the list. The average shows up at the top of the view, just under the header for the column (see Figure 8.23).

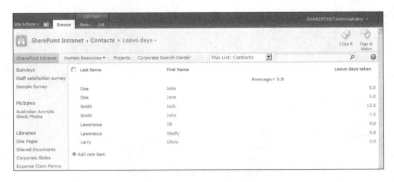

FIGURE 8.23
A view showing the average of a column.

Totals are also supported in the datasheet view type, and the totals appear as a row in the bottom of the view (see Figure 8.24).

FIGURE 8.24
A datasheet view showing the average of a column.

To specify a total for one or more columns, scroll down to the Totals section in the view creation page and expand it by using the plus sign next to the section title. You then see a list of all the columns selected under the Columns section (see Figure 8.25). For each one, you can open the drop-down and choose the calculation that will be done for it.

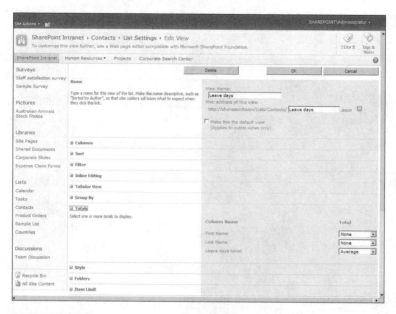

FIGURE 8.25
Creating a view with an average total on a column.

You can specify only one calculation per column. If you want to do different calculations, you must create a separate view for each calculation.

> **TIP** You can add a total to a column only if it appears in the view. If the column to which you want to add a total does not show up under the Totals section, you need to make sure it is selected under the Columns section.

Specify a Different Item Style for a View

> **Scenario/Problem:** You want to change how a view displays items so that the view does not show them in the regular tabular way in which views normally present items.

Solution: Some view types support displaying items in different styles. This means that instead of showing items in a simple table, you can have the view display the items in a different manner that may make the view easier to read.

A common example is the Shaded style, which shows every other row in the table with a different shade or background color (see Figure 8.26).

FIGURE 8.26
A view showing contacts with the Shaded style.

Another example is the Boxed style, which displays each item in a box (see Figure 8.27).

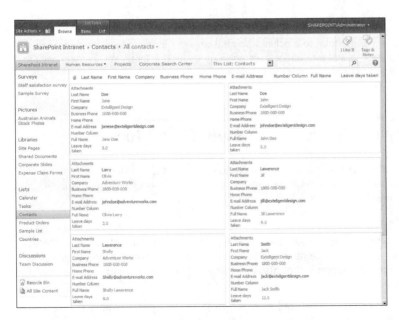

FIGURE 8.27
A view showing contacts with the Boxed style.

To specify the style for the items in a view, scroll to the Style section of the view creation page and expand it by using the plus sign next to the section title. When you see a list of the styles available for that view type (see Figure 8.28), simply select the style that you want.

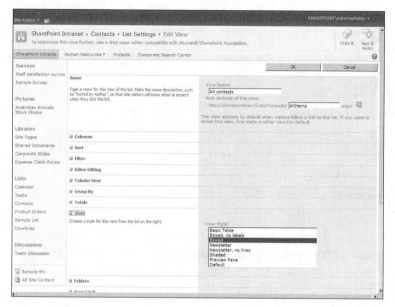

FIGURE 8.28
Specifying the Boxed style for a view.

> **TIP** Try the different view styles. You might find that one of them is better suited for your purpose than the default one.

Specify How Folders Will Be Used in a View

Scenario/Problem: You want to choose whether a view should display the folders in a list or library or should display all the documents and list items without folders.

Solution: You can choose whether a view shows the contents of the document library or list in folders or shows all the items and files as if there were no folders. A view that is configured to show the items without folders is known as a *flat view*. By default, views will show folders and files within folders (see Figure 8.29).

FIGURE 8.29
A view of a document library showing folders.

To specify that a view should not display folders, scroll to the Folders section in the view creation page and expand it by using the plus sign next to the section title. You then have the option of specifying whether the view should display the items in folders (see Figure 8.30).

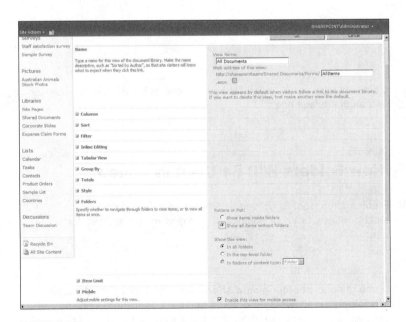

FIGURE 8.30
Configuring a flat view.

A flat view displays all the items that are in the list or document library, even if they are not in the root folder of that list or library (see Figure 8.31). Essentially, this view makes it look as if there are no folders in that list or library.

FIGURE 8.31
A flat view of the document library shows all documents from all folders.

TIP A flat view can be difficult for users who create or upload documents or list items because the flat view does not display the folders, and the user can't specify in which folder a document or list item should be created. It is recommended to create this kind of view only in addition to a view that displays the folders.

Specify the Item Limit for a View

Scenario/Problem: Because there are many items in a list or library, you do not want the view to display them all in one page. Displaying them all can cause the page to take a long time to load and makes it harder for users to find what they are looking for.

Solution: You can specify an item limit on a view. An item limit on a view enables you to either specify the maximum number of items that are displayed in the view or specify the maximum number of items that are displayed in each page in a view.

For example, suppose you have an announcements list that is used a lot. With at least three announcements made every day, after a year, the list will contain more than 1,000 announcements. Displaying all the announcements in one page makes it difficult for users to focus on the current announcements.

A common solution to this problem is to create a view with an item limit that displays, for example, only the last three announcements (see Figure 8.32). To do this, you need to make sure the view sorts the announcements by their creation dates (or modified dates) and then set the item limit to 3.

FIGURE 8.32
An announcement list showing only the last three announcements.

To specify an item limit for a view, scroll to the Item Limit section in the view creation page and expand it by using the plus sign next to the section title. You then have the option of specifying how many items should be displayed and whether the view should limit itself to that number or display the items in groups of that number (see Figure 8.33).

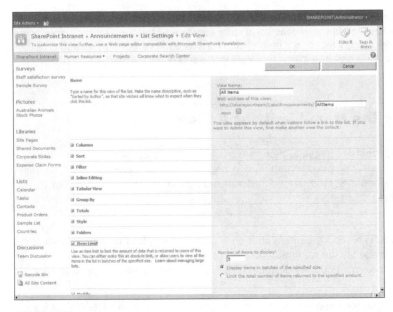

FIGURE 8.33
Specifying the item limit on a view.

If you want to let users see the old announcements, you can choose the Display Items in Batches of the Specified Size option. This makes the view show the items in pages and allows the users to go back and forth between the pages, showing at one time only the number you specified (see Figure 8.34).

FIGURE 8.34
An announcement list showing the announcements in groups of three.

Enable or Disable Inline Editing in a View

Scenario/Problem: You want the users of a view to be able to quickly edit a list item without opening dialogs or switching to datasheet view.

Solution: An advanced option available for standard views is to allow inline editing. This option changes the view to allow users to edit the details of a list item or a document without opening the Edit Properties dialog. (See "Use the Inline Editing Interface" in Chapter 6, "Creating and Managing Files, List Items, and Forms in SharePoint," for more details.)

To turn this option on or off when creating or editing a view, expand the Inline Editing section of the view settings page by using the plus sign next to the section title and set the Allow Inline Editing check box to the setting you want (see Figure 8.35).

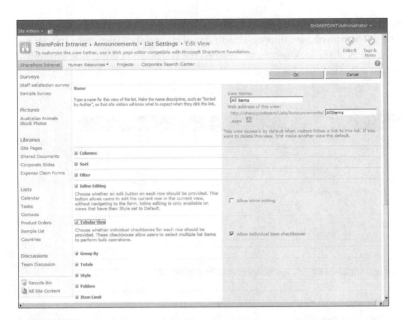

FIGURE 8.35
Disabling the Allow Inline Editing and enabling the Allow Individual Item Checkboxes options when creating a view.

Enable or Disable Selecting Multiple Items in a View

Scenario/Problem: You don't want users to be able to delete, check out, or check in several files or items at the same time by using the check boxes method described in Chapter 6.

Solution: You can disable (remove) the check boxes in a view and prevent users from selecting multiple items. To do so, expand the Tabular View section in the view creation or edit page by using the plus sign next to the section title and either enable or disable the check boxes option by setting Allow Individual Item Checkboxes to the setting you want (refer to Figure 8.35).

Create Mobile Views

Scenario/Problem: Today, many people have mobile phones and other small mobile devices capable of displaying websites. However, the size of a device's screen and its resolution limits how much a user can see.

Solution: It is often a good idea to create special views that show information in a more compact way to enable mobile device users to see that information more clearly and to more comfortably navigate in it (see Figure 8.36).

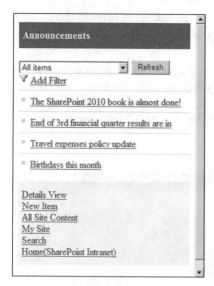

FIGURE 8.36

A mobile view for an announcement list is designed to be more user friendly for mobile device users.

SharePoint attempts to identify whether a device is a mobile device and then switches to a default mobile view that is optimized for that purpose. Nonmobile devices see the view as if it is a regular view. Each mobile view has a special URL that the mobile device is redirected to.

To specify that a view should have a mobile URL, scroll to the Mobile section in the view creation page and expand it by using the plus sign next to the section title. You can create a view and specify it to be the default mobile view for the list (see Figure 8.37), or you can just leave it as another new view in the list.

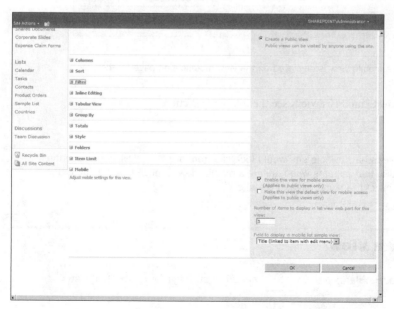

FIGURE 8.37

Creating a mobile view.

Additional options you can set for the mobile view are how many items to show (because you may want to trim a list for a mobile view) and what column to display as the title in the mobile view.

If you don't have a mobile device yourself, and you want to see what the view looks like after it has been created, you must manually type the URL that SharePoint creates for the mobile view. To find out what that URL is, go into the view modification page and scroll down to the Mobile section. The URL for the mobile view appears there as text (see Figure 8.38).

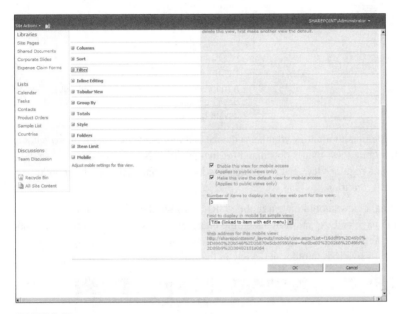

FIGURE 8.38
The URL of a mobile view is displayed on the view modification page for the view.

To learn how to modify a view, see the following section.

> **TIP** To see what a whole site would look like from a mobile device, you use the second URL that appears when editing a mobile view. That URL is the link to the mobile view of the home page of the site.

Modify a View

> **Scenario/Problem:** You want to change the settings for an existing view.

Solution: The easiest way to change a view is to switch to the view that you want to modify, and then click the view name in the breadcrumbs (in the Browse dialog) and choose Modify This View (see Figure 8.39). You can also access this option from the Modify View button in the Library ribbon or List ribbon (see Figure 8.40).

FIGURE 8.39
To modify a view, use the Modify this View link in the breadcrumbs menu.

FIGURE 8.40
To modify a view, you can also use the Modify View button in the List ribbon or Library ribbon.

Selecting Modify This View or Modify View opens the view editing page, which enables you to modify every setting about the view except its type (see Figure 8.41). If you want to switch a view to a different type (for example, change it from a standard view to a calendar view), delete the view and create a new one. For more information about deleting a view, see the next section.

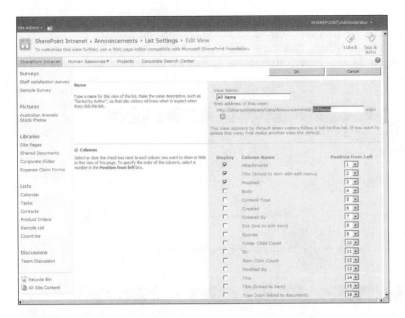

FIGURE 8.41
To change a view's file name, use the Web Address of This View box.

One difference between the view creation page and view editing page is that in the view editing page, you can define the name of the file that the view uses as well as the name of the view itself.

Delete a View

Scenario/Problem: If a view becomes obsolete, you may want to delete it. Or you might want to create a view with the same name as an existing view but with a different type, and you need to delete the existing view before you can achieve that.

Solution: To delete a view, navigate to the view's modification page (see the preceding section), and then use the Delete button at the top of the page. You are prompted to confirm that you want to delete the view. If you click Yes, the view is deleted.

NOTE You cannot delete the default view for a list or library. If the view you want to delete is the default view, you need to make another view the default view first by editing the view and selecting the option Make This the Default View, as shown in Figure 8.25. Then you can delete the view you wanted to delete.

CHAPTER 9

Authoring Pages

You can modify the contents that SharePoint pages display. SharePoint pages include the home page of a site and other pages that you can add to the site's document libraries and wiki page libraries. By default, a SharePoint site has only one page that you can edit: the home page. However, you can create many more pages and add links to them. Usually, the additional pages are in document libraries or wiki page libraries in the site.

This chapter explains how you can create new pages in a site and how you can edit and author the content in those pages. It covers topics such as editing controls, which are controls that exist on some pages to enable you to specify their content, and some common web parts that you can add to the pages.

Create a New Page

Scenario/Problem: Often, as a site manager, you want to add more pages to a site. These pages can be used to show information you don't want to display on the home page of the site and can be focused to specific uses, such as articles (where each article is a page) or news items (where each news item is a page).

Solution: You add pages to SharePoint sites by creating new pages in document libraries or new wiki pages in wiki page libraries. In most sites, the option to create a new page is shown under the Site Action menu as New Page. Clicking that option usually opens a dialog that asks for the page's name and then creates a wiki page.

However, if that option isn't shown, or if you want to create a page of a different type, open the Create dialog (shown in Figure 9.1). Refer to "How to Open the Create Dialog for Lists and Libraries" in Chapter 7, "Creating Lists and Document Libraries," for instruction on how to open this dialog and how to filter it to show only options for creating pages. Figure 9.1 shows how this dialog looks if you have Microsoft Silverlight installed.

FIGURE 9.1
The Create dialog with Silverlight, filtered to show only page types.

If you do not have Microsoft Silverlight installed, the Create dialog shows options to create different types of pages under the Pages and Sites section, as shown in Figure 9.2. Choose one of these options to continue.

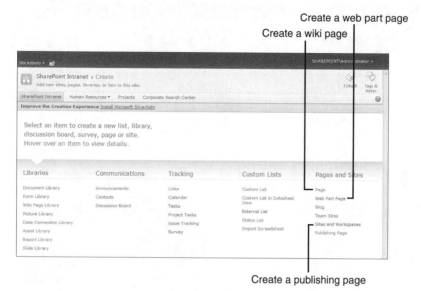

FIGURE 9.2
The Create dialog without Silverlight, showing options for creating different types of pages under Pages and Sites.

In either version of the Create dialog, you find by default either two types of pages in SPF or three types if the site you are using is running on SharePoint Server and has the publishing feature activated. The three, as shown in Figures 9.1 and 9.2 are Page, Web Part Page (available on all types of sites), and Publishing Page (available only on sites running on SharePoint Server with the publishing feature). Developers and administrators may create additional types of pages, so you may have more options available to you. The section "The Differences Between Different Types of Pages," later in this chapter, explains the difference between the three default types.

The following sections explain the process of creating each type of page.

TIP Short file name (URL names) make the best site names. Try to choose a short file name when you create a page. Some options allow you to specify the file name for the new page (see Figure 9.12, later in this chapter), but even if the interface does not allow you to specify a URL name (for example, see Figure 9.5, later in this chapter), you should choose a short name as the page's name. You can rename the title for the page later on! (See "Edit the Properties of a Page," later in this chapter.)

The Differences Between Different Types of Pages

The Page option creates a blank page with room for text and web parts. This allows you to type text freely into the page and add components as required (see Figure 9.3).

Other tasks in this chapter explain in detail the difference of how to perform different tasks in the different types of pages.

FIGURE 9.3
A new wiki page allows you to freely type text in the page, as well as add other components.

The Web Part Page option creates a web part page. This kind of page does not allow you to type text anywhere in the page but instead requires you to add web parts to the page in zones that are defined by the page's layout (see Figure 9.4). This helps enforce a certain layout for pages in the site.

FIGURE 9.4
A new Web Part Page allows you to add web parts in prespecified zones.

> **NOTE** Some web parts allow you to write text in them (such as the Content Editor web part, which is covered later in this chapter, in the section "Use Built-in Web Parts" section). Other web parts show different information or functionality.

The Publishing page option is available only in certain sites with certain features. These pages are designed to enforce certain layouts on the pages in the site and therefore are preferred for sites that need strict structure and consistency between the pages. These pages are usually slightly more complex versions of wiki pages or web part pages or a mix of the two (for example, a wiki page with web part zones in certain places). An example for one of these layouts is the (Article Page) Summary Links layout. A page based on this layout looks similar to a wiki page but with additional controls:

- A link list on the right of the page
- A control to easily change the page's title
- A control to easily change the article date
- A control to easily define a byline
- A control to set a rollup image (an image that will be displayed by rollup web parts that list what pages are there on the site)

Figure 9.5 shows an example of such a page using that layout.

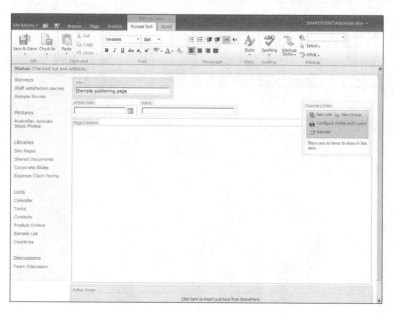

FIGURE 9.5
A publishing page using the (Article Page) Summary Links layout.

Create a New Wiki Page

When you choose to create a new wiki page (using the option Page in the Create dialog shown in Figures 9.1 and 9.2), the name box appears on the right side of the Create dialog with Silverlight or, if you are using the Create dialog without Silverlight, a New Page dialog appears, asking for the name for the new page.

After you type the name for the new page, click the Create button. The name for the page is important because it is used for both the name of the file (which the users type in the address bar of their browsers to open the page) and as the title of the page (which the users see in the navigation bar and in the top of their browsers). You should select a short but meaningful name for the page. You can rename it later, but that can cause links to the page to break.

> **NOTE** For more information on how to rename a wiki page, see the section "Edit Properties of a Wiki Page," later in this chapter.

When you click Create, SharePoint checks whether it has a fitting library into which to put the wiki page. If it doesn't, you are prompted that two new libraries will be created: a wiki page library for wiki pages and a site assets library for any images or other types of files you want to upload and display as part of the page (see Figure 9.6). For example, if you add an image to a wiki page, that image gets uploaded to the asset library. These kinds of files are referred to as *assets*.

If you click Create, SharePoint create two libraries: Site Assets (for the assets) and Site Pages (for wiki pages).

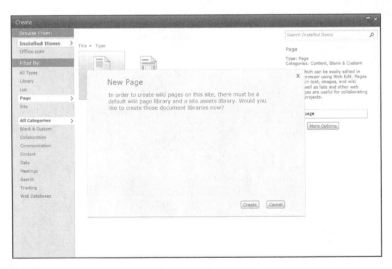

FIGURE 9.6
The prompt asking for permission to create libraries in the site for pages.

If a default library already exists for wiki pages in the site, you are not prompted. Instead, the page is immediately created and opens in editing mode. For more information about editing the contents of pages, see the section "Edit the Contents of a Page," later in this chapter.

Create a New Web Part Page

When you choose the Web Part Page option in the Create dialog with Silverlight (refer to Figure 9.1), the only option you have in the dialog is the Create button. Clicking this button opens the settings page for the web part page—the same one that opens when you click Web Part Page in the Create dialog without Silverlight (refer to Figure 9.2).

In this page you must choose a name for the file that will be created for the page. You also choose the layout template for the web part zones on the page and the document library to put the page in, as shown in Figure 9.7.

FIGURE 9.7
Creating a new web part page.

The different web part zone layout templates are shown in the page under the Choose a Layout Template. Each option in the list box describes the page that will be created in the form of where the web part zones will be located. For example, the layout template called Full Page, Vertical has only one web part zone, spread across the entire page, and any web part that is added to it is vertical, spreading the entire width of the page. Other web parts can be either above it or below it. If you click on the different layout templates, the image on the left change to show a wireframe of the web part zones layout, as shown in Figure 9.7.

> **TIP** Choose the layout template carefully because it is not possible to change the layout of a web part page after it is created (unlike with a publishing page, as explained later in this chapter). If you create a page with the wrong layout, you have to delete it and create it again with the correct layout.

If there are any document libraries in the site, you can choose them from the Document Library option at the bottom of the page. By default, all pages in a site go to either the Site Pages library or the Pages library, if one exists. If you want to create the page in a different library, you can choose it from the box.

After you picked the title, layout template, and document library, click Create. The new page is created in the document library and opens in editing mode. For more information about editing the contents of pages, see the section "Edit the Contents of a Page," later in this chapter.

Create a New Publishing Page

In a site that supports publishing pages, an option to create a page should appear under the Site Actions menu as Create Page. However, if it doesn't, it is with the other page options, as described earlier. The process of creating the page is slightly different when you choose the Create Page option from them menu, however, in that you are not asked what page layout you want for your page, and a default page layout is used. This is very useful for site managers who want to make it easier for users to always create the same kind of page, while leaving a more flexible option to create different types of page by using the Create dialog.

If you choose to create a publishing page by using the Create Page option in the Site Actions menu, you are prompted for a page name only, and the page is created with the default layout. You can change the layout of the page later (see the section "Change the Page Layout of a Publishing Page," later in this chapter). The name you choose for the page is used to generate the page's file name (which is displayed to the user in the address bar of the browser). You can change this name later, but changing it breaks users' favorite lists and links to the page, so it is not recommended. The name is also used to set the page's title, which can be changed later with no issues.

You might want to choose the page layout before creating the page, set its description, and set the file name and the title separately. You can do this by creating the page using the Create dialog, as explained earlier in this chapter (refer to Figures 9.1 and 9.2).

When you choose the Publishing Page option from the Create dialog, you have only the Create button available to you. Click on this button to open the Create Page settings page, where you can enter the new page's title, description, and URL name (the name for the file, as just explained), as well as the page layout for the page, as shown in Figure 9.8.

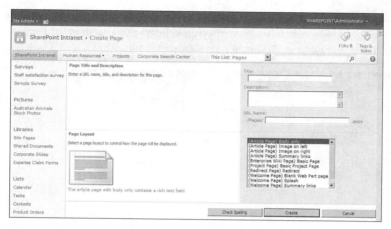

FIGURE 9.8
The Create Page settings page for a publishing page.

Because page layouts can be created by developers or removed by administrators, you might see more or fewer options for layouts than you see in this chapter. You should review the options available and choose the one that's closest to what you want to achieve with your page. Remember that a page is just a file in a document library, and you can always delete the page if you choose the wrong layout—just as you would delete any other file in a document library. (See "Delete a File or List Item" in Chapter 6.)

After you selected a title, a URL name, and a page layout, click the Create button to create the page and open it in editing mode. For more information about editing the contents of pages, see the section "Edit the Contents of a Page," later in this chapter.

Edit the Properties of a Page

Scenario/Problem: You want to change properties such as the page layout of a publishing page and the title of the page (that is displayed at the top of the user's browser and in the navigational breadcrumbs, and possibly in other locations on the site), the caption for the page, the page's description, and the page's image (which also may appear in different locations on the site).

Solution: How you change the properties of a page depends on what type of page you are editing. The following sections cover the different options.

Edit Properties of a Wiki Page

A wiki page by default does not have any properties except for the file name, which is also shown as the page's title. It is very important to select a good file name for a wiki page because renaming the page breaks links to it.

To rename a wiki page, open it in your browser and switch to the Page ribbon. Then click on the Edit button to switch to editing mode, and then switch again to the Page ribbon and click on the Rename Page button, as shown in Figure 9.9.

FIGURE 9.9
The Rename Page button for the wiki page.

If the wiki page library is configured to have properties for the pages, the Edit Properties button in the Page ribbon becomes available. If you click it, you see a page where you can edit the properties of the page.

Edit Properties of a Web Part Page

To edit the properties of a web part page, open the page in your browser and switch to the Page ribbon. In the ribbon, click the Title Bar Properties button in the Page Actions section of the ribbon. A panel opens on the right of the page, allowing you to set the page's title, caption, description, and image (see Figure 9.10). (To set an image, type the link to the image in the Image Link box.)

FIGURE 9.10
Editing the properties of a web part page.

Edit Properties of a Publishing Page

To edit the properties of a publishing page, open the page in your browser, switch to the Page ribbon, and click the Edit Properties button, as shown in Figure 9.11.

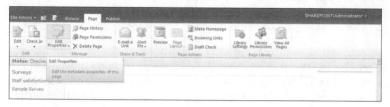

FIGURE 9.11
The Edit Properties button in a publishing page.

The properties page for the page opens (see Figure 9.12). This page allows you to change all the properties set for the page, just as if you were editing a file. You can edit the page's content type, title, and other properties that may be required for that type of page (depending on the selected content type). When you're done, either click the Save button at the bottom of the page or use the Save button in the Edit ribbon at the top of the page.

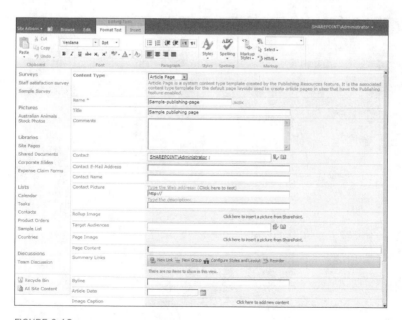

FIGURE 9.12
Editing the properties of a publishing page.

Change the Page Layout of a Publishing Page

Scenario/Problem: You might want to change the page layout that was selected when the page was created. For example, say that a page was created with the "body only" layout, and you want to change it to a layout that includes a web part zone or an image on one side of the text.

Solution: To change the layout of an existing publishing page, open the page in your browser and switch to the Page ribbon. There, click on the Edit button to switch the page into editing mode. This enables you to click on the Page Layout button in the ribbon.

NOTE In some publishing sites, the ribbon is hidden by default. To get to the ribbon, open the Site Actions menu and select Show Ribbon from that menu to expose the Page ribbon.

The Page Layout button then shows the various available page layouts for you to choose from (see Figure 9.13).

FIGURE 9.13
Choosing a new page layout for a publishing page.

After you click on the layout that you want, you can see it change the page. It is important to note that switching layouts may remove web parts from the page because the web parts are tied to a specific web part zone, and if the new layout does not have the same web part zone, the web parts that belonged in that zone will be removed.

If you are happy with the new layout, click the Save & Close button in the Page ribbon. (The page might still need to be published. See "Publish a Page," later in this chapter.) If you want to revert to the layout that you had before, open the menu under the Check In button and click Discard Check Out. This retracts all the modifications you've made to the page since the last time you checked it out, including the page layout change.

Edit the Contents of a Page

Scenario/Problem: As a site manager, you want to change what is displayed on a specific page in a site.

Solution: To change the display, you must view the page in editing mode—a mode that enables you to edit the page. You can make such changes after you switch to editing mode. (You'll learn how to make specific changes, such as changing text or a picture or a web part, later in this chapter.)

When you have the permissions to edit a page, and if the page is not currently checked out by someone else, you edit the page by navigating to it in the browser, opening the Site Actions menu, and choosing Edit Page, as shown in Figure 9.14.

FIGURE 9.14
Opening the Site Actions menu and choosing Edit Page to get to page editing mode.

NOTE If the page is checked out to another user, the Edit Page menu option is not available until that page is checked in.

When the page is in editing mode, it looks different than it looks normally, showing either web part zones (where you can add web parts) and/or editing controls, depending on the type of page (refer to Figure 9.5). For example, a wiki page by default has only the page body control—a control in which you can type. Publishing pages may have additional controls, depending on their layouts, while web part pages show web part zones to allow you to add web parts, as well as the existing web parts for you to edit.

When you are finished editing the page, save your changes. How you do this depends on the configuration of the library the page is in. In libraries that do not keep track of page versioning and do not require checking in or checking out the page, you can just click the Stop Editing button on the Page ribbon. In libraries that maintain version control over pages, use the Save & Close button in the Page ribbon, along with a Check In button. If publishing is required in the document library, you have a Publish ribbon with buttons for publishing the page after you check it in. For more information, see "Publish a Page," later in this chapter.

Use the Text Editing Control in a Page

Scenario/Problem: When authoring a page, you want to enter or change the text that appears on the page.

Solution: Some pages have text editing controls embedded in them. This is true of all wiki pages and most publishing pages. You can type rich text in these controls, including pictures, videos, links, tables, and even web parts. The following sections explain how you can use this type of control to add or change these elements.

NOTE Some pages do not have text editing controls. To add text to or edit text in those pages, use the Content Editor web part, as explained in the section "Use the Content Editor Web Part," later in this chapter.

Edit and Format Text

To edit text in a text editing control, simply click anywhere in the control. When you do that, the ribbon switches to the Editing Tools ribbon, with the subribbon Format Text selected, allowing you to format the text as required (see Figure 9.15).

FIGURE 9.15
The Format Text subribbon of the Editing Tools ribbon allows you to set formatting for the text in a text editing control.

You use the ribbon and control as you would use any word processor; for example, to make part of the text bold, highlight it and click the Bold button (labeled B).

Add a Hyperlink

To add a hyperlink to text, highlight the part of the text that you want to make a hyperlink and switch to the Insert subribbon of the Editing Tools ribbon, as shown in Figure 9.16. In this ribbon, you can either click the Link button or open the menu under it to reveal the From SharePoint and the From Address options, as shown in Figure 9.16.

FIGURE 9.16
The Link button's menu.

Selecting the From SharePoint option or just clicking the Link button opens a dialog that enables you to choose where the hyperlink will link to (see Figure 9.17). In this dialog, you are presented with the content in the current site, and you can navigate to content in subsites. You can double-click any site, list, or library to view what is in it, or click a site, a list, a library, or the items in them to add the link to the selected item to the Location box at the bottom of the dialog. Click OK to close the dialog, and the link is added to the text.

The dialog for adding a hyperlink from SharePoint.

Selecting the From Address option shows a much simpler dialog that asks you for the text to display for the link and the address that the user will be directed to when clicking on it (see Figure 9.18).

FIGURE 9.18
The dialog for adding a hyperlink from address.

After you have added the link, clicking on it in the text editing control allows you to switch to the Link Tools ribbon (see Figure 9.19). Here you can either remove the link or edit its properties (including the description that is shown when a user hovers over the link). You can also configure how it should behave, such as whether it should open in a new tab (or a new window) and whether it should show an icon next to the text to further signify that this is a link. You can change the icon's image later (see the following section for information about changing existing pictures).

FIGURE 9.19
Editing a link using the Link Tools ribbon.

Add and Edit a Picture

To add a picture to a text editing control, place the cursor where you want the picture to be added and switch to the Insert tab in the Editing Tools ribbon. Open the drop-down menu under the button to expose the options to upload an image from your computer (From Computer), select an image somewhere else on the web using its address (From Address), or select a picture that was already uploaded to the site (From SharePoint), as shown in Figure 9.20. This last option is not always available and may be either missing from the menu or disabled, depending on the configuration of the site. The following sections describe these options in detail.

The Insert Picture button

The three Insert Picture options

FIGURE 9.20
The Picture button and the drop-down menu.

After you add a picture to the page, click the picture to expose the Picture Tools ribbon (see Figure 9.21). On this ribbon you see the Change Picture button, which works like the Picture button. You also have the option to set the alternative text for the image (for users whose browsers do not support images, or in case the image cannot be loaded) using the Alt Text box. You can also configure the image's size by typing a custom size, and you can resize by dragging and dropping the borders of the image.

This ribbon also enables you to choose a border for the image (using the Image Styles button drop-down) and the position for the image.

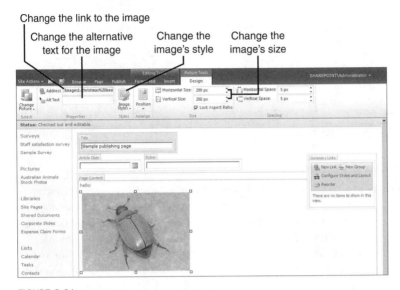

FIGURE 9.21
The Picture Tools ribbon shows when you select a picture.

Use a Picture from Your Computer

To use a picture you have on your computer in a page, choose the From Computer option in the Picture drop-down described in the preceding section. This opens the Select Picture dialog, which allows you to specify the picture to upload from your computer and the library in SharePoint to upload it to.

> **NOTE** If the From SharePoint option is not available in the site you are using, From Computer is the default behavior for the Picture button, so you can simply click the button instead of opening the drop-down menu.

You choose the file you want by clicking the Browse button, choose the library, and click OK to upload. Depending on the settings for the library you chose, a dialog may ask for the picture's properties. After you fill in the required properties and click Save, the picture is uploaded to the library and added to the page.

Use a Picture Using an Address

To use a picture that exists on the web (that is, was already uploaded to the site or on another website), you open the Picture drop-down (refer to Figure 9.20) and select the From Address option. This opens the Select Picture dialog, which allows you to specify the picture's address and the alternative text that will be displayed if the picture is not available or if the user's browser doesn't support images (see Figure 9.22).

FIGURE 9.22
Adding a picture from a known address.

Use a Picture from SharePoint Server

The last option for inserting a picture is to select one that already exists in SharePoint. (You can use this option only with SharePoint Server, not with SPF.) You can use the From Address option to achieve the same result if you already know the address of the image file, but usually typing the address is a lot harder than browsing to the image file and selecting it, which is what this option allows.

To see the dialog for browsing to an image in the current site, open the Picture drop-down (refer to Figure 9.20) and choose the From SharePoint option. This option may be missing from the site if the site does not have all the publishing features enabled. This means that sites that are not running on SharePoint Server—that is, SPF sites—do not have this option at all, and sites that are running on SharePoint Server may still have this option disabled if the publishing features are not enabled on the site.

> **NOTE** If the From SharePoint option is available in the site you are using, it is also the default behavior for the Picture button. It allows you to simply click the button instead of opening the drop-down menu.

Clicking the From SharePoint option opens the Select an Asset dialog, which allows you to browse for a picture that was uploaded to the site. This dialog is the same as the one for adding a hyperlink from SharePoint (refer to Figure 9.17) but is meant to be used to find images.

In the Select an Asset dialog you can select the picture by clicking it once and clicking OK, or you can navigate through the sites to find the picture you want. The links on the left side go to the picture library in the current site and to the library in the root site. If the picture you are looking for is in a different location, click the Up button to see all the contents of the site. Then you can navigate through the site and subsites and look in different picture libraries (or document libraries) to select the picture you want. To select a picture, either double-click it or click it once and then click OK.

Add and Edit a Table

To add a table in a text control, place the cursor where you want the table to be added. Then switch to the Insert subribbon in the Editing Tools ribbon and click the Table button. Clicking this button opens a submenu that allows you to quickly add a table by choosing how many rows and how many columns will be in the table by clicking on the squares (see Figure 9.23). Above this quick option is the Insert Table option, which opens a dialog that allows you to specify the number of rows and columns using numbers instead.

FIGURE 9.23
The Insert Table button menu

After the table has been added, you edit it by clicking inside it, and then the Table Tools ribbon shows up, with two tabs. The Layout ribbon (see Figure 9.24) allows you to customize the table's layout (inserting/removing rows and columns, specifying width and height for the table and for each row and column, and so on), and the Design tab (see Figure 9.25) allows you to choose styles for the table and specify settings for the current row and column.

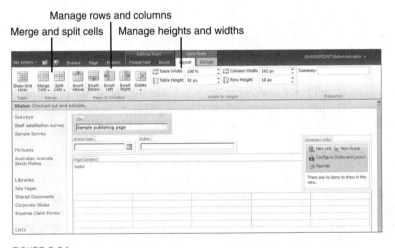

FIGURE 9.24
The Layout tab in the Table Tools ribbon.

FIGURE 9.25
The Design tab in the Table Tools ribbon.

Use Wiki Syntax to Link to Existing Content and Create Pages

Scenario/Problem: When authoring a page, you realize that a certain piece of text should be linked to a page that is not yet created. You do not want to stop authoring your page, or maybe you are not the right person to author the other page you want to link to.

Solution: Wiki syntax offers quick and easy ways to link to existing content and also to mark a piece of text as one that should have a page created for it. SharePoint then turns terms into special links, that, when clicked, allow the user to create pages for the terms. The following sections explain how to use wiki notation to achieve these two simple tasks.

Linking to Existing Content

To link to existing content while typing text in a wiki page, type [[. This opens a pop-up menu that shows a list of existing pages available in the site (see Figure 9.26). To link to one of these pages, simply select it from the menu and add]]. The item is added to the text as [[*pagename*]], and when you save the document, this is transformed into a link to that page.

FIGURE 9.26
Typing [[a wiki page opens a pop-up menu that allows you to quickly link to another page.

The menu also offers two special options at the bottom: List and View. Selecting one of these is the same as typing [[List: or [[View:. You can then start typing either the name of the list or the view that is in the current site, and SharePoint autocompletes the name of the list as you type it or allows you to choose a list and then an item or view (depending on whether you selected List or View in the first level, as shown in Figure 9.27).

FIGURE 9.27
When you start typing the list name, SharePoint shows you the lists you can choose from.

As before, the text shows as [[List:*listname*]], and this transforms into a link to the list or view when you save the page. For example, [[List:Sample List]] shows up in the page as the name of the list (Sample List), and it is linked to the list. Typing [[List:Sample List/1|sample item]] links to the item in the list Sample List with the title Sample Item, as shown in Figures 9.28 and 9.29.

FIGURE 9.28
The syntax to link to a list item in a list.

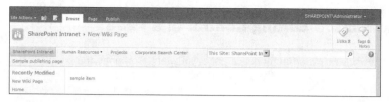

FIGURE 9.29
The link is shown as the list item's title.

> **TIP**   If the pop-up menu does not appear, press Ctrl+space to force it to show up.

Creating New Pages

If you are writing something and realize that a certain word or term in your text should link to a page that needs to be created, you don't need to stop and create it right away. Instead, you can use the wiki syntax to mark it as a link and then create it later—or let someone else create it. To do this, simply type the term you want to make into a link inside double square brackets. For example, if you write [[Product X]], the words Product X appear on the page as a link, even if there is no page for that product.

When you save the page, the link looks different from other links; it is underlined with a black dotted line, as shown in Figure 9.30. Clicking this link opens the New Page dialog, which allows you (or other users) to quickly create a page for the word (or words) you wrote, as shown in Figure 9.31.

FIGURE 9.30
A link to a page that doesn't exist yet is marked with a black dotted underline.

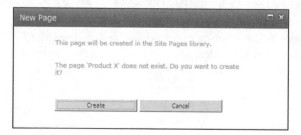

FIGURE 9.31
The New Page dialog for a wiki link.

Use the Picture Editing Control in a Page

Scenario/Problem: When authoring a page, you want to change the picture that appears on the page, but the picture is not in a text editing control.

Solution: A page may have a picture editing control embedded in it. If a picture is not defined for the picture editing control, a link shows in that control when the page is in editing mode, allowing you to insert a picture. Clicking this link opens the Edit Image Properties dialog (see Figure 9.32). This dialog allows you to browse for the picture and specify properties for the picture, such as its alternative text, its layout and size, and whether it should be a hyperlink (and if so, whether it should be opened in a new window).

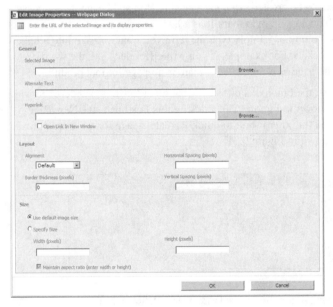

FIGURE 9.32
The Edit Image Properties dialog opens when you use the picture control to insert a picture.

Clicking the Browse button opens the dialog shown earlier in this chapter in Figure 9.17. To edit the properties of a picture after it is added, you use the same method described in the section "Add and Edit a Picture," earlier in this chapter.

NOTE Some pages do not have a picture editing control, and the pictures displayed in them are stored in web parts. For information about how to modify web parts, see the sections "Use the Image Viewer Web Part" and "Modify a Web Part," later in this chapter. For information on adding a picture as part of the text in a text control, see "Add and Edit a Picture," earlier in this chapter.

To change or edit an existing picture in a picture control, follow the same instructions as if the picture is in a text control. (See the "Add and Edit a Picture" section, earlier in this chapter.)

If you want to clear a picture control (that is, remove the picture and not replace it), click the picture in the picture control and press the Delete key. The picture is removed, and the next time you enter editing mode for the page, the link to add a picture reappears.

Add a Web Part

Scenario/Problem: When authoring or editing a page, you want to add different kinds of content to different sections of the page.

Solution: Some pages enable you to add web parts to them. To add a web part to a page, you first need to decide where on the page you want it. Depending on the type of page, there may be several web part zones you can add web parts to, or you may have the option to add a web part to a text control in the page.

Add a Web Part to a Text Editor Control

To add a web part as part of the text in a text editor control, place your cursor in the location where you want the web part to be and switch to the Insert tab of the Editing Tools ribbon. (See "Edit the Contents of a Page," earlier in this chapter, for instructions on how to do so.) In this ribbon, click the Web Part button to open a new pane under the ribbon that allows you to select the web part you want to add (see Figure 9.33).

The categories   The Web Part button   Description of the selected web part

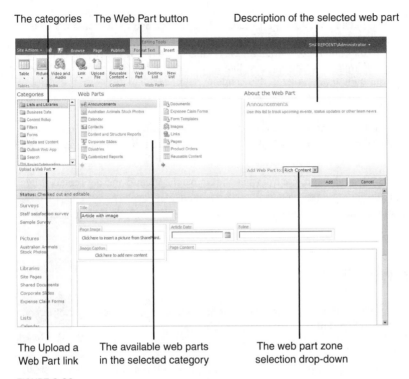

The Upload a   The available web parts   The web part zone
Web Part link   in the selected category   selection drop-down

FIGURE 9.33
The web part selection pane.

For more information about how to use this pane and how to find the web part you want, see "Choose a Web Part," later in this chapter.

Add a Web Part to a Web Part Zone

In pages where there are web part zones, a zone is shown on the page as a rectangle, with the zone name above the top-left corner of the rectangle. If a web part zone is empty, the zone has another rectangle inside the zone with a link that says Add a Web Part. If the zone already has one or more web parts in it, the Add a Web Part link appears above the existing web parts.

After you decide to which zone you want to add a web part, click the Add a Web Part link in that zone. When you click this button, the web part browsing pane appears, allowing you to select the web part you want. For more information on using this pane to add the web part, see the following section.

Choose a Web Part

The web part selection pane allows you to find the web part you want, based on the web part's category (shown on the left of the pane) and the list of available web parts in the middle of the pane. When you click one of the web parts, you see the web part's description on the right side of the pane (refer to Figure 9.33).

The pane shows all the web parts available in the current site. Some sites offer different web parts than others. You can browse the categories by clicking on them, and the choices in the middle of the pane change to reflect the category you clicked.

The first category, Lists and Libraries, shows all the lists and libraries that exist in the current site. If you want to add a view of one of those lists or libraries, you can select the list or library from the list of web parts. This kind of web part is known as the List View web part, and you can find more information about it later in this chapter, in the section "Use the List View Web Part." For more information on some of the other commonly used web parts, see the next section.

To add the web part you selected to the page, click the Add button in the pane. SharePoint adds the web part to the location you chose when you started the process. If you want to add it to a different location, open the drop-down box with the different zones under the About the Web Part section of the pane. For information about changing the location of a web part or its settings, see "Modify a Web Part," later in this chapter.

Use Built-in Web Parts

Scenario/Problem: When authoring or editing a page, you want to add different content to different sections of the page.

Solution: The following sections explain some of the choices you have when adding a web part to a page. Although there are many more web parts for you to choose from, the ones described here are the most common ones.

Use the List View Web Part

There are two ways to add a list view web part to a page. The first is to click the Existing List button instead of the Web Part button in the Insert ribbon. The second is to select the Lists and Libraries category in the web part selection pane. Both options show you the list of all the lists and libraries available in the current site as web parts. The only difference is that clicking the Existing List button hides the categories, showing you only the web parts that belong to the Lists and Libraries category.

By selecting one of the lists or libraries and adding it to the page, you actually add a List View web part to the page. After you add the web part to the page, the page displays the items in the list or library that you selected. What view is displayed by default depends on the type of list.

If you want to change what information is displayed, you can do this by using the same method you use to edit a view in a list or library. To edit the view the web part is displaying, you hover over the web part with your mouse. Doing this exposes a check box that allows you to select the web part in the web part's title row. When you check the check box, you see the List Tools ribbon or Library Tools ribbon, with the List or Library tab available. To modify the view shown in the web part, you follow the same instructions as in "Modify a View" in Chapter 8, "Creating List Views."

> **NOTE** The view you will be modifying does not exist in the list but instead is config-
> ured in the web part. So even if it looks like you are editing the default view of the
> list itself, you needn't worry: You are only modifying the view of the web part and not
> the view used in the list.

In addition to changing the view, there are additional settings you can configure for the
web part, using the web part's settings pane. For more information about how to modify
a web part and get to its settings pane, see "Modify a Web Part," later in this chapter.

When you're viewing the editing pane for a list view web part, you can select from the
list of views that were created for the list or library different views for the web part.
You can also create a view just for the web part by clicking the Edit the Current View
link if you want the web part to display a view that was not created in the list or
library. This has exactly the same result as editing the view using the method described
earlier.

You can also select the toolbar type for the web part. This setting defines whether the
web part displays a summary toolbar (that is, a link at the bottom for adding a new
item to the list or creating a new document in the library), no toolbar, or a full toolbar.
A full toolbar is used only for picture libraries and surveys because they do not have
ribbons.

FIGURE 9.34
The List View web part's settings pane.

Use the Content Editor Web Part

You can type any kind of text in a Content Editor web part, including scripts. To add a
Content Editor web part to a page, switch the web part selection pane to the Media and
Content category and select the Content Editor web part from the list of web parts.

After you add the web part, it does not appear with any text. Instead, you see an
instruction telling you that you need to add text (content) to the web part by opening
the tool ribbons for the web part. To do so, click the link in the text. The web part
switches into text editing mode, exposing the Editing Tools ribbon, with the Format
Text and Insert tabs (see the section "Use the Text Editing Control in a Page," earlier in
this chapter).

However, unlike the text editing control, the content editor web part does not support inserting some types of content, such as web parts and video and audio. If in the future you would like to change the text, you can. See "Modify a Web Part," later in this chapter, for details.

Use the Image Viewer Web Part

The Image Viewer web part enables you to display just an image. To add an Image web part, select it from the list of available web parts under the Media and Content category.

When you add the web part to the page, it doesn't have any image set. Instead, it offers instructions on how to specify the image: by clicking the Open the Tool Pane link. If you need to change the image later, you can, as described in the section "Modify a Web Part," later in this chapter.

When the tool pane is open, you can specify the link to the image that should be displayed, as well as some settings for how it will be displayed (see Figure 9.35).

FIGURE 9.35
The tool pane for the Image Viewer web part.

The first setting is the link to the image. You just type (or paste) the link into the Image Link box. Then click the Test Link hyperlink above the box to make sure the link you typed is correct and points to the correct picture. If the link is fine, the picture opens in a new window, which you can then close.

In the Alternative Text box, type the text that you want to appear in the web part if the user who is browsing the site is using a browser that doesn't support images or has that option turned off. This text is also displayed when the user hovers the mouse cursor over the picture.

Use the Media Web Part in SharePoint Server

You use the Media web part to either display a video or play an audio file in a page. You can find the Media web part under the Media and Content category in the web part selection pane.

After you add the Media web part to a page, the web part is shown with a Click Here to Configure link in it, as shown in Figure 9.36.

FIGURE 9.36
The Media web part before it is configured.

NOTE This web part uses Silverlight to play the audio and video and also to configure itself. If you don't have Silverlight installed, the link to configure might not work.

When you click the link, the Media ribbon appears. On this ribbon, you can select the media file by opening the drop-down menu under the Change Media button and set different options for the media itself, such as whether it should start automatically and how it should look.

Selecting a media file (audio or video) is the same as selecting an image, as explained in "Use the Picture Editing Control in a Page," earlier in this chapter.

TIP Media files, especially video files, are often big. You should take note of the size of a file before uploading it. If it is bigger than the size allowed by the system administrator, SharePoint prevents you from uploading it. If you need to be able to upload a large file and are unable to, you should contact your site administrator and ask for a bigger size quota.

When a file is selected, the web part allows users to click Play. Or, if you chose the option to start the media automatically in the Options ribbon (see Figure 9.37), it starts playing the file each time the page opens.

Use the Content Query Web Part in SharePoint Server

The Content Query web part is one of the most useful web parts. It is used to display information in the current site or in other sites in the current site collection, based on a query. For example, if you want to show an aggregation of all the announcements from all the sites, this web part does it. It is a quite complex web part with a lot of options (some of which must be configured by a developer), but most of them are easy to set up, as shown here.

FIGURE 9.37
The Media web part's Media ribbon.

The Content Query web part is available only in publishing sites and is not available in sites that are not at least under a root publishing site.

The Content Query web part can be found under the Content Rollup category in the web part selection pane. After it is added, this web part displays a link to open the web part's tool pane to configure the query it should perform.

To modify the query that the web part performs and display a different kind of content, click the link to open the tool pane for the web part (see Figure 9.38).

FIGURE 9.38
The tool pane for the Content Query web part.

In the tool pane, expand the Query section to see the options to specify what content should be displayed and from where (see Figure 9.39).

FIGURE 9.39
The Query section of the content query web part tool pane.

You can specify whether the query will be on all sites in the site collection, on a specific site and its subsites, or on just a specific list. For the last two options, use the Browse button to open a dialog that enables you to select the site or list in question (see Figure 9.40). Click OK to return to the Content Query web part tool pane.

FIGURE 9.40
Selecting a list for the Content Query web part.

In the List Type selection box, you can define what kind of list type the web part should look in for its content. This includes document libraries, pages libraries, picture libraries, and all other list templates.

The Content Type section enables you to select what content types the web part will limit its query to. If you don't want to specify a specific content type, you can leave it at the default All Content Types. Otherwise, you can limit it to a group of content types (for example, all the document content types) and to a specific content type). To do that, select the content type group (for example, document content types) and then either select All Content Types in the second drop-down or select the specific content type that you want.

Next, you can set the filters (see Figure 9.41). You can specify that the web part will display only list items or documents that have specific values in specific columns by setting up to three filters on the web part. To do so, scroll down in the tool pane to the Filters section, and under Show Items When, you select the column you want, the kind of filter you want, and the value to filter on. For example, select Company Is Equal to AdventureWorks or Article Date Is Equal to Today.

FIGURE 9.41
The Filter section in the Content Query web part, with a filter specified on Article Date Is Equal to Today.

In addition to configuring the query itself, you can modify how the items will be displayed by expanding the Presentation section of the pane. You can specify how many items should be displayed; how they should be sorted, grouped, or styled; and which columns to display (see Figure 9.42).

FIGURE 9.42

The Presentation section in the Content Query web part.

Modify a Web Part

Scenario/Problem: When editing a page, you want to change the settings for existing web parts on that page.

Solution: The following sections explain how to get a web part into editing mode. These sections discuss some of the common settings you can modify for a web part in each mode, such as modifying the web part's title, its display settings, and the web part's position on the page.

To modify a web part of any kind, switch the page to editing mode (see "Edit the Contents of a Page," earlier in this chapter). Then select the web part whose properties you want to edit by hovering your mouse over the web part and selecting the check box that appears at the top-right corner of the web part (on the title row). Doing so should reveal the Web Part Tools ribbon, with a tab called Options, as shown in Figure 9.43.

FIGURE 9.43
The Options tab in the Web Part Tools ribbon and a web part's properties pane with the Appearance section expanded.

This tab has the Web Part Properties button at the top left. Clicking this button opens the tool pane for the web part. Different web parts have different tool panes with different settings, but all of them have some basic settings that you can modify.

> **TIP** Another way to get to the web part's properties pane is to open the web part's drop-down menu, as described in the section "Reuse a Web Part (Export/Import)," later in this chapter.

Modify a Web Part's Title

To modify a web part's title, expand the Appearance section in the web part's tool pane (refer to Figure 9.43). The first option in the Appearance section is the title of the web part. Simply type in the title you want and click OK to save it.

Modify a Web Part's Title Bar and Border Settings

To modify whether a web part displays the title bar and whether it displays a border line around its contents, expand the Appearance section in the web part's tool pane and scroll down to the Chrome Type selection (refer to Figure 9.43).

Chrome Type can be set to one of these options:

> ▶ **None**—The web part does not display a title bar or border. This is typical for Image Viewer web parts, where you want the picture to appear without a title bar above it and without a border around it, as if it is part of the page and not in a web part (see Figure 9.44).

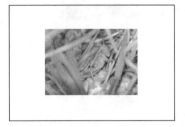

FIGURE 9.44
The Image web part with the None chrome type.

▶ **Title and Border**—The web part displays the title bar and a border around the content (see Figure 9.45).

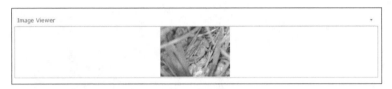

FIGURE 9.45
The Image web part with the Title and Border chrome type.

▶ **Title Only**—The web part displays the title bar without a border around the content (see Figure 9.46).

FIGURE 9.46
The Image web part with the Title Only chrome type.

▶ **Border Only**—The web part does not display the title bar but does display a border around the content (see Figure 9.47).

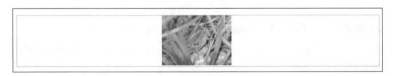

FIGURE 9.47
The Image web part with the Border Only chrome type.

Modify or Remove the Link for the Web Part's Title

In some web parts, you want the title to be a link that the users can click. To set that link or remove it (some web parts have a link by default), expand the Advanced section in the web part's tool pane and scroll down to the Title URL box. In this box, type the link that you want for the web part's title or clear the box to remove the link.

Move a Web Part in a Page

To move an existing web part in a page, switch the page to editing mode (see "How to Edit the Content of a Page" earlier in this chapter), and then just drag and drop the title of the web part to the location where you want it to appear. To do so, just hover the mouse cursor over the web part's title; then hold down the left mouse button and, without releasing it, move the mouse cursor to the place where you want the title— either in the same web part zone or in another, or to a different location in the text (if you are editing the contents of a publishing page or a wiki page).

The location of your mouse cursor is displayed by the title of the web part you are moving. When you are hovering the mouse cursor over a web part zone, the place in that zone where the web part will be added is signified by a bold line above or below or between the existing web parts already in that zone (see Figure 9.48). When you have the mouse cursor where you want the web part to be, you release the mouse button.

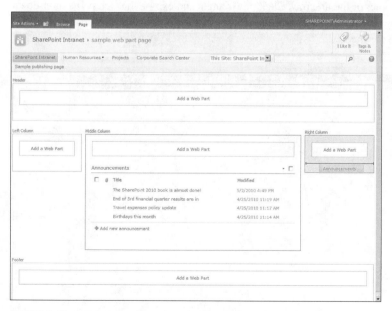

FIGURE 9.48
Dragging and dropping the Announcements web part.

Reuse a Web Part (Export/Import)

Scenario/Problem: After you have configured a web part to your liking, you want to save that web part and use it again in another page with similar settings.

Solution: To save the web part and use it again, you must export the web part and then import it to the other page. The following sections explain how to export a web part and then import it to another page.

Export a Web Part

Exporting a web part involves saving the web part's settings as a file to your computer. Not all web parts support this option, and in some web parts, the owner of the page may choose to disable this option. In those cases, you should look in the options in that web part's properties tool pane (see "How to Modify a Web Part," earlier in this chapter) to see whether the option to allow the web part to be exported is enabled. (Not all web parts have this option; some web parts cannot be exported.)

To export a web part that allows exporting, switch the page that has the web part to editing mode (see "Edit the Contents of a Page," earlier in this chapter) and then hover your mouse over the web part's title row. Doing so exposes a small black triangle on the right corner of the title row. Click this triangle and expose the web part's drop-down menu, shown in Figure 9.49. If the web part allows exporting, the Export option appears on the menu.

FIGURE 9.49
The web part's drop-down menu.

After you select the Export option, a File Download dialog appears, allowing you to save the web part to your computer. You can save the file anywhere on your computer so that you can import it later (see the following section).

Import a Web Part

To import a web part that you have previously saved to your computer, open the page in editing mode (see "Edit the Contents of a Page," earlier in this chapter) and click the web part zone where you want the web part to be added, as if you were adding a new web part. However, when the dialog with the list of web parts appears, instead of selecting a web part from the list, click the Upload a Web Part link shown under the Categories box (refer to Figure 9.33). When you click this link, you see a button to browse and a button to upload the file you have exported, as shown in Figure 9.50.

The Upload a Web Part menu

FIGURE 9.50
The Upload a Web Part menu appears under the list of categories.

Once the web part is uploaded, it is added to the Imported Web Parts category in the web part selection pane. To add it to the page, simply follow the instructions from the section "How to Add a Web Part," earlier in this chapter, and select the Imported Web Parts category to find the web part you have uploaded.

Publish a Page

Scenario/Problem: When a page is located in a document library that requires publishing—something that is common when you're using the publishing features (where all pages in a site are in the Pages library)—you must publish the page in order for users to be able to see it.

Solution: Publishing can be accomplished from the document library itself, just like publishing any other file that is in a document library (see "Check In and Check Out a File or List Item" in Chapter 6). You check in the page and then publish it, going through any approval process that might be required. (Again, refer to Chapter 6 for more information about the publishing and approval process.)

However, publishing pages is different from publishing regular files in that you can publish pages directly from the pages themselves. When you are editing a page that requires publishing, a Publish ribbon appears, with buttons designed to assist you in publishing the page (see Figure 9.51). If the library where the page is located does not require approval, simply click the Publish button to publish the page for everyone to see.

The Publish button

FIGURE 9.51
The Publish button is available if approval is not required.

However, if the library requires approval before publishing, you see the Submit button instead, as shown in Figure 9.52.

The Submit button

FIGURE 9.52
The Submit button is available if approval is required.

When you submit for approval, most users are not able to see your changes, but the people who have permissions to approve items in the document library can view your changes and approve or reject them. If an approver approves the page, it is published for other users to view. Approvers who navigate to the page can also use the Publish ribbon to approve or reject the page from the page itself, as shown in Figure 9.53.

The Cancel Approval button

The Approve button

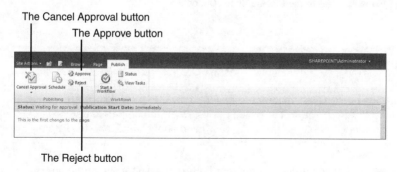

The Reject button

FIGURE 9.53
An approver gets buttons to approve or reject a page.

Discard the Check-out of a Page

Scenario/Problem: Often you start editing a page and then either change your mind or regret a change and want to roll back and start again.

Solution: To start over, just discard the check-out of the page. This section explains how to accomplish that.

The option to discard a check-out is available only when the page is in a document library that tracks versions and requires a check-out, such as in publishing websites. Pages that are not in such document libraries do not give you the option, and any change you make is saved; therefore, you must manually roll it back.

To discard the check-out of a page, use the built-in Discard Check Out option for that page from the library view, exactly as you would discard a check-out of a file in a document library (see "Check In and Check Out a File or List Item" in Chapter 6). However, an easier and more accessible way to discard the check-out of the page is through the Page ribbon. In the Page ribbon, open the drop-down menu under the Check In button, and then select the Discard Check Out option, as shown in Figure 9.54.

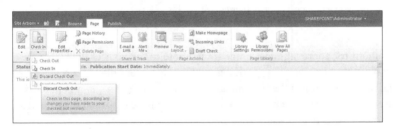

FIGURE 9.54
Using the Page menu to get to the Discard Check Out option.

Compare Versions of a Page

Scenario/Problem: Often you want to restore a page to a previous state (before some changes were made to the page), but you want to compare differences between the versions before making up your mind about which one to restore.

Solution: Pages that reside in a document library that supports versioning enable you to restore previous versions of the pages, just like any other files in document libraries that support versioning. However, with pages, you also get the option to view the changes that were made to them between each version and compare them.

> **NOTE** Page changes that are tracked by versioning include changes to add and remove web parts and edit content in the page's editing controls, such as the text editing control and image editing control. However, changes made to the contents in the web parts on the page do not count as part of the page's contents and are not restored when you restore a previous version. They are also not shown in the comparison of versions.

To compare the changes between versions of a page, switch to the page's Page ribbon and click the Page History button in the ribbon.

The page that opens shows the changes made in each version. The list of versions is in the left pane, and the current text with change tracking is in the right pane (see Figure 9.55).

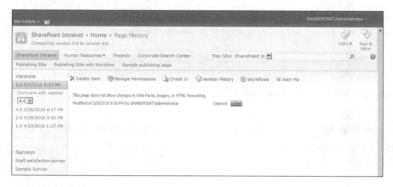

FIGURE 9.55
The version comparison screen.

When a change is made to a piece of content in the page (for example, the text in a text editing control on the page), the section in the version comparison page shows the old value and the new value, indicating what editing was done (see Figure 9.56). New text is highlighted, existing text appears as regular text, and text that was deleted appears in red strikethrough.

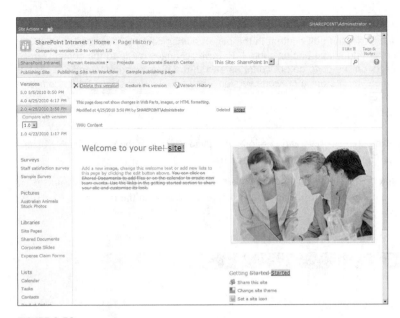

FIGURE 9.56
The text in the text editing control was changed.

You can browse the other versions of the page by clicking the version date and time on the left. You can delete or restore the version by using the toolbar in the page.

CHAPTER 10

Managing Security

If you are in charge of managing a list or library, you should learn how to manage the security on either the list or library or on the single items in them. This chapter covers some basic tasks related to security of lists, libraries, and list items.

See What Permissions Are Set

Scenario/Problem: You want to see what permissions are given to whom in a list or library or on a specific list item. For example, you want to know who can read, write, or delete files in a document library. Alternatively, you want to know who has permissions to read a specific document or to edit it.

Solution: The following sections explain how to check what permissions are defined for files, list items, document libraries, and lists.

Check Permissions on Files and List Items

To check what permissions are set on a file or list item, you must have the right to manage permissions on the file or item. If you don't have the appropriate permissions, the option to manage them is not available.

To manage the permissions on a file in a document library or a list item in a list, select the file or item. Then, in the Documents ribbon or Items ribbon, click the Document Permissions button or the Item Permission button, as shown in Figure 10.1.

FIGURE 10.1

The Document Permissions button in the Documents ribbon is available only when you have the required permissions on the file or item.

Clicking this button opens a page that shows the permissions for the file or item you're looking at (see Figure 10.2). On this page, you can see what permissions each user or group of users has on the file or item. This page is explained later in this chapter, in the section "Read the Permissions Page."

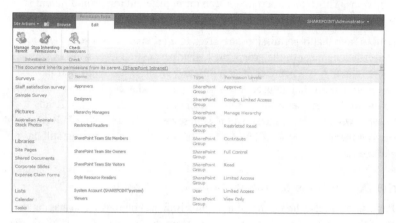

FIGURE 10.2
The manage permissions page for a document.

Check Permissions on Lists and Libraries

To be able to check what permissions are set on a list or library, you must have the permissions to manage the list or library. If you do not have the appropriate permissions, the button to manage permissions is not available. To manage the permissions on a list, switch to the List ribbon and click the List Permissions button in the Settings section. In a document library, switch to the Library ribbon and click the Library Permissions button. The page that opens is the same as the one for a document or a list items (refer to Figure 10.2 and see the following section). However, in a list and library, there is an additional button in the ribbon called Manage Access Requests. For more information about this button, see "Configure Access Requests for Lists and Libraries" later in this chapter.

Read the Permissions Page

The name of the file or title for the item, list, or library appears in the page's title after the word Permissions. This information helps you make sure you are viewing the permissions for the right file or item. The name of the user or group is in the first column, and the type (identifying whether it is a user or group) is in the second column. In the last column, you can see the permission set that the user or group has on the item, file, list, or library. Depending on the configuration of your server, other columns with more information about the user or group may also appear.

For example, in Figure 10.2, people in the SharePoint Team Site Visitors group can only read the file or item because they have only the Read permission, whereas SharePoint Team Site Owners can do everything to the file or item (including manage the permissions on it, delete it, and so on) because they have the Full Control permission set. The System Account (SHAREPOINT\system) group is shown to have Limited Access permissions. This type of permission can mean different things in different sites but usually means read-only permission.

It is important to note that if permissions are given to a group and then separately to a user, if that user is a member of the group, the higher permission level wins. For example, suppose user A is a member of group B, and group B has Full Control permissions on an item. Although user A was given just Read access, because user A is a member of group B, that user also has full control of the item and not just Read access. The same would apply if the situation were reversed: If user A has Full Access and that user is a member of group B, which has Read-Only access, the user still has full access to the item.

Check the Permissions for a Specific User or Group

A page's Permission Tools ribbon, shown in Figure 10.2, has buttons for managing the permissions of the parent (if the file or item is inheriting from a parent), to stop inheriting permissions, and to check permissions. Clicking on the Check Permissions button opens a dialog that allows you to check what kind of permissions a certain user or group has on the file, item, list, or library, as shown in Figure 10.3.

FIGURE 10.3
The Check Permissions dialog.

To use the dialog, simply type the user name or group name in the User/Group box and click the Check Now button. The dialog then shows you what permission levels that person or group has on the file, item, list, or library, as shown in Figure 10.4.

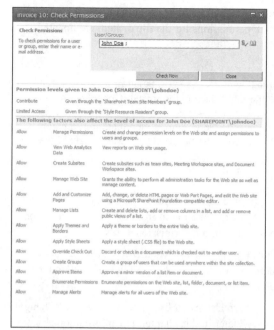

FIGURE 10.4
The Check Permissions dialog, showing what permissions John Doe has on a document.

NOTE For more information about groups, see the section "See Who Is a Member of a SharePoint Group," later in this chapter.

Grant Permissions to a File or List Item

Scenario/Problem: You want to change the permissions a certain user or group of users has on a file or list item. Because permissions for items are inherited from the list or library they are in, the items or files have the same permissions as the list. Sometimes you want to set different permissions on documents or items than for the list. For example, say you want to upload a document to share with several colleagues but not with other people who have access to the document library.

Solution: To assign permissions on a file or list item, you need to get to the manage permissions page of that file or list item (see "Check Permissions on Files and List Items," earlier in this chapter).

When you're on the manage permissions page for the file or item, you might be able to immediately change permissions, or you might have to first disconnect the permission inheritance for that file or item. Permission inheritance is on by default for all files or items in SharePoint. It means that the file or item inherits its permissions from the list or library in which it is located and has exactly the same permission sets. If the permissions for the list or library change, the permissions for the file or item are updated automatically.

NOTE If a file or an item is inheriting permissions from its list or library, which in turn is inheriting permissions from the site (which in turn may be inheriting from its parent site), the permission management page shows a yellow bar below the ribbon (refer to Figure 10.2). This bar says that the file or item is inheriting from a parent and displays a link to where you can manage the permissions—at the level of the list, library, site, or parent site.

While inheritance is active, it is not possible to set a different permission level on a file or an item (refer to Figure 10.2). To stop a file or an item from inheriting permissions, click the Stop Inheriting Permissions button in the Permission Tools ribbon.

If you want to change the permissions for the parent—whether it's a list, library, or site—you can click the Manage Parent button in the ribbon or click the link to the parent in the yellow bar shown in Figure 10.2.

For more information about managing permissions on lists and libraries, see "Change a User's Permissions on a List or Library," later in this chapter. For information about managing permissions for sites, see Chapter 14, "Managing Site Security."

After you click the Stop Inheriting Permissions button, a prompt appears, asking you to confirm that you want to disconnect the permissions inheritance from the list or library. The prompt also explains that after you do so, changes to the permissions of the list and library will not affect the file or item you are managing. This means, for example, that if a certain user is granted permissions to edit files or items in the list or library after you disconnect the inheritance of permissions, that user still can't edit the specific list item or file that you managed unless you (or someone else) explicitly give that user the permissions to edit that document.

If you are sure that you want to manage the permissions for a file separately from the permission of the list or library, click OK. The page changes and allows you to manage the permissions for the file or item.

If the file's or item's permission inheritance was already disconnected in the past, by you or by someone else, you see the screen shown in Figure 10.5 when you click Manage Permissions for the file or list item. You can change your mind and switch the file or item back to inherit permission using the Inherit Permissions button on the ribbon.

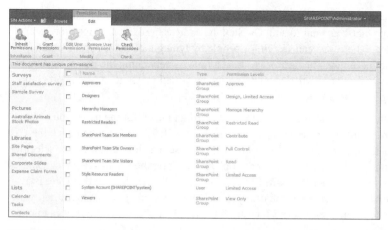

FIGURE 10.5

The edit permissions page for a list item or file when permission inheritance is disconnected.

Now you can manage the permissions on the file or item. To add permission to a user or group that doesn't already have permissions, click the Grant Permissions button in the Permission Tools ribbon. This opens the Grant Permission dialog, which enables you to select either a user or group and select what permission levels should be given (see Figure 10.6).

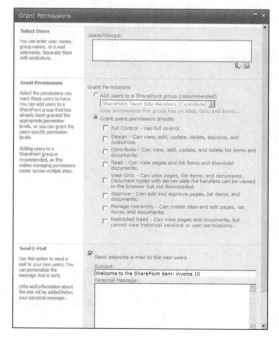

FIGURE 10.6

Granting permissions to a new user or group.

In the Select Users section, type the name (or part of a name) or e-mail address for the user or group that you want to add. Or click the address book icon to open the people search dialog, where you can search for people by typing a name or part of a name. You can add more than one user or group at a time by separating the names with semicolons. This is similar to when you are writing an e-mail message in Microsoft Outlook and you choose who you want to send the e-mail to.

If you use the Check Name icon and there is no exact match for the name you entered, a red underline appears beneath the name (see Figure 10.7). You can then click the name to open a menu that shows users who are a close match to that name or select to remove the name. For example, typing "Joh" and clicking the Check Name icon causes a red line to appear under the name "Joh." When you click it, you see that there is a user called John Doe. If this is the user you're looking for, click the name. If not, you can either click Remove to delete John from the text box or click More Names to open the search dialog.

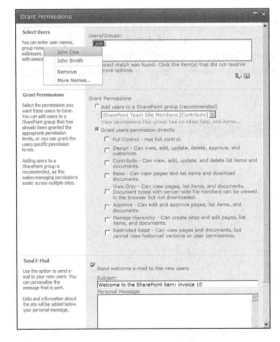

FIGURE 10.7

Typing part of a name in the text box.

The search dialog enables you to search for people. You just type part of the name of the person or group that you want, as shown in Figure 10.8, and click the Search icon. A list of possible matches appears. To select one of them, double-click the name, and it is added to the box at the bottom of the dialog. After you have chosen all the users and groups, click OK to close the dialog and return to the Add Users page.

FIGURE 10.8
Typing part of a name in the people search dialog.

After you have found the users and/or groups that you want to add to the list, select the permissions they should have by selecting one or more of the check boxes in the list of permissions under Grant Users Permission Directly (refer to Figure 10.6). Selecting options here gives the users the permissions you selected. As before, the higher permission level wins, so if you give someone the Read and Contribute permissions, the user can edit the file as well as read it because of the Contribute setting.

Alternatively, you can add the users or groups to a SharePoint group. If you do, they get whatever permission level the SharePoint group has. This is a useful mechanism for controlling permissions. For example, if you decide that all the users who have Contribute (edit) permissions on a document should now have read-only access, you have to edit each user's permissions. Instead, by using SharePoint groups, you can add users to a SharePoint group that has the Contribute permission level, and when a change is required, you change the permissions only on that SharePoint group and not on each user individually. You can add both users and security groups to the SharePoint group.

To add users or groups to a SharePoint group, click the Add Users to a SharePoint Group option and then select from the drop-down list the SharePoint group to which you want to add the users and/or security groups (see Figure 10.9). Click on View Permission This Group Has to open another dialog that shows what permissions the group has on the different sites and lists.

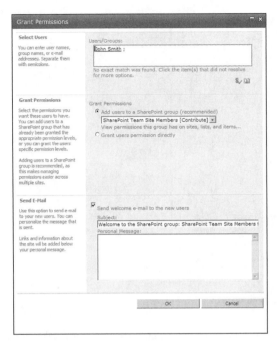

FIGURE 10.9
Adding users and groups to a
SharePoint group.

If the server hosting the SharePoint site supports sending e-mail messages, another
option appears, allowing you to send e-mail to the users to tell them that they have
permissions on the file or item (refer to Figure 10.6). You have the option to select not
to send the e-mail, or if you select to send it, you can change the title and body of the
message.

When you are done selecting all the options, click OK to save the new permissions.

Change a User's or Group's Permissions
on a File or List Item

Scenario/Problem: You want to change an existing permission that was
granted to a user or group on a file or list item—perhaps to give that user more
permissions or remove that user's permissions altogether.

Solution: To change permissions on a file or an item, open the manage permissions page for that file or item and select the name (or names) of the user or group
for which you want to change the permissions. Then click the Edit User Permissions
button in the Modify section of the Permission Tools ribbon. The Edit Permissions
dialog appears, enabling you to select permissions for that user or group (see
Figure 10.10).

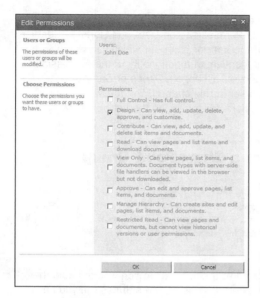

FIGURE 10.10
Changing a user's or group's permissions.

In the Edit Permissions dialog, you can select one or more permission levels. For example, if you select Contribute and Approve, the user will be able to both edit the document or list item and approve it but will not be able to set the permission on the file or item. When you are done selecting permissions, click OK.

Grant Permissions on a List or Library

Scenario/Problem: You want to change the permissions on a list or library. For example, you want to add a user to the list or library as a reader or as an author.

Solution: To assign permissions on a list or document library, you need to get to the manage permissions page of that list or document library (see "Check Permissions on Lists and Libraries," earlier in this chapter). This page is identical in functionality to the permission management page described in the section "Grant Permissions to a File or List Item," earlier in this chapter. Follow the instructions in that section to grant permissions to the list or library.

Change a User's Permissions on a List or Library

Scenario/Problem: You want to change the permissions that a user or group has on a list or library. For example, you might want to remove permissions altogether or grant more permissions.

Solution: To change permissions on a list or library, open the manage permissions page for that list or library (see "Check Permissions on Lists and Libraries," earlier in this chapter) and click the name of the user or group for which you want to change the permissions. This page is identical in functionality to the permission management page described in the section "Change a User's or Group's Permissions on a File or List Item," earlier in this chapter. You follow the instructions in that section to change permissions for a user on the list or library.

See Who Is a Member of a SharePoint Group

Scenario/Problem: SharePoint groups contain several users. You want to see who belongs to a group before you assign permissions to that group. (You may later want to add users to or remove them from a group; this task is explained in "Assign Users' Permissions on a Site" in Chapter 14.)

Solution: SharePoint groups are defined at a site level. To see who is a member of a SharePoint group, you need the right permissions on the site itself. If you have those rights, you can open Site Actions and select Site Settings (see Figure 10.11).

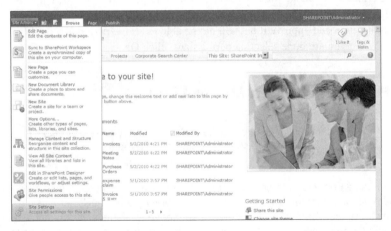

FIGURE 10.11
Selecting the Site Settings option.

Selecting this option opens the settings page for the site (see Figure 10.12). Here, click the People and Groups link under the Users and Permissions header. The page that opens is the one used to manage security on a site (see Figure 10.13). The SharePoint groups are listed in the left navigation pane, under the Groups header.

FIGURE 10.12
Clicking on the People and Groups link
in the site settings page.

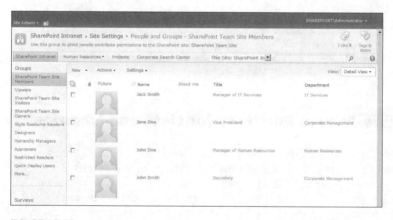

FIGURE 10.13
You can view the groups and who is in which group on this page.

> **TIP** The Site Actions menu might be hidden in some sites. To get to the manage
> site security page, you add /_layouts/people.aspx to the end of the site path.
> For example, if your site is at http://sharepoint/sample, type http://sharepoint/
> sample/_layouts/people.aspx in your browser to get to the page.

Click the link with the name of the group for which you want to see the members.
Doing so shows a list of members—either users (such as John Doe) or security groups
(such as Human Resources). Not all users have display names set, so some of them
might not have anything under the Name column.

If you want to see who the user with the missing name is, just click that user's picture to open the user information page (see Figure 10.14).

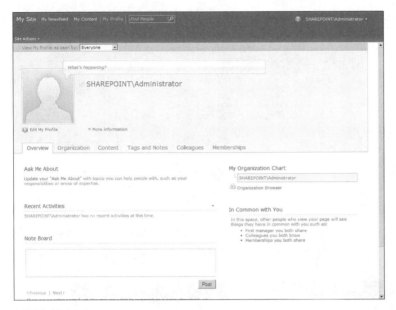

FIGURE 10.14
The user information page for the administrator shows the user's details in the personal site for that user.

Configure Access Requests for Lists and Libraries

Scenario/Problem: You are managing the security of a list or library, and you want to configure the access requests for it. Access requests are sent when a user who doesn't have permission to a list or library wants to have permission. When users who don't have permission try to get to the library, if access requests are configured, they are presented with a dialog that enables them to request access (see Figure 10.15).

FIGURE 10.15
Users who don't have access to a library see this dialog when they try to open the library.

As you can see, the users can request access by using the Request Access link. That request takes them to a dialog where they can explain why they think they should have access (see Figure 10.16). This information is then sent as an e-mail message to the library owner.

FIGURE 10.16
The Request Access dialog appears when the Request Access link is clicked.

Solution: To enable or disable access requests, open the document library or list and get to the manage security page for that library or list (see "Check Permissions on Lists and Libraries," earlier in this chapter). On this page, click the Manage Access Requests button in the Manage section of the Permission Tools ribbon (see Figure 10.17).

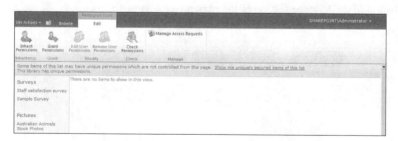

FIGURE 10.17
The manage permission page for a list, showing the Manage Access Requests button.

NOTE The Manage Access Requests button might not appear if SharePoint is not configured to send e-mails. If you do not see this button, contact your administrator and request this feature.

When you click the Manage Access Requests button, a dialog opens, allowing you to select whether access requests should be enabled or disabled (see Figure 10.18).

FIGURE 10.18
The Manage Access Requests dialog.

In some instances, the Allow Requests for Access option is not available, and you see the check box grayed out. To enable this option and to select which e-mail address should receive the access requests, you need permissions to manage permissions on the site. If you have those permissions, and you want to change the e-mail address that will get the requests, open the Site Actions menu and click the Site Permissions option to get to the site permissions management page.

If you started from a subsite and that site is inheriting the permissions from a parent site, click the Manage Parent button in the ribbon to go to the page for managing the permissions for the site that isn't inheriting its permissions.

If the site you are on is not inheriting permissions, you should see the Manage Access Requests button in the Manage section of the ribbon (see Figure 10.19).

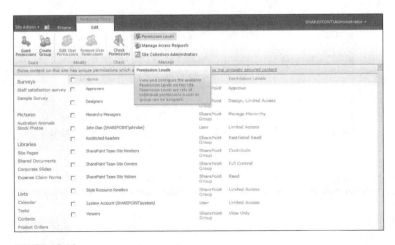

FIGURE 10.19
The Manage Access Requests button in the site permission management page.

Clicking this button opens a dialog that allows you to disable or enable the access requests for the site. If it is disabled, the Manage Access Requests dialog in the document libraries and lists in the site (refer to Figure 10.16) shows a disabled button. The other option on this page sets the e-mail for the person (or a group) that access requests will be sent to (see Figure 10.20).

FIGURE 10.20
The Manage Access Requests dialog for a site.

> **NOTE** It is important to note that the e-mail setting in this dialog affects all document libraries and lists in the site, as well as access requests to the site itself and any subsites (and their lists and libraries) that are inheriting permissions from the site you are configuring.

CHAPTER 11

Workflows

A developer can create a workflow to automate a process for files or list items. As an author or a contributor for a list or document library, you might be required to start a workflow or participate in one. This chapter covers basic workflow-related tasks, explaining how to start a workflow, track its progress, and attach a workflow to a document library or list that you are managing.

Start a Workflow

Scenario/Problem: When a workflow has been attached to a list or document library, it can be configured to start automatically when someone changes an item or file, or it can be configured to require the user to manually start the workflow. If it is configured to start manually, you might have to start it yourself.

Solution: To manually start a workflow on a list item or file, select the item's or file's row in the list or library view to switch to the Documents ribbon or Items ribbon. If there is at least one workflow associated with the document library that allows you to manually start it, the Workflows button is available in the ribbon (see Figure 11.1).

FIGURE 11.1
The Workflows button in the Documents ribbon.

Clicking this button opens the Workflows screen, which has options for starting a workflow associated with the list or document library on the specific item (see Figure 11.2).

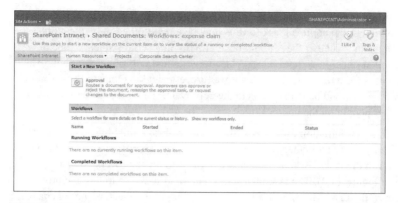

FIGURE 11.2
The Workflows screen.

In the Start a New Workflow section of the Workflows screen, choose from the list of workflows that you can apply to the list item or file. Click the one you want to start to open the page that the workflow specifies as its initiation page (see Figure 11.3). This page appears every time you initiate a workflow on an item, and each different workflow may have a different page. Some workflows do not have an initiation form at all.

FIGURE 11.3
The Approval workflow's initiation page.

In the case of the Approval workflow, the initiation page asks for one or more approvers to assign the approval task to (this may be already filled in by the workflow's settings) and whether they should be approving in a serial sequence (one after another) or all at once. It also provides a place to write text describing your approval request and asks for a due date for the approval process and how long each person in the approvers list should have to complete the approval. Finally, it provides an option to notify other people on the approval process, in the CC section.

After you fill in the initiation form, click Start. The workflow might take a while to start, and then you are redirected to the list or library. The approval workflow then creates a task in the tasks list in the site and assigns it to the approvers you have selected (see Figure 11.4). The task then sends an e-mail message to those approvers, telling them of the task. The approver has options to approve, reject, request a change, or reassign, as shown in Figure 11.4.

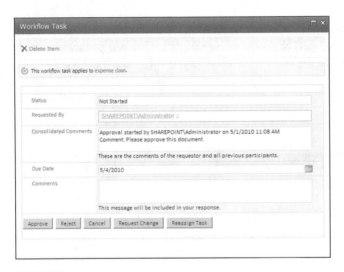

FIGURE 11.4
The Approval workflow creates tasks for approvers to approve.

Track the Progress of a Workflow

Scenario/Problem: You want to see the progress of a workflow that was started on a list item or file.

Solution: Select the item or file and click the Workflows button in the Items ribbon or Documents ribbon (refer to Figure 11.1). The workflows page that opens shows the running workflows as well as the completed ones (see Figure 11.5).

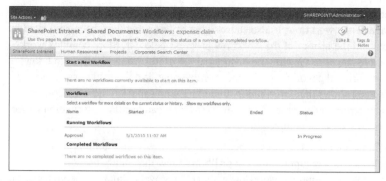

FIGURE 11.5
The running and completed workflows appear in the Workflows section.

Click the name of a workflow or its status to get to the status summary page that is relevant to the workflow on the current item (see Figure 11.6).

FIGURE 11.6
The status summary page for a workflow.

NOTE Figure 11.6 shows what the workflow information page looks like with Microsoft Silverlight installed. Without Microsoft Silverlight installed, the page looks slightly different.

The workflow's status summary page shows where the workflow is by displaying a graphic image of the workflow. It also shows a list of tasks that have been generated by the workflow and the history of the workflow progress below it. More complex workflows have more steps, so viewing the history can be useful when you want to know who did what during the workflow runtime. For example, if a workflow was canceled, the history screen shows that information, including who canceled the workflow. If there were any errors in any of the workflow steps, you can use this information to see why the workflow was not completed.

Some workflows offer quicker ways to get to the workflow status summary window. These workflows add a column to the list or library view that shows the status in that view. For example, the approval workflow adds an Approval column to the views of the list or library, showing you the status of the workflow and enabling you to click the status to get to the status summary page (see Figure 11.7).

FIGURE 11.7
The Approval workflow adds a column showing the status.

Associate a Workflow with a List or Library

Scenario/Problem: You want to assign a workflow to a list or library so that users can select it from the list of available workflows. Or you might want to define a workflow that starts automatically when a document or list item is added or modified in the library or list.

Solution: To attach different workflows to a list or library, you need the Manage list or Manage library permission on that list or library. If you have those permissions, switch to the Library ribbon or List ribbon and click on the Workflows button (see Figure 11.8).

The Workflows button

FIGURE 11.8
The Workflows button in the Library ribbon.

Clicking the Workflows button opens the Workflow Settings page for the list or library. This page enables you to associate a workflow with the list or library (see Figure 11.9).

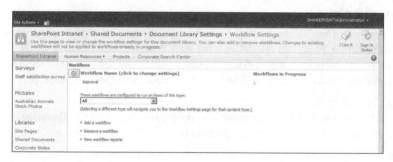

FIGURE 11.9
The Workflow Settings page for adding a workflow.

The list of workflows that were already added to the list or library appears at the top of the page (under the Workflows title). The option to add a workflow is shown as a link at the bottom of the page. Click this link to open the Add a Workflow page, shown in Figure 11.10.

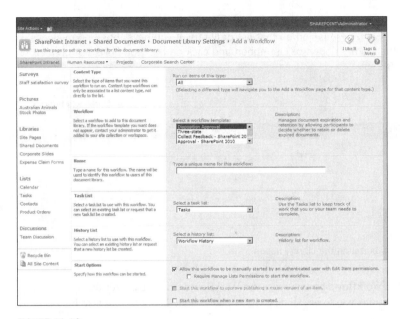

FIGURE 11.10
The Add a Workflow page.

In the Add a Workflow page, you can define what workflow you want to create on the list or library by selecting from the workflow box that lists the available workflows. By default, the only workflows available in SharePoint Server are the five built-in workflows:

- **Disposition Approval**—Allows starting a workflow to manage document expiration and retention. As part of the workflow, people involved with the file or list item are required to decide whether to retain or delete expired documents.

- **Three-State**—Tracks the progress of approval of a document or a list item through three states: Active, Ready for Review, and Complete.

- **Collect Feedback**—Allows starting a review workflow for a document or list item in the list or library. Reviewers can provide feedback, which is compiled and sent to the owner of the file or list item when the workflow has completed.

- **Approval**—Allows starting an approval workflow on the list's or library's items, where approvers can approve or reject the document or list item, reassign the approval task, or request changes to the document.

- **Collect Signatures**—Allows starting a workflow for collecting signatures that are required to complete a business process on a document. Note that this workflow can be started only from within a Microsoft Word 2007 or Microsoft Excel 2007 client, and then only from certain versions of Microsoft Office 2007 (Ultimate, Professional Plus, and Enterprise). If you cannot start this workflow from your Microsoft Office client, you should check the version of your Microsoft Office and upgrade if necessary.

In SPF, only the Three-State workflow is available by default.

After you choose a workflow, choose a name for it. Because more than one workflow of any type can be attached to the document library or list, each must have a unique name so that the users can recognize it in the list of workflows. For example, a document library might require two approval workflows: one for expense claims and one for travel expenses. To create those two, you need to add them both as approval workflows—but each one with a different name.

The next choice is what task list the workflow should use to create tasks associated with it. As you saw earlier in this chapter, the Approval workflow creates tasks for approvers to approve the file or list item when the workflow starts. You can point each workflow to a specific task list or tell the workflow to create a new task list for itself.

The History List section enables you to define where the workflow reports its progress, for the purpose of storing the history. As you saw earlier in this chapter, when viewing a workflow's progress, you can see the history of steps taken in the workflow. Here, you can define in which list that history is kept. By default, the history is kept in a hidden list called Workflow History that the users do not ordinarily see. If you want to store the information in another list, you can define that here.

Finally, the last section of the page, Start Options, enables you to specify when the workflow starts (see Figure 11.11).

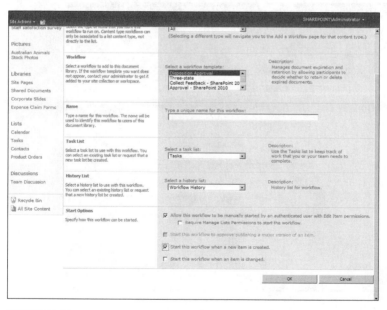

FIGURE 11.11
Creating a new approval workflow that starts automatically for new items.

With the first option, Allow This Workflow to Be Manually Started, users can start the workflow manually. The third option, Start This Workflow When a New Item Is Created, causes the list or library to start the workflow automatically when a new item or file is added to the list or library. As you can see in Figure 11.11, if you choose to let the users start the workflow manually, the users must have the Edit Items permission on the list or library; otherwise, they can't start the workflow on any item. Select the Require Manage Lists Permissions to Start the Workflow check box to allow only managers of the list to be able to start the workflow.

You can use the second option, Start This Workflow to Approve Publishing a Major Version of an Item, only if the list or library has versioning set to allow major and minor versions. If this option is selected, this workflow starts when a user submits a file or list item for approval to get published as a major version. The last option causes the workflow to start when an item or a file is changed in the list or library.

When you are finished configuring the workflow, click Next to open the workflow's association form (if the workflow has one). A workflow association form is different for each workflow type and is used to configure settings that are specific for that workflow type (see Figure 11.12). For example, the Approval workflow's association form enables you to set whether the approval is done in parallel or in a serial manner. Parallel approval means that all the approvers get an e-mail message at the same time, whereas serial approval means the first approver on the list must approve before the second one gets the request to approve, and so on.

FIGURE 11.12
The Approval workflow's association form.

When you are done setting the configuration for the workflow, or if there are no additional configuration settings, click OK. If you selected that users can start the workflow automatically, your new workflow is added to the list of workflows the user can start.

CHAPTER 12

Creating Subsites

If you are a site manager, you might want to create subsites under the site you are managing. For example, you might have a site called Projects, under which you will create a subsite for each project to hold the project's files and details. This chapter explains how to create subsites, including the different templates for subsites that come with SharePoint.

This chapter also includes instructions for how to use the special Meeting Workspace subsites.

Create a Subsite

Scenario/Problem: You want to create a subsite under an existing site. For example, you want to create a site for a team, or a blog site for a certain person, or a wiki site for a specific topic.

Solution: The following section explains how to create a site in general and then gives examples of creating three types of sites.

To create a subsite under an existing Microsoft SharePoint 2010 site, open the Site Actions menu and choose the New Site option. If this option is not in the menu, you might have to go through the More Options option to open the Create dialog. As explained in Chapter 7, "Creating Lists and Document Libraries," how this dialog looks depends on whether you have Microsoft Silverlight installed.

Create a Subsite with Microsoft Silverlight Installed

If you have Microsoft Silverlight installed, when the Create dialog opens, you can filter it to show only site templates, as shown in Figure 12.1.

FIGURE 12.1
The Create dialog, filtered to show only sites.

In this dialog you can choose the kind of site you want to create from the list of available templates (which may be different from site to site). Choose the template you want from the middle section of the dialog, and on the right side, type the title for the new site. The title is displayed on the top of the site and in the navigation links pointing to the site. You can change this title at any time from the site settings.

Next, choose and type the URL name for the site. This name determines how the link to the site will look. It is recommended that you consider this name carefully because, although it can be changed after the site is created, if it changes, shortcuts that your users have created and links that point to that site break (without considerable work by the SharePoint administrator). Keep this text as short as possible, and you shouldn't use spaces and special characters in the URL name of a site.

NOTE To change any of the first three settings in the Create dialog, see "Change the Name, Description, Icon, or URL of a Site" in Chapter 13, "Customizing a SharePoint Site."

Choose the template you want, and then click the More Options button. In the dialog that appears, in addition to the title and the URL name, you can also specify the description for the site (see Figure 12.2).

FIGURE 12.2
The Create dialog, showing more options for creating a site.

This information is normally displayed under the site's title or in the site's home page (depending on the design of the site) and can also be changed at any time. Next, in the dialog, choose options in the Permissions section (refer to Figure 12.2). You can define whether the site will have the same permission set as its parent site (the site you are currently on) or unique permissions. If you are happy with the new site having the same permissions as the current site, you can leave the default setting, Use Same

Permissions as Parent Site. If you choose Use Unique Permissions, you must set permissions on the site after it has been created. You can modify the permissions of the site at any time. See Chapter 14, "Managing Site Security," for more information about changing the site's permissions.

Finally, choose in the Navigation Inheritance section whether the site should have the same top navigation bar as the parent site or whether it should have a navigation bar of its own. This section lets you create subsites that look either like part of the top site or like separate sites altogether. You can change these settings later (see "Modify the Top or Left Navigation Bar" in Chapter 13).

Create a Subsite Without Microsoft Silverlight Installed

When you don't have Microsoft Silverlight, the Create dialog offers some popular site templates under the Pages and Sites category, and it also has the link Sites and Workspaces. Clicking this link opens a page that allows you to select a template and specify the new site's settings, as shown in Figure 12.3.

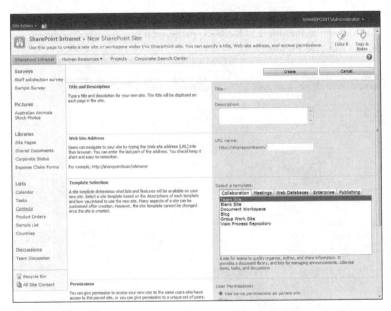

FIGURE 12.3
The site creation page when you don't have Microsoft Silverlight installed.

All the settings in this page are the same as the settings in the More Options dialog explained earlier, with the exception that in this page you also select the template for the new site. To choose the template, click on the tabs for the template categories, and then choose a template from the list of available templates shown here. For example, under the Collaboration tab shown in Figure 12.3, you can choose the Team Site template to create a team site, or switch to the Publishing tab to choose the Publishing Site template or the Enterprise Wiki template.

When you are finished setting the options for the new site, click the Create button to create the site. The new site opens unless you have chosen to have unique permissions for the site. In that case, the permissions setting page for the site opens first (see Figure 12.4). For more information about setting these permissions, see Chapter 14.

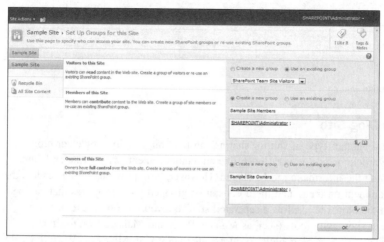

FIGURE 12.4
The permissions setting page for a site with unique permissions.

Create a Team Site

A team site is a simple site with a document library, an announcements list, a calendar list, a links list, a tasks list, and a team discussion board. To create a team site, select the Team Site template in the Create dialog (refer to Figures 12.1 and 12.3) and fill in the site's title and URL name (and, if you wish, other parameters, such as the description, using the More Options button, as shown in Figures 12.2 and 12.3). Then click Create.

Create an Enterprise Wiki Site in SharePoint Server

A wiki site is a site for managing and sharing information. This type of site is used mostly to share ideas and knowledge among many people. The Enterprise Wiki Site template enables users who use the site to easily change the pages and create new pages. It also comes with a ratings system that allows users to rate each wiki article and a categories system that enables grouping of articles by categories.

To create a wiki site, select the Enterprise Wiki Site template (refer to Figure 12.1), fill in the parameters for the site as explained earlier in this chapter, and click Create. When the site is created, it has only one page, the home page for the site. The page has some default text explaining what a wiki is. It also has an Edit This Page button on the top that allows users to edit the content of the page (see Figure 12.5).

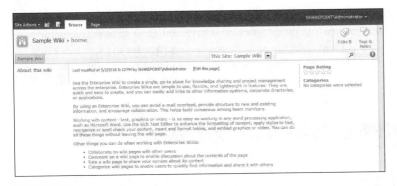

FIGURE 12.5
A new enterprise wiki site.

Create a Blog Site

A blog site is another type of site for sharing information, usually articles or blog posts. Each article or post is very much like an announcement, with a title and some text containing the information to be shared. However, blog posts also offer readers the option to comment on them, and the posts can be grouped into categories that can be managed in the blog site itself as a separate list. The layout of a blog site is customized to show blog tools (such as Manage Posts and Manage Comments), as shown in Figure 12.6. A blog site also offers integration with Microsoft Word to easily create posts in that application using the Launch Blog Program to Post link.

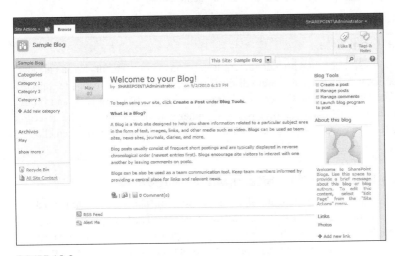

FIGURE 12.6
The home page of a new blog site.

To create a blog site, select the Blog option (refer to Figures 12.1 and 12.3), fill in the details, and click Create. After you create the site, the home page of the blog shows a sample post that explains what a blog is and displays a list of actions you can perform on the blog, including creating a new post and managing the posts and comments (refer to Figure 12.6).

Create an Event with a Website

Scenario/Problem: You want to create a site for an event. An event in a calendar list can have an associated subsite that is used to store more information about the event and help the people managing the event to get ready for it. For example, when planning a meeting, you might want to collaborate with other people on the agenda of the meeting. You might also ask several people who are scheduled to speak in the meeting to upload their presentations and supporting documents before the meeting so that the other attendees can read them on time. The attendee list for the meeting can also be managed on the site; it can list not just who was invited but who actually came to the meeting.

This capability is not exclusive for meetings but can also be used to track information about an event—for example, a conference for which some people must prepare and collaborate.

Solution: To create an event site, you can use the regular method of creating a site, as explained earlier in this chapter, and choose one of the event meeting templates available (refer to Figure 12.1). This way, you can create an event site but not link it to the calendar event item itself; you can do the linking later.

You also can create the site directly from the calendar event item itself. To do so, simply open the calendar event item for which you want to create a site or you create a new calendar event item (see Figure 12.7) and select the Workspace option. Then click Save.

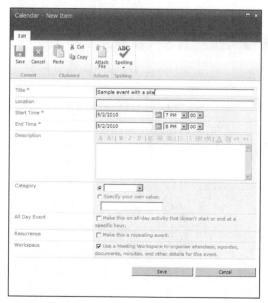

FIGURE 12.7

Creating a new calendar event item with the option to create a meeting workspace for the event.

When you click Save, the page shown in Figure 12.8 appears. It enables you to specify the settings for the new site.

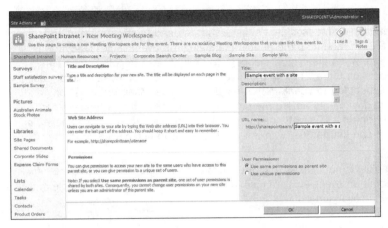

FIGURE 12.8
Creating an event site from a calendar event item.

In this page, you can either create a new site (which is the default behavior). Or, if there are already subsites available, you see the Link to an Existing Meeting Workspace option. If you choose this option, you only need to click OK to associate the event list item with the meeting workspace because the site was already created and configured.

If you choose to create a new site, click OK to be redirected to the template selection page. On this page, you see the available meeting workspace templates to choose from (see Figure 12.9).

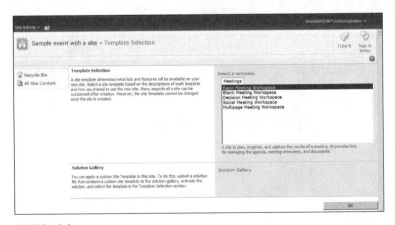

FIGURE 12.9
Choosing a template for the new meeting workspace.

After you select a template and create the site, a new site is created from that template. Different templates offer different lists in the site. The most common one is the basic meeting workspace, which offers management of objectives, agenda, attendees, and a document library to hold documents related to the event (see Figure 12.10).

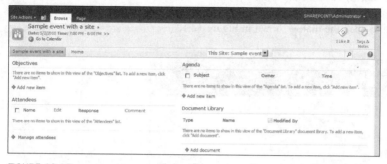

FIGURE 12.10
A new basic event workspace.

Create an Agenda

In a basic event workspace, you create an agenda by adding items to the Agenda list. A web part with the agenda usually appears on the home page. To add an item, simply click the Add New Item link under that web part. The page for adding an agenda item then opens (see Figure 12.11). Here, you can specify the subject of the agenda item, who owns it, the time spot allocated to it, and any notes required.

FIGURE 12.11
Creating a new agenda item.

You manage an agenda as you would in any other list. For more information about managing lists (for example, deleting or editing items), see Chapter 6, "Creating and Managing Files, List Items, and Forms in SharePoint."

Invite Attendees

If you are the owner of an event workspace site, you can manage the attendees list of the event by clicking Manage Attendees under the Attendees web part on the home page. Selecting this option opens a special list to which you can add people as attendees, specifying whether each person replied to the invitation and whether he or she is required to attend. To add a new attendee, switch to the Items ribbon and click the New Item button to open the dialog shown in Figure 12.12.

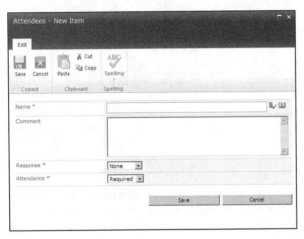

FIGURE 12.12
Adding a new attendee.

CHAPTER 13

Customizing a SharePoint Site

When you are in charge of a SharePoint site, you will want to customize it to fit your view of how it should look and behave. Such customization includes changing the site's title, the way the site looks (using themes), the page used as the home page for the site, the site's navigation, the site's search settings, and more.

This chapter covers these topics and explains how to accomplish some of the most common site customization tasks.

Open the Site Settings Page

Scenario/Problem: You want to change a site's settings.

Solution: To change a site's settings, access the Site Settings page by opening the Site Actions menu and choosing Site Settings, as shown in Figure 13.1.

FIGURE 13.1
Opening the Site Settings page.

Different types of sites have more settings than others (see Figures 13.2 and 13.3). A root-level site has more settings than a subsite, and publishing sites have additional settings. The settings available on a page vary based on the permissions you have on the site. For example, in a root-level site, the link to the settings for the site collection (see Figure 13.3) is displayed only if you have site collection administrator privileges.

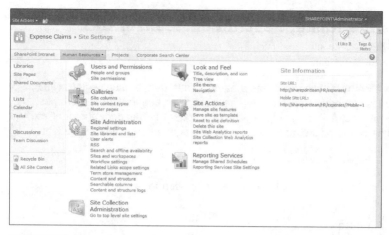

FIGURE 13.2

The Site Settings page for a subsite.

FIGURE 13.3

The Site Settings page for a root site that is a publishing site.

Change the Name, Description, Icon, or URL of a Site

Scenario/Problem: Every site has a name or title that is usually displayed on all the pages, generally above the top navigation bar and in the breadcrumbs. The description of a site sometimes appears under the breadcrumbs or at the top of some of the pages, and the icon usually appears next to the title (see Figure 13.4).

You might want to change the title, description, or icon for a site.

The site's icon or logo
The site's title   The site's description

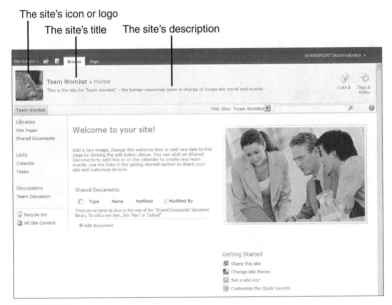

FIGURE 13.4
The site's title, icon, and description.

Solution: To change these settings, open the Site Settings page, as explained earlier. In the Site Settings page, click the Title, Description, and Icon link in the Look and Feel section of the page (refer to Figure 13.2).

The Title, Description, and Icon settings page opens, as shown in Figure 13.5, allowing you to change the settings.

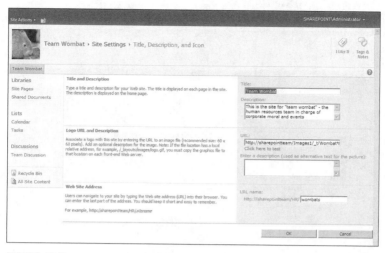

FIGURE 13.5

The Title, Description, and Icon settings page.

TIP Although you can change the URL name of the site from the Title, Description, and Icon page, it is not recommended that you do so after users have begun using your site. If you change the URL name, any link or bookmark that users have created pointing to the site is broken.

Change the Look of a Site by Using Themes

Scenario/Problem: Themes change how a site looks by applying different styles to the site. Themes feature different color schemes and different fonts. You might want to change how a site looks by using themes.

Solution: To apply a different theme to a site, open the Site Settings page, as explained earlier. In the Look and Feel section of the page, click the Site Theme link. This selection opens a page that enables you to pick a theme for the site (see Figure 13.6).

FIGURE 13.6
Picking a site theme.

When you click the available options for themes in the box, the image next to it is changed to show the color scheme used by the theme, with examples of what hyperlinks, headings, and body text look like in the theme.

In a subsite, you can choose to inherit the theme from the parent site (the default behavior) or specify a different theme.

If no theme uses the color scheme you want, you can choose the theme that is closest to what you want and then use the Customize Theme section of the page to specify the colors you want to change. For example, you can specify that you want the heading to be in a different font than the built-in scheme. Modifying these options doesn't modify the built-in theme; the customized theme is only applied to the site. You can reset a theme back to the original by choosing Default Theme.

To preview the site with the new theme, click the Preview button. A dialog appears, showing how the site looks with the chosen configuration. To apply the theme, click the Apply button. You can also select to have the theme applied to all subsites of the current site. If you choose this option, any subsite that has a different theme is reset to inherit the theme you selected and customized.

Change the Home Page of a Site

Scenario/Problem: You want to change which page is opened when a user types in the address of the site or clicks the site's link in the navigation bar.

Solution: If the site you are working on has multiple pages, you can choose which page in the site is the home page (also known as the welcome page) for the site. For information about creating pages, see Chapter 9, "Authoring Pages."

To select a page to be the home page, navigate to that page and switch to the Page ribbon. If you have sufficient permissions on the site, you see the Make Homepage button in the Page Actions section of the ribbon. To make the page the home page, click the Make Homepage button and confirm the action in the pop-up prompt that shows up.

Alternatively, in publishing sites, click the Welcome Page link in the Look and Feel section of the site. (Again, this option appears only in publishing sites.) This selection opens the Site Welcome Page setting page, which enables you to specify which page should be opened (see Figure 13.7). Simply type in the link or use the Browse button to browse to the page in the site that you want to be the home page.

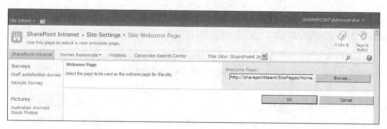

FIGURE 13.7
The Site Welcome Page setting page.

> **NOTE** The browsing function allows you to select a list or library in the site. However, if you select a list or library and try to save it as a new welcome page, SharePoint will not allow it and will tell you that the selection is not valid. You can only select pages or list items as the welcome page for a site.

Modify the Top or Left Navigation Bar

> **Scenario/Problem:** You want to modify the links shown on the top or left navigation bar. For example, you might want to add a tab to the top navigation bar or remove a link from the left navigation bar.

Solution: How you modify the links shown on the top or left navigation bar depends on the type of site you are using. The following sections provide the details.

Modify the Top or Left Navigation Bar in a Non-Publishing Site

In a non-publishing site, the navigation settings for the top and left navigation bars are in two separate locations. The link to the top navigation management page is called Top Link Bar in the Site Settings page, and the link to the left navigation bar management page is called Quick Launch.

Clicking on either link opens a page where you can add links, edit existing links, and reorder the links (see Figure 13.8).

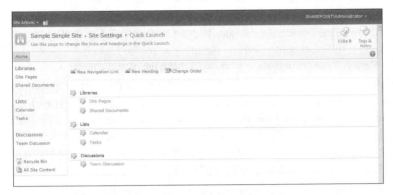

FIGURE 13.8
The Quick Launch (left navigation bar) management page.

The following sections explain how to manage the navigation options in these pages.

Add a Link to the Top Navigation Bar

To add a link to the top navigation bar in a non-publishing site, navigate to the Top Link Bar management page, as explained earlier, and click the link New Navigation Link. This opens a page with an option to type the link's web address and description, as shown in Figure 13.9.

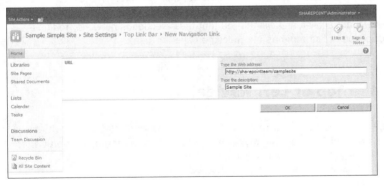

FIGURE 13.9
Adding a link to the top navigation bar (Top Link Bar) in a non-publishing site.

Add a Link to the Left Navigation Bar

To add a link to left navigation bar in a non-publishing site, navigate to the Quick Launch management page, as explained earlier, and click the link New Navigation Link (refer to Figure 13.8). This opens a page with the option to specify the link's web address and description, as well as the heading under which to place the new link (see Figure 13.10).

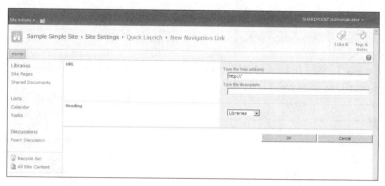

FIGURE 13.10
Adding a link to the left navigation bar (Quick Launch) in a non-publishing site.

Add a Heading to the Left Navigation Bar

A heading in a non-publishing site's left navigation bar is a navigation link that can have other links under it. When you add a link to the left navigation bar (see "Add a Link to the Left Navigation Bar," earlier in this chapter) you have to choose under which heading that link should appear.

To add a heading to the left navigation bar in a non-publishing site, navigate to the Quick Launch management page, as explained earlier, and click the New Heading link (refer to Figure 13.8). This opens a page with the option to type the link's web address and description. This is similar to the page for adding a link to the top navigation bar (refer to Figure 13.9). (Note that a heading cannot be under another heading.) When you click OK, the heading is added to the list, and you are able to add links under it.

Edit a Link in the Top or Left Navigation Bar

To edit a link in one of the navigation bars, open the management page for that bar, as explained earlier in this chapter. In the management page, locate the link you want to edit and click the Edit icon next to the link (refer to Figure 13.8). The page that opens allows you to edit the settings for that link.

> **NOTE** For some of the built-in options (such as the built-in headers in the left navigation bar), you can't change the web address.

Remove a Link from the Top or Left Navigation Bar

To remove a link in one of the navigation bars or to remove a header in the left navigation bar, open the management page for that navigation bar, as explained earlier in this chapter. In the management page, locate the link you want to delete and click the Edit icon next to the link (refer to Figure 13.8). In the page that opens, you can delete the link or header by using the Delete button.

> **NOTE** Deleting a heading that has links under it also deletes the links. You might want to move the links to another heading by editing each link and changing the heading setting.

Modify the Top or Left Navigation Bar in a Publishing Site

In a publishing site, the navigation settings for both navigation bars are in the same page. To get to the navigation management page, open the Site Settings page and click the Navigation link in the Look and Feel section of the page. The Site Navigation Settings page opens, as shown in Figure 13.11.

FIGURE 13.11
The Site Navigation Settings page.

On the Site Navigation Settings page, you can define what links and headings each navigation bar will have—and you can add, remove, or change the order of those links. The top navigation bar is referenced on this page as Global Navigation, and the left navigation bar is called Current Navigation.

In a subsite, this page has more options, as you can see in Figure 13.12. Here, you can set whether the site should display the same top or left navigation options as its parent site or whether it should have its own set of navigation bar links.

FIGURE 13.12
The Site Navigation Settings page for a subsite.

The first option on the page is whether the navigation bars should show subsites under the current site and whether the navigation bars should show pages.

Add a Link to the Top or Left Navigation Bar

To add a link to either navigation bar, click the Global Navigation node (for the top navigation bar) or Current Navigation node in the Navigation Editing and Sorting box. Then click the Add Link option in the menu. This selection opens a dialog where you can specify the link to be added (see Figure 13.13).

FIGURE 13.13
Adding a link to a navigation bar.

In the Title box, you can specify what text the link displays to the user. Also, you can either type in a link or browse to a page in the site by using the Browse button. You can also specify whether the link is opened in a new window when clicked.

Add a Heading to the Top or Left Navigation Bar

In a publishing site, you can add headings to both the top and left navigation bars. A heading in a publishing site can be a link or just text that can have other links under it.

> **NOTE** Unlike a heading in the left navigation bar in a non-publishing site that must be a link, in a publishing site the heading doesn't have to be a link. Instead, a heading can just be a container for links, without allowing users to click it in the navigation bar.

To add a heading, simply click the Global Navigation node (for the top navigation bar) or Current Navigation node in the Navigation Editing and Sorting box. Then click the Add Heading button in the menu. The dialog that pops up is the same as the one for adding a link (refer to Figure 13.13), but unlike with adding a link, in this case you can keep the URL setting empty if you don't want the heading to be a link.

Edit a Link or a Heading in the Top or Left Navigation Bar

To edit a link or heading from either navigation bar, click the link or heading in the Navigation Editing and Sorting box, and then click the Edit button on the toolbar. The dialog for the link's setting opens, allowing you to specify how this link should behave (refer to Figure 13.13).

Remove a Link from the Top or Left Navigation Bar

To remove a link from either navigation bar, click the link in the Navigation Editing and Sorting box, and then click the Delete button on the toolbar.

Change Which Heading a Link Is Under

To select the heading for a link in a publishing site, move the link up or down in the Navigation Editing and Sorting box until it is under the heading you want. Select the link, and then use the Move Up and Move Down buttons (refer to Figure 13.11) to move the link in or out of headings.

> **NOTE** Unlike links in the left navigation bar in a non-publishing site that must be under headings, in a publishing site you can have a link exist in the root (not under a heading). Simply move the link to be under either Current Navigation or Global Navigation.

Create a Site Column

Scenario/Problem: You want to create a site column.

Solution: To create a site column, open the Site Settings page, as explained at the beginning of this chapter, and then click Site Columns in the Galleries section of the page. This selection opens the Site Columns gallery page, where you can create new site columns or edit or remove existing ones (see Figure 13.14).

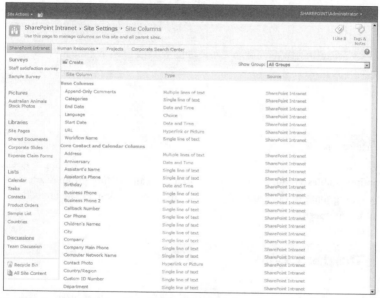

FIGURE 13.14
The Site Columns gallery page.

To create a new column, click the Create button on the toolbar. This selection opens a page where you can define the column's name and type (see Figure 13.15), as well as additional settings—just like creating a list column (see Chapter 7, "Creating Lists and Document Libraries"). The one difference from creating a list or library column in this page is that site columns can be added to a group to make finding the columns from the list of site columns easier.

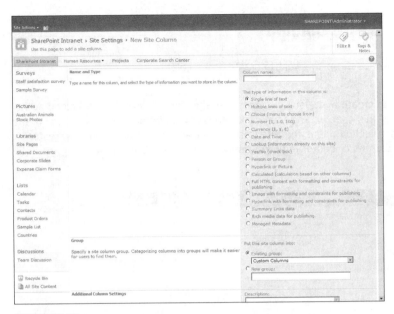

FIGURE 13.15
Adding a new site column.

The Group option enables you to either add the column to an existing group or create a new group by typing that group's name. By default, the columns you create are added to the Custom Columns group.

Create a Content Type

Scenario/Problem: You want to create a content type and define what columns are included in the content type.

Solution: As explained in Chapter 1, "About Microsoft SharePoint 2010," a content type is a collection of site columns and additional settings that can be created for a site. To create a new content type in a site, open the Site Settings page, as explained at the beginning of this chapter, and click Content Types in the Galleries section of the page. This selection opens a page where you can create or modify content types (see Figure 13.16).

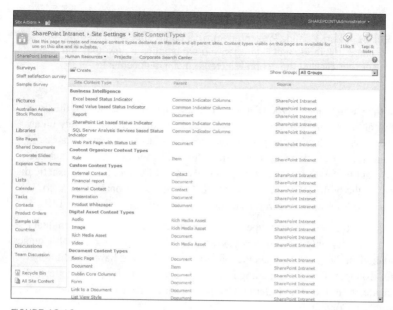

FIGURE 13.16
The Site Content Types gallery page.

Click the Create button on the toolbar to create a new content type. The page shown in Figure 13.17 opens. The first setting you need to set for a content type is the name for the content type, followed by its description. The name and description appear in the New drop-down in the document library or site when the user opens it to select a content type.

FIGURE 13.17
Creating a new content type.

> **TIP** It is wise to name a content type in singular form (for example, Corporate Financial Report, Board Meeting Presentation). This name appears under the New button for document libraries and lists when you are creating a new item and signifies to the user that clicking the option will create a single document.

Next, select the parent content type. This step is important because most of the time, you do not want to start the content type from scratch but instead want to rely on an existing content type. Selecting the parent content type is also important because changing it can (but does not necessarily) affect the child content type. For example, suppose you want to create a content type named External Contact that has exactly the same settings as the built-in Contact content type, but with additional columns to capture the contact's company address and company description (see Figure 13.18).

If you specify that the new content type is the child of the existing Contact content type, you must specify only the columns you want to add on top of the default Contact columns. Also, if in the future you decide that all contacts should have an additional column—for example, Birthday—adding it to the parent content type Contact can also add it automatically to the child External Contact, as shown later in this chapter in the section "Modify a Content Type."

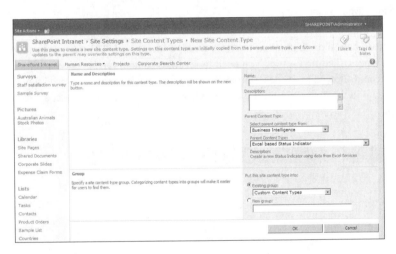

FIGURE 13.18
Creating a new content type named External Contact that inherits from the Contact content type.

After you select the content type main settings, click OK to create the content type. This selection opens the page where you can define the additional settings for the content type. For example, you can add, edit, or remove columns; set workflow settings; and perform other advanced settings (see Figure 13.19).

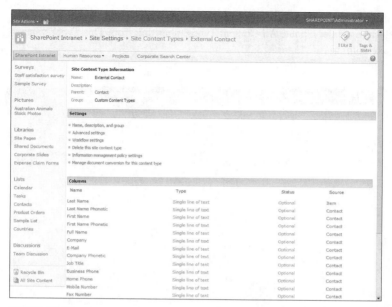

FIGURE 13.19
The settings page for a content type.

To add a column to a content type, scroll down to the bottom of the page shown in Figure 13.19, where you can find links to either create a new site column for the content type or add a column from the list of available site columns.

Modify a Content Type

Scenario/Problem: You want to modify an existing content type by changing its name or perhaps adding or removing a column and other settings.

Solution: To modify an existing content type, open the Site Settings page, as explained at the beginning of this chapter, and click Content Types in the Galleries section of the page. This selection opens a page where you can modify content types (refer to Figure 13.16).

Click the name of the content type you want to change to open the content type's setting page (refer to Figure 13.19). To edit the content type, change any setting available on this page, including the content type's name, description, and group; its workflow settings; its columns; and more advanced settings.

With every setting you change, you have an option to also update all content types inheriting from the content type. Updating them ensures that a change you make is also made to other content types created with the current content type as their parent. For example, if you add a Birthday column to the Contact content type and you want the change to also affect any other content types that inherit from Contact, such as External Contact, select Yes under Update All Content Types Inheriting from This Type? when adding the site column (see Figure 13.20).

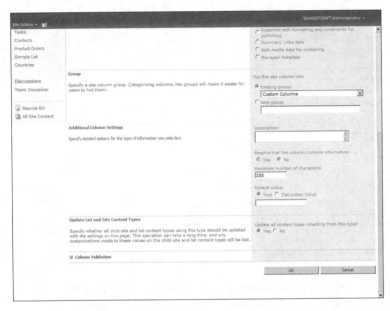

FIGURE 13.20
Adding a site column to a content type and updating the child content types.

CHAPTER 14

Managing Site Security

When you own a SharePoint site, you might want to restrict or allow different users to do different tasks. For example, you might want certain users to be able to add items to lists and upload files to document libraries, while allowing other users to only read those items. You might want to give permission to approve items and files to a group of people, and you might want to allow another group to create new lists and libraries or even manage the site together with you.

When you are managing SharePoint security, it is important to remember that you can set the permissions for either a specific user or group of users from the corporate directory or from other forms of external user databases (depending on the configuration on the server). The corporate directory groups or groups in other external databases are defined by the administrators of those directories or databases and not as part of SharePoint. You can give them access to your SharePoint site (or restrict them) without having to manage the members of the group. For example, most organizations have a group for each division or team.

Furthermore, for security reasons, you might want to create groups that you manage on a site-by-site basis. These are called *SharePoint groups*, and SharePoint sites usually have several such groups set up—for example, the group of "visitors" who are allowed only to read content in the site and the group of "members" who are allowed to add content to the site. Most of the time, you should add users and groups to SharePoint groups to simplify changing the permissions later.

This chapter explains how to manage the security aspects of SharePoint sites. All these tasks assume that you have the required permission to manage the security of the site you are browsing.

Get to a Site's Permission Management Page

Scenario/Problem: You want to manage the security in a site.

Solution: To get to a site's security settings page, open the site's Site Actions menu and click the Site Permissions option, as shown in Figure 14.1.

If the Site Permissions option is not in the Site Actions menu, you can get to the permission management page by using the Site Settings page (click the Site Settings option in the menu, as shown in Figure 14.1) and then clicking the Site Permissions link under the Users and Permissions heading (see Figure 14.2).

Either method opens the site permission management page, where you can manage the permissions for the site (see Figure 14.3).

NOTE A list, library, or list item in a site may have unique permissions—that is, someone might have changed the permissions on it and broken its inheritance from the site. In this case, a yellow bar warns you that changes made in the site level will not impact those items, as shown in Figure 14.3.

FIGURE 14.1

Opening a site's permission management page from the Site Actions menu.

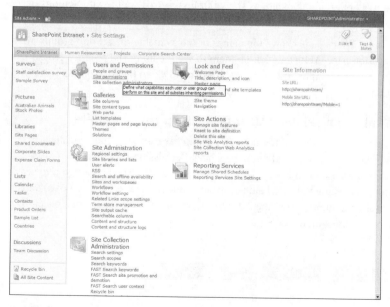

FIGURE 14.2

Opening a site's permission management page from the Site Settings page.

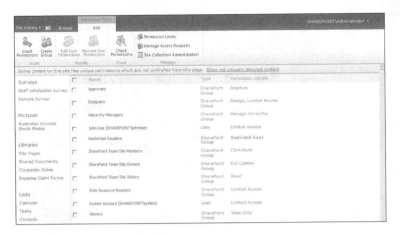

FIGURE 14.3
A site's security management page.

Get to a Site's People and Groups Settings Page

A useful page when managing security on a site is the People and Groups settings page. This page allows you to browse through the groups available in the site and see which users and security groups are assigned to each SharePoint group.

To get to a site's People and Groups page, open the site's Site Actions menu and click the Site Settings option in the menu, as shown in Figure 14.1. In the Site Settings page, click on the People and Groups link (refer to Figure 14.2).

The People and Groups page shows the names of the available SharePoint groups in the left navigation pane. You can click on them to see the users and security groups that belong in them. For example, Figure 14.7 shows John Doe in the SharePoint Team Site Visitors group.

Check What Permissions a User or a Group Has on a Site

To check what permission a specific user or a group has on a site, open the site's Permission Management page and click the Check Permissions button in the Check section of the ribbon (refer to Figure 14.3). The dialog that appears allows you to select a user or group by typing the user name or group name in the User/Group box. You can also find a user or group by using the Address Book link and then perform a check by using the Check Now button (see Figure 14.4).

SharePoint Intranet: Check Permissions

Check Permissions
To check permissions for a user or group, enter their name or e-mail address.

User/Group:

Check Now   Close

FIGURE 14.4
The Check Permissions dialog.

When you click Check Now, the dialog displays the permission levels the user or group has and through which group. In Figure 14.5 you can see that the user Jane Doe has been given some permissions directly, and she has other permissions because she belongs to a group.

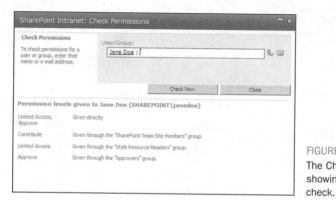

FIGURE 14.5
The Check Permissions dialog, showing the results of a check.

Assign Users' Permissions on a Site

Scenario/Problem: You want to assign a user or a group permissions to a site or add a user to an existing group.

Solution: To allow users to view a site to which they previously didn't have access, you can either add them to one of the SharePoint groups or add them to the site directly, without adding them to a specific group. The following sections explain how to perform these options.

TIP As mentioned earlier in this chapter, it is recommended that you always add users to SharePoint groups because doing so makes the permissions easier to manage in the future.

NOTE A site normally inherits permissions from its parent site (unless the site is a root site and doesn't have a parent). Therefore, you might not be able to edit a site's permissions unless you break the site's inheritance, using the Stop Inheriting Permissions option in the Permission Tools ribbon in the site's security page. You might want to manage the security of the parent site and not the current site, so you should make sure you want to break the inheritance.

Add or Remove Users in a SharePoint Group

To add a user to a security group in a site, navigate to the site's permission management page, as explained earlier in this chapter. In the Permission Tools ribbon, click the Grant Permissions button. The Grant Permissions dialog appears, allowing you to select the user or group and to which group that user or group should be added (see Figure 14.6).

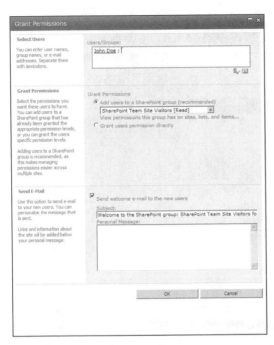

FIGURE 14.6
FIGURE 14.6
The Grant Permissions dialog allows you to add users to a site group.

On the Grant Permissions page, you can either use the Add Users box to type the names of the people you want to add (separated with semicolons—for example, John doe;Jane smith) or click the Address Book icon to search and select the people from the directory. For example, to add a person as a visitor to the site, type that person's user name in the Users/Groups box and select the visitors from the Grant Permissions drop-down (refer to Figure 14.6). When you are finished selecting the users and the group to which they should belong, click OK.

The page showing the people in the group is updated to show the people you added (see Figure 14.7). For instruction on how to see who is in a SharePoint group, see "Get to a Site's People and Groups Settings Page," earlier in this chapter.

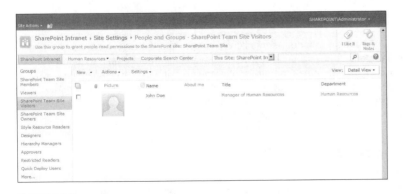

FIGURE 14.7
A user has been added to the group.

To remove people from the group, navigate to the page for that group (see "Get to a Site's People and Groups Settings Page," earlier in this chapter) and select the check boxes next to their names. Then open the Actions menu on the toolbar and select Remove Users from Group (see Figure 14.8).

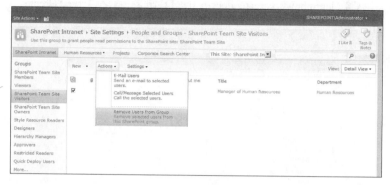

FIGURE 14.8
Removing a user from a group.

Add Users' Permissions Directly to or Remove Them from a Site

You might not want to add a user to a SharePoint group in a site but instead might want to give a user a specific set of permissions unrelated to a specific group. In this case, navigate to the site's security page and click the Grant Permission button in the Permission Tools ribbon (refer to Figure 14.3). In the dialog that appears, select the users and select what permissions they have on the site by choosing the Give Users Permission Directly option (refer to Figure 14.6).

You can either type the names of the people you want to add in the Users/Groups box at the top or click the Address Book icon to use a people search dialog to select the users. Then select the permission levels you want the people to have on the site. You can select more than one permission level; for example, if you select Contribute and Approve, you allow the users you selected to add list items and files to the site and approve documents that they or other people have added. Remember that the higher permission always wins, so the user or security group has all the permissions from all the permission levels. To learn how to create a customized permission level, see "Create Permission Levels for a Site," later in this chapter.

To remove users from a site, open the site's permission management page (see "Get to a Site's Permission Management Settings Page," earlier in this chapter) and select the users in the page. Then click the Remove User Permissions button in the Modify section of the ribbon. This removes the users from the site, including any SharePoint groups the users belonged to.

Change Permissions of Users or SharePoint Groups in a Site

To change the permissions that are allocated to a user or group in a site, navigate to the site's permission management page, as explained earlier in this chapter. To change the permission levels, select the users or groups that you want to change and click the Edit User Permissions button in the Modify section of the ribbon.

The Edit Permissions dialog that opens allows you to set what permissions those users or groups will have (see Figure 14.9). After you select them, click OK to set the permission levels. To learn how to create a customized permission level, see "Create Permission Levels for a Site," later in this chapter.

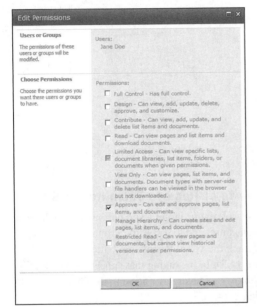

FIGURE 14.9
Selecting the permissions users and/or groups should have.

Create a SharePoint Group for a Site

Scenario/Problem: You want to create a SharePoint group so that you can manage who is in the group. Then you want to assign permission to everyone in the group to sites, lists, libraries, and list items.

Solution: By default, when you create a site, SharePoint automatically creates some groups for you to use in that site. To create a new SharePoint group, open the site permissions settings page, as shown earlier in this chapter, and then click the Create Group button in the Grant section of the ribbon (refer to Figure 14.3).

The page for creating a new SharePoint group has several options you can set for the group (see Figure 14.10). You can modify all these settings later by editing the group's settings.

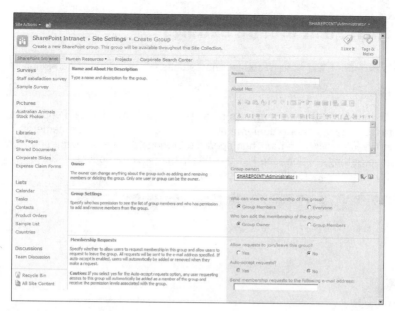

FIGURE 14.10
The SharePoint group creation page.

The first options are the name for the group and its description. The next option is the owner of the group. This setting defaults to you, but you can choose any other user. You just need to make sure the user you choose has permissions to access the site. The owner can add and remove users from the group, as well as change the group's settings, even if the owner doesn't have permissions to manage the site itself. This means you can make anyone an owner of a group without giving that user permissions to manage other aspects of the site.

In the Group Settings section, you can define who can see the list of people who have been added to the group; the options are everyone or just the people who are members of the group. Also, you can define whether only the owner can add and remove members or whether anyone who is a member can do so (effectively making the group self-managing).

The next section on this page, Membership Requests, enables you to define whether people can send requests to join or be removed from the group. If you want to enable this option, you must specify an e-mail address to which the requests will be sent. Users then have the option of sending requests to join the group when viewing it. You can also choose that if a user requests to join the group, the request should be automatically accepted.

Finally, in the last section of the page, you can define what permission levels the group will have on the site. To learn how to create a customized permission level, see "Create Permission Levels for a Site," later in this chapter.

Edit a SharePoint Group's Settings

Scenario/Problem: You want to change the settings for an existing SharePoint group.

Solution: To change a SharePoint group's settings, navigate to the site's People and Groups settings page, as shown earlier in this chapter, and then click the name of the group in the left navigation bar. Then open the Settings drop-down menu and click the Group Settings option (see Figure 14.11). The page that opens enables you to modify the settings for the group (see Figure 14.12).

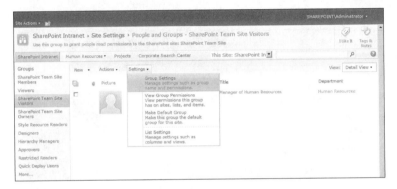

FIGURE 14.11
Getting to a SharePoint group's settings page.

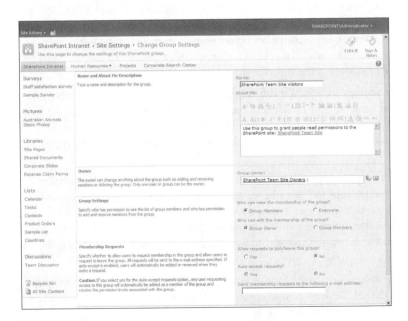

FIGURE 14.12
A SharePoint group's settings page.

NOTE Although the group's settings page allows you to modify the settings for the group, it does not provide an option to change the group's security settings. To do that, use the method described in "Change Permissions of Users or SharePoint Groups in a Site," earlier in this chapter.

Create Permission Levels for a Site

Scenario/Problem: Earlier in this chapter, you saw that to assign permissions to users or groups, you can choose from a predefined list of permission levels, such as Readers, Contributors, and Approvers. If you want to create a permission level that differs from the existing permission levels, you can create a custom permission level. For example, you might want to create a permission level that enables users to view and delete items or files but not edit them. Or maybe you want to create a permission level that allows users to view the site and be able to create subsites but not edit items in the site.

Solution: To create permission levels, open the site's permissions management page and click the Permission Levels button in the Manage section of the ribbon (refer to Figure 14.3).

NOTE If you are working on a subsite, by default the permission levels are inherited from the parent site. Although you can still edit them (an action that breaks the inheritance), you should make sure this is what you actually want to do. If you want to make sure you are editing the permission levels in the top site, use the Manage Parent option in the Inheritance section of the Edit ribbon of the permission management page to get to the parent site's permissions management page.

On the Permission Levels page, you can see and manage all the existing permission levels (see Figure 14.13).

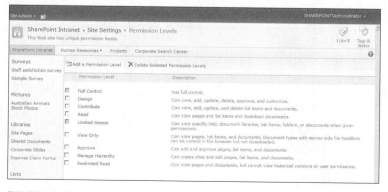

FIGURE 14.13
The Permission Levels page.

To create a new permission level, click the Add a Permission Level button on the toolbar. The Add a Permission Level page opens (see Figure 14.14). On this page, you can define the name for the new permission level and what permissions set it should include. Simply select the permissions you want the permission level to include and click the Create button at the bottom of the screen.

FIGURE 14.14
The Add a Permission Level page.

APPENDIX A

Common Keyboard Shortcuts

Sometimes using the keyboard is more effective than using the mouse, especially if the graphical designer of the page moved things around and you are not certain where on the page they are. Knowing the keyboard shortcuts can help you quickly get where you want to go.

Like the rest of this book, this appendix is useful both to anyone using a SharePoint site and to those who are adding or editing content in a SharePoint site. Also, some of these shortcut combinations work in all pages, while others are unique to certain types of pages. Each section lists where the shortcuts can be used.

Using Keyboard Shortcuts

The keyboard shortcut combinations are described in this book as a series of keys that you need to press. If you must press several keys at the same time, this is expressed with the + sign. If after pressing a certain key combination you must release the keys before pressing another, this is expressed with "and then." For example, if you want to switch a calendar view to the daily view (instead of the monthly view), use the shortcut Alt+period and then Enter, which should be read as instructions to hold down the Alt key and the period key (.) at the same time, and then release them and press Enter.

Keyboard Shortcuts for Anyone Using a SharePoint Site

General Shortcuts

The Home link	Alt+1 and then Enter
Skip to main content	Alt+X and then Enter
Help	Alt+6 and then Enter
Go to the search box	Alt+S
The personal settings menu	Alt+W and then Enter

Site Actions menu	Alt+/ and then Enter
All Site Content	Alt+3 and then Enter
Move to next web part	Alt+W

Top Navigation

The top navigation tab	Alt+1 and then Enter
The next navigation tab	Tab and then Enter
The previous navigation tab	Shift+Tab and then Enter

List or Library Views

(Calendar view) Previous day, week, or month	Alt+Shift+< and then Enter
(Calendar view) Next day, week, or month in a view	Alt+Shift+> and then Enter

Ribbon Shortcuts

Skip ribbon commands	Alt+Y and then Enter

Keyboard Shortcuts for Authors and Editors

Editing List Items or File Properties

Cancel button	Alt+C
Save button (or OK button)	Alt+O
Save and Close button (in a survey response)	Alt+S
(Date picker control) Previous month	Alt+Shift+< and then Enter
(Date picker control) Next month	Alt+Shift+> and then Enter

Editing Pages in a Web Part Tool Pane

OK button	Alt+O
Apply button	Alt+Y
Cancel button	Alt+C

All Site Content Page

Create button	Alt+N and then Enter (or because the Create button is selected by default when you load the page, simply press Enter when the page is loaded)
View menu, Site Workflows button	Alt+W until the correct option is selected and then Enter

Using the Rich Text Editor

Right-to-Left text direction button	Ctrl+Shift+<
Left-to-Right text direction button	Ctrl+Shift+>
Bold button	Ctrl+B
Copy button	Ctrl+C
Center button	Ctrl+E
Italics button	Ctrl+I
Align Left button	Ctrl+L
Increase Indent button	Ctrl+M
Decrease Indent button	Ctrl+Shift+M
Font Size menu	Ctrl+Shift+P
Align Right button	Ctrl+R
Underline button	Ctrl+U
Paste button	Ctrl+V
Background Color menu	Ctrl+Shift+W
Cut button	Ctrl+X

APPENDIX B

Useful Links

This appendix contains a collection of useful links that you might want to use to quickly get to a certain place in a SharePoint site. In this appendix, the placeholder {Site} is used for the site path. For example, if you want to get to the View All Site Content page of a site, the link would be written as {Site}/_layouts/viewlsts.aspx. To get to that page for a site with the path http://sharepoint, you replace the {Site} placeholder with the path http://sharepoint and add the rest of the text to complete the link: http://sharepoint/_layouts/viewlsts.aspx.

Similarly, some links include the path to a specific page, in which case the placeholder {Page} is used. You simply replace the placeholder with the full path to that page.

Useful Links for Anyone Using a SharePoint Site

The View All Site Content page	{Site}/_layouts/viewlsts.aspx
My Memberships page	{Site}/_layouts/mymemberships.aspx
My Links page	{Site}/_layouts/myquicklinks.aspx
Add a Link to My Links page	{Site}/_layouts/quicklinks.aspx
My Site page	{Site}/_layouts/mysite.aspx
My Alerts page	{Site}/_layouts/MySubs.aspx
Site Content and Structure page	{Site}/_layouts/SiteManager.aspx
Search Current Site and Below page	{Site}/_layouts/OSSSearchResults.aspx

Useful Links for Authors and Editors

Manage Content page	{Site}/_layouts/mcontent.aspx
List of last content you edited	{Site}/_layouts/myinfo.aspx
Create a new page (in a publishing site)	{Site}/_layouts/CreatePage.aspx
Web part page maintenance	{Page}?contents=1

Useful Links for Site Managers

Manage Site Settings	{Site}/_layouts/settings.aspx
Manage Sub Webs Page	{Site}/_layouts/mngsubwebs.aspx
Manage Navigation Options	{Site}/_layouts/navoptions.aspx
Modify Top Navigation	{Site}/_layouts/AreaNavigationSettings.aspx
Manage People and Groups	{Site}/_layouts/people.aspx
Create New Subsite	{Site}/_layouts/newsbweb.aspx
Manage Alerts	{Site}/_layouts/SiteSubs.aspx
Delete	{Site}/_layouts/deleteweb.aspx

Index

A

HOW-TO

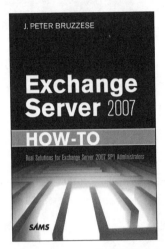

Exchange Server 2007 How-To
ISBN-13: 978-0-672-33048-3

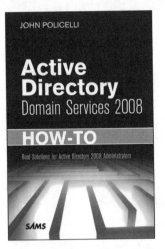

**Active Directory Domain Services
2008 How-To**
ISBN-13: 978-0-672-33045-2

SharePoint 2007 How-To
ISBN-13: 978-0-672-33050-6

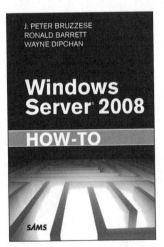

Windows Server 2008 How-To
ISBN-13: 978-0-672-33075-9

How-To series books are available at most retail and online bookstores. For more information or to order direct visit our online bookstore at **informit.com/store**

Online editions of all How-To series titles are available by subscription from Safari Books Online at **safari.informit.com**

FREE Online Edition

Your purchase of **SharePoint 2010 How-To** includes access to a free online edition for 45 days through the Safari Books Online subscription service. Nearly every Sams book is available online through Safari Books Online, along with more than 5,000 other technical books and videos from publishers such as Addison-Wesley Professional, Cisco Press, Exam Cram, IBM Press, O'Reilly, Prentice Hall, and Que.

SAFARI BOOKS ONLINE allows you to search for a specific answer, cut and paste code, download chapters, and stay current with emerging technologies.

Activate your FREE Online Edition at
www.informit.com/safarifree

> **STEP 1:** Enter the coupon code: MASOHAA.

> **STEP 2:** New Safari users, complete the brief registration form.
> Safari subscribers, just log in.

If you have difficulty registering on Safari or accessing the online edition, please e-mail customer-service@safaribooksonline.com